D1613408

SERVING THE PEOPLE
SOCIAL SERVICES AND SOCIAL CHANGE

ANN WITHORN

SERVING THE PEOPLE

SOCIAL SERVICES
AND SOCIAL CHANGE

COLUMBIA UNIVERSITY PRESS
NEW YORK   1984

Library of Congress Cataloging in Publication Data

Withorn, Ann, 1947–
  Serving the people.

  Includes bibliographical references and index.
    1. Public welfare—United States.   2. Radicalism—
United States.   3. United States—Social policy.
4. Social service—United States.   5. Social change.
I. Title.
HV95.W575 1984   361'.973   84-3160
ISBN 0-231-05560-9 (alk. paper)

Columbia University Press
New York   Guildford, Surrey
Copyright © 1984 Ann Withorn
All rights reserved

Printed in the United States of America

Clothbound editions of Columbia University Press Books are
Smyth-sewn and printed on permanent and durable acid-free paper

Book design by Ken Venezio

To the students,
the faculty,
and the staff
of the College of Public and Community Service
University of Massachusetts, Boston

CONTENTS

INTRODUCTION

Tᴴɪѕ book is written while social services are under fundamental attack. President Reagan calls basic social programs "fiscal free rides" and urges us to regain our economic and social independence by learning to live without them. David Stockman argues that there are no "entitlements" to services, no rights to welfare or social services. A stream of disappointed liberals and neoconservative and Moral Majority writers accuse all social welfare programs of failure, of destroying the family, of creating a culture of dependence, and of weakening the nation's moral fiber.

In the face of such widespread criticism, many human service advocates muster only a frightened defense of their favorite programs or strive to show how little is actually spent on services. Recipient groups organize to protect their bottom-line benefits, not to assert that everyone should benefit from a full-scale system of social programs. Few feel able to insist that well-organized, caring services are political and social necessities, much less to argue that they are a fundamental demand of any movement for social and economic justice. To assert such a vision seems unrealistic, out of touch with the conservative temper of the times.

A basic argument of this book, however, is to demand that we go beyond contemporary notions of "realism" in our thinking about human services. Service programs are vulnerable now, in part, because progressives have failed to recognize and demand them publicly as an essential (if complex and contradictory) component of our political agenda. Activists often focus only on the bureaucratic and social control aspects of public services, seeing them merely as establishment responses to popular pressure. In doing so they abandon the field to liberals who present social programs as essentially apolitical, obligatory functions of an expanding industrial society. Leftists thereby deny radical social service workers a self-conscious, legitimate role as co-builders of a better society, even as liberals refuse to allow them serious complaints regarding the social control aspects of their work.

In this book I argue that human service workers need to admit—even proclaim—the fundamentally political nature of their work, and also to embrace the radical potential for human services to be one means of achieving a more equitable and caring society. We need to inject such a position into the current debate about the role of the public sector, both as a means of properly expanding the terms of the discussion *and* as a means of deepening our own political and social analysis. Instead of being defensive proponents of change with no social program of our own, we can reinterpret popular opposition to public services as a protest against inaccessibility and lack of humanistic content. From this perspective, we can begin to respond to the envy behind often-heard complaints, "I have to suffer without day care/food stamps/medical support—why should I pay for someone else to get them?" Now may be the time to recognize such complaints as demands for more, and better, services—not for less.

A positive, politicized view of the potential for human services will allow us to be critical of the limited, apolitical, half-hearted, and ill-conceived ways in which services have been provided without undermining demands for better services in the future. Indeed, we should begin to see that services have been provided so poorly in part to discredit their progressive political potential, to keep people from recognizing and demanding them as rights, as mutual benefits accruing to all citizens of a more caring society. Now is the time to regain our memory of the way in which a more socially responsible society has been one part of the goals of all twentieth-century progressive movements and to allow radical service workers to acknowledge and embrace their natural role as social change activists in achieving those goals.

In spite of "realistic" admonitions to cut our losses and to take the safest possible course, then, I will argue here that what is needed is not surrender but a vision, a vision of a society where it is no shame to acknowledge one's needs, where people can all admit their inter-

dependency and devote major social energies into developing radically different, humane, and responsible ways to care for each other.

ORIGINS

This book probably began when, as a member of a radical Boston-
area student group in 1969, I felt drawn to do "support work" for
the local welfare rights chapter. Somehow it seemed important to find
a way of linking my anger at "the system," which was waging global
and domestic war, with acts of solidarity and caring for others. Later,
in teaching and social service jobs, I began to feel an even stronger
urge to combine my emerging socialist and feminist analysis with my
daily practice. Here I encountered disapproval from political comrades who viewed service programs as social control and, therefore,
as worthy only of principled opposition. Also, some co-workers
thought my attempts to view the job politically were unnecessary and
risked reducing my effectiveness with individuals. Thus, although I
had become a socialist and a feminist because I wanted a society where
people could treat each other better, I found that most people on
the left *and* in human services wanted me to split my two concerns.
Either I was to be political—hard and critical in my analysis of the
welfare state—and to suppress my sense that some services had the
potential to be good, desirable things, or I was to try to help individuals and groups with their problems without so much as a peep of a
broader analysis. When I pushed harder, sympathetic left friends did
suggest that I could perhaps organize a union of my co-workers, and
colleagues did allow that certain economic and feminist principles
could be included in training sessions.

Faced with such a dilemma I returned, like many refugees from
the real world before me, to graduate school and a set of questions
which seemed to require study and a more detached analysis. There
I spent some important years studying social services and social
movements and discovered that I was not alone with my concerns.
Early feminists, Wobblies, communists, socialists, and labor movement activists had provided services from a political perspective.
During the 1930s and 1940s, social workers had organized unions
concerned with quality services. One, Bertha Reynolds, had written
extensively about the overlapping issues. And, groups within recent

movements had also self-consciously provided services, groups such as the United Farm Workers Union and the women's health movement. This investigation provided me with a dissertation topic and a conviction that I was beginning to make sense of the questions which bothered me.[1]

I have spent the last six years trying to combine what I learned with a growing awareness of the problems faced by concerned human service workers. I teach at the College of Public and Community Service at the University of Massachusetts/Boston. It is an alternative undergraduate college where adult human service workers earn degrees in their fields and spend time trying to discover what they want to achieve and can accomplish in their work. During my time here I have written an oral history/organizational study of the Massachusetts human service system, with the help of students, and have begun to explore related questions of the "politics of social services."[2]

I now find myself able to combine my interest in the lessons learned from movement-provided services, with my sense of the tensions faced by committed human service workers like my students, and with my developing analysis of the many functions of social services in the capitalist welfare state. Through it all I have tried to remember the advice given me by Bertha Reynolds in 1975:

You must always remember that good social work must be political, not because we try to indoctrinate anybody, but because if we help people help themselves better and understand the world they are in better, then they will be more able to help everyone else make the better world we all need. We can only do this well if we view the world from a social perspective. To be a good social worker you have to be a progressive thinker.[3]

CHALLENGING THE CHOICES

The assumption underlying this book is that the 1980s are the time to alter our perspective and begin to see service delivery and the political quest for basic social change as unalterably intertwined, not irrevocably separate. There are four major reasons why this can be done now.

First, the nature of the current attacks on social programs indicates that the New Right, at least, understands the underlying political potential of many human service programs. Conservatives fear that—despite how badly they are administered and their demeaning method of delivery—the provision of services will raise social expectations, build links among people, give people some hope for a better life and allow women, especially, to have more options than the narrow choices available within the family.[4]

We can respond with more than a defensive posture if we acknowledge and praise many of the "dangers" for which services are criticized. We can, thereby, force a long-needed public discussion regarding what citizens have a right to demand from the state and each other. From this position of advocacy we can also criticize existing social service programs, because they fail to live up to the high standards which are the people's right. Existing social programs have failed in large part because they have not been in touch with community need, because they have not seen themselves as responsive to a constituency, but instead have usually represented the planning-in-a-vacuum approach of middle-class social welfare professionals, and been limited by fiscal "realities" of the capitalist state. Because we are now demanding more politicized, better services we can also criticize the social control aspects of existing programs while insisting that the truly responsive services on our agenda will not so readily serve the interests of the ruling class. Since we offer our proposals as political activists and not as a "responsible professional elite," we need not worry about the costs of our demands to capitalism. Such concerns only allow us to raise issues about military spending and arms buildup.

In short, the New Right and the current attack on the state allow us the chance to practice what Andre Gorz has called "revolutionary reforms," demands which do not, like reformist reforms, "subordinate objectives to the criterion of rationality and practicability of a given system" but which are, instead, "conceived not in terms of what is possible within the framework of a given system and administration but in view of what should be made possible in terms of human needs and demands."[5]

Second, the changing roles and backgrounds of human service workers make our strategy more feasible. During the past fifteen years "human services" has replaced "social welfare" as the term of choice to describe the whole network of social programs. The unified influence of professional social work associations over all activity supported by public and private social programs seems to have lessened. Instead there are now youth workers, mental health workers, counselors, and many others providing services without the same class background and the same elitist training.[6] Such workers are important for a number of reasons. They are less resented by the communities they work with, often coming from and living in the same neighborhoods in which they work. Often they are more amenable to unionizing and to an identification as workers. In addition they often still see themselves involved in the practice of social change, although the younger workers have less experience with political activity than in prior periods.[7] Therefore, many of the very workers whose jobs are most in jeopardy due to fiscal cutbacks are the people who will be most liked by the communities in which they work and may prove most willing to fight a broad, rather than a narrow, campaign for their jobs.

Third, the past fifteen years have already seen changes in service delivery patterns which provide a solid base for our strategy. As I shall argue in chapter 3, the Poverty Programs began the changes. Never remotely able to end poverty, what they did was begin to provide services in a different manner than those provided by traditional agencies. They talked about the links among organizing, the community, and services. Whatever their ultimate flaws, the Poverty Program services, in their accessible storefront office staffed with neighborhood workers, began to offer another model for what social services can be that cannot be dismissed as a leftist fantasy.

The deinstitutionalization of mental hospitals and schools for the retarded has also produced more services in the community, no matter what we may think of the way the overall program has been carried out. It is now more likely that your average citizen will meet a retarded or mentally ill person (it is to be hoped, not someone who has just been dumped into the community). Such encounters remind all of us that people have real needs which are not related to weakness or personal failure, and may create a base of support for public discussion of social services which could not occur when everyone with extreme needs was locked away.

Similarly, another politically questionable change of the 1970s, the contracting out of public services to private providers, may, at least, bring a wider range of people into the net of public services. As I will argue later, contracting out has created fundamental confusions over what is public and what is private, confusions that undermine attempts to organize a united workforce. On the other hand, people who would never have worked as a state bureaucrat or civil servant are now involved in social services in ways that may contribute new energy and strength to a political strategy. Similarly many "private" service recipients go to agencies which receive state contracts, so they may be more likely to see their fate linked to that of the public service system.

The growth of recipient advocacy groups during the 1970s also has already begun the process of politicizing service delivery. Elderly and disabled groups, women, and many others have organized to achieve social services. Indeed, those groups see services as their right and have been concerned not only with receiving service money but also with the quality of the service provided. The task for activists is to join with such groups in order to keep fighting for services but also to see the links with other services and to set the issue of services in a wider framework.

The self help movement is a final area of social service change which lends support to our strategy. Since the mid-sixties, self help groups of all types have emerged all across the country. The range of issues is astounding and the degree of political radicalism varies greatly. All, however, offer a hopeful component of the campaign to politicize service delivery; they all embody some criticism of professionalism and some sense that mutually provided services are highly desirable goods in this society.[8] Again, I will discuss self help later, but the insights into the meaning of service activity that have come out of the self help movement provide a critical new dimension to demands for services. We can call for expanded and better services without feeling that we are simply calling for more jobs for social workers. Instead our demands may include self help options and material supports.

Fourth, the final support for our strategy comes out of the experience of the contemporary women's movement. Over the past fifteen years feminists have been working together to redefine the links between personal and political concerns. This work is reflected in feminist services, as discussed in chapter 3, but feminist theory also provides the intellectual base for a revitalized left movement that will honestly value the substance of good service work, not just see services as good mobilizing issues.

There are many aspects of feminism's new definition of what is political that will help us. In the most general sense, feminism's recognition that family life, sexual life, and general human interaction embody political values that can be studied, criticized, and changed is basic to a movement which will argue for quality services, not just more services. Similarly, the growing feminist awareness of the need for complexity in understanding social class and its implications for human interactions will help activists examine their nervousness about relations between "middle-class" service providers and "working-class" clients. Finally, feminism's recognition that services are needed for women to achieve liberation from the limiting demands of family life should help us to overcome lingering doubts about the political value of service work.

Taken together, the New Right attack, the changing social service workforce, recent structural changes, and the insights of contemporary feminism provide a base for a new left strategy. This strategy will be able to demand services without compromising quality and see service workers as people within a "critical industry" for social change efforts.

METHOD

The method by which this book was written is eclectic and represents the fruits of different intellectual pursuits over a span of eight years. First there was historical research into the origins of traditional and radical social services from the beginning of this century until the 1960s. This research drew mainly on secondary sources and some primary materials available in Boston's major libraries: Harvard's Widener and Schlesinger Libraries, the Brandeis Library, and the Simmons School of Social Work Library. Most of this work was done for my dissertation and was completed from 1974 through 1975. The study of contemporary radical services was conducted between 1975 and 1977 and involved extensive review of primary materials as well as interviews with United Farm Workers Union members and feminist health movement members. The fruits of this research are extensively presented in my 1977 dissertation and are summarized and abbreviated here.[9]

Since 1977 I have been consulting, teaching, and writing about the problems facing contemporary service workers, especially those who desire basic social change. As part of the work for writing a book on Massachusetts human services I interviewed over forty service workers and reviewed much of the contemporary literature on service delivery.[10] Finally, in explicit preparation for this book I reviewed the British and U.S. literature on radical social work and interviewed seven more Boston area human service activists.

Most of the interviews cited here, from those conducted for the dissertation to the later studies, were not tape-recorded. Instead, I interviewed people and kept extensive process notes which were then cited, without direct attribution in most cases. The goal was never, at any stage of the research, to conduct a rigidly scientific review of data but instead to provide a human backdrop to a speculative review of the issues facing people involved in human service work—as radicals or simply as traditional workers and administrators. From the beginning my hope has been to bring my experiences and values into an analysis of the politics of social services that will help others with similar goals and problems, not to put forward any definitive research findings. As the work has progressed through different stages it has been reviewed by a number of academic and political associates. Their comments—ranging from editorial suggestions to political critiques—have consistently informed the development of this analysis, which finally might be described as a long historical and strategic essay on the potential of development for a more political understanding of social services and social service work.

AUDIENCE

This book is written for all service workers who see their work as one way to bring broader social change. Most may be people whose experiences with providing services makes them seek to do more than help individuals and, instead, to achieve wider, if ill-defined, goals. Others may be activists whose service work has merged with community work or union involvement. And some may be self-conscious radicals who have developed a political analysis based on years of study and political practice.

When I speak of, and for, such an audience I am assuming a certain, limited unity of analysis and practice. First, I assume that all understand a criticism of the social welfare system in this country that links its flaws to the economic and social demands of the dominant social order—even though many may not be ready to accept any particular political label. Second, I assume that my readers are seeking ways to develop an analysis and practice that links them with clients and other workers, rather than a professional identity which allows them to distance themselves from both. Third, I assume that all share a desire to be more immediately helpful to the individuals and groups of clients they work with as well as to link their daily work more closely to broader social goals.

Members of such an audience may feel distant from many self-defined radicals, leftists, or feminists because they may feel that their daily work is not politically valuable. This book is written to help such service workers show other radicals the natural links between their political work and more "militant" activity. It is also written in the hope that committed service workers can become less apologetic and can begin to assert more forcefully the important political insights which they can bring to a general progressive analysis and strategy.

On the other hand, this book is written to help its readers understand the distance they may feel from certain colleagues, supervisors, or teachers. There may be many shared concerns with such people—especially regarding our desire to do "good work." But, whether always understood or not, critical differences emerge around conceptions of whether service work is "political." By this I mean that to see one's daily work, as well as the structural and economic patterns of social policy, as inextricably linked to the larger social, racial, sexual, and economic processes of this society, is to have a political view of the world. Those who do not accept such a perspective—indeed who see it as bringing "bias" to service work and who argue that one cannot bring politics into a technical job without hurting clients and "polarizing" the workplace, usually oppose an explicitly political stance. Such differences can be confusing and upsetting to all concerned.

A central argument of this book is that the world of human services will be healthier when everyone, from all political vantage points, comes to see service work as political at all stages and as worthy of open, acknowledged debate about its goals, systems of delivery and daily tasks. Until we can have such debates the tensions will remain and a good deal of valuable work will remain undone.

PLAN

The first chapter provides an overview of the historical and ideological nature of the perceived split between the development of a political conception of social change and the conception of social services that has characterized left and professional activity in this country. It attempts to lay the groundwork for developing a notion of political practice in the social services which will seek to avoid the choice so long forced on radicals and others—that one must either help people every day *or* be a committed advocate of political change. In chapter 2 we review the early history of services provided by social movements in order to suggest that there is a natural link—often suppressed by radical movements and the social work profession—between commitment to progressive goals and the delivery of services. Chapter 3 suggests that the political developments of the 1960s served to provide a rationale for a more political conception of service work—through the activity of feminists, farm workers, Black Panthers, new leftists, and even poverty program workers and self help proponents.

In chapter 4, we discuss the individual options available to service workers today who wish to create a political practice without the friendly environment of a movement service, but drawing on the lessons of such services. Chapter 5 refers back to the professional development elaborated in chapter 1 and suggests how and why professionalism is a major barrier to an effective political practice. It discusses ways to fight professionalism while retaining a sense of pride and power in one's work. In chapter 6 we discuss the possibilities available for effective political practice within bureaucracies, and how the modern state forces us to a new conception of political analysis and goals for service work. Finally, in chapter 7 we return to our general argument regarding the natural and necessary affinity between providing caring social services and the creation of a viable and desirable political vision which will answer the current challenge of the right and go beyond the limited welfare state models that have developed in Europe.

Although this book attempts to offer no definitive answers to the political questions facing service workers today, it is intended to give us hope and a sense of special purpose. In these times, when the "vision" of a powerful conservative movement can lead only to the demise of any mutual social responsibility and the creation of a nation without social hope, it may be that sensitive, politically self-aware service workers have a critical and unique social role to play. It may be we, and not comrades with complex economic analyses and more narrowly materialistic conceptions of change, who can best articulate a political ideology and appeal to the masses of people who are feeling personally isolated and without permission to acknowledge their basic social needs. Because we share a real sense of their pain we may have a special chance to develop relationships that will suggest positive social connections and the beginning of a more liberating personal life. If we can do this, service workers may be able to create one part of a popular basis for radical change that goes beyond what has been offered by a mean-spirited and hate-filled right *or* by an overly rationalistic and future-oriented left. With stakes like these we cannot help but try.

SERVING THE PEOPLE
SOCIAL SERVICES AND SOCIAL CHANGE

1

THE FORCED CHOICE: MAKING CHANGE VS. HELPING PEOPLE

C<small>HOOSE</small>. Choose between long-range and short-range goals. Choose between revolution or reform. Choose between technical advancements in service delivery and raising popular consciousness about social responsibility. Choose to damn social work completely or to accept its practice uncritically. Choose only to help those in need or to advocate structural changes which would alter the sources of need. Choose between policy and practice. Choose.

The message comes to human service workers from all directions. Professional leaders assume that interest in policy issues should transcend concern for questions of everyday service delivery. Clinically oriented counselors insist that attention to broader issues will limit one's ability to help individuals change. Left theoreticians explain that we must take the long view and avoid the fruitless response to daily crisis. Liberal lobbyists tell us that if we raise the broader implications of new programs we will never get our legislation passed. Conservatives criticize the interventionist state for imposing political values that weaken individual independence. Activists dismiss Band-Aid programs. Often practitioners, social workers, administrators, and direct service workers accept the dichotomy and see themselves excused from thinking about politics, policy, and other issues which are not their concern and are "over their heads." Meanwhile planners, policy analysts, and serious leftists feel little obligation to dirty their hands with the daily business of caring for others.

Sometimes the choice becomes uncomfortable. Service workers see their best efforts consistently defeated by the continuing presence of broader social problems. Professional planners and policy makers find themselves distrusted or even despised by the very clients and workers for whom they design programs. Radicals discover that their vanguard has no rear guard because the masses they would lead see them as impractical and out of touch with reality. All are caught by their categories, by the forced separation of concern for what is political, long range, and large scale from attention to activities which must occur every day, over and over again if people are to care for each other.

There have, however, been efforts to avoid the choice. Often in the past, service work has occured under the aegis of groups whose explicit goals were to make political, large-scale change in the society. Some social workers have, at all levels, tried to define their work as one part of a broader effort to achieve political and social change. More recently, organized attempts have been made by feminists, blacks, and progressives to link their analysis of what is wrong with the system to both large and more individualized change efforts. And today many human service workers are struggling, alone and collectively, to find ways to combine their broader political values and goals with a daily practice that both reflects and furthers those goals.

The results of such efforts suggest that it is both possible and necessary to link a commitment to long-range political goals with efforts to alleviate pain and respond to human needs. Indeed, many have come away from such attempts with a sense that their desires to achieve broader social goals and to provide services stem from the same, not separate, political values, which can only be developed by continuous merging of daily caring with wider analysis. Finally, some have come to argue that good service work depends on a broader political vision—or it degenerates into a charity that only enhances the power of the service provider and the existing social order—and that the best political strategy must be informed by an awareness of everyday needs in order to maintain its legitimacy. In other words, good services must be politicized and good politics must value and push for services as one aspect of a broad social agenda.

To accomplish this, both those who work at all levels in human services and those who seek broad social change must expand their definition of what it means to be political. Often both groups have only defined political questions as involving overt struggles for power among organized groups or concerning issues of basic economic allocation. Questions of the quality of daily life, or the manner of caring for others in the society, have been seen as private, or as questions for technical policy development which was only affected in the most general way by broader "political" struggles among groups in power. Liberals, social democrats, and socialists might generally be more in favor of social programs for economic redistribution or social security, while conservatives and moderates might be more in favor of private resolution of economic and social problems; but specific policies, much less methods of delivery, were not proper subjects for political passion. They were issues for experts to work out based on "evidence" and "fiscal realities."

In calling for services to be seen as more political, I use the term to suggest that everything which reflects and affects the social, economic, and power relations in this society is political, and therefore the appropriate subject for open public debate, disagreement, and struggle. Further, I suggest that all concerned about social welfare issues should view all service activity as explicitly political in both its outcomes and processes—that it can reflect a range of political values and that, therefore, we have a right to push for our service work and all social programs to reflect our political goals.

However, to suggest that all service workers, as well as professional leaders, see daily service delivery and social policies as political is *not* to demand or expect that all share the same political values. Rather, it means that if human services were politicized, at all levels, then conservatives and liberals, social democrats and socialists could have open conflicts over the relative political value of one type of program or the other, of one type of delivery model or the other. Ordinary citizens could consider how such debates affect their lives and could begin to think about social welfare programs as rights over which they had some natural voice, not as technological interventions applied to them or their families when they were judged to be in "need." Hopefully, the politicization of social welfare at all levels would mean an end to the current approach where all daily practice and most policy issues are viewed as technical decisions to be made by experts, rather than as the proper subject for widespread debate and political decision making.

The effects, then, of the choices mentioned above are great and should be understood before we consider specific means of overcoming them. We need to consider the reasons why both service work and most social welfare issues have come to be viewed as outside the parameters of political debate and, indeed, why it is so threatening to many people to suggest that they be politicized. In order to justify efforts to combine overt political goals with both daily practice and policy development we need to look in more detail at the result of separating them. Finally, we should consider how the current political climate, which threatens to destroy even the technical and apolitical conception of social welfare, forces us to reconsider how we present ourselves as service workers and as proponents of social programs. Perhaps then the real political difficulty will be clear. The danger comes not from "politicizing" social welfare and service work but from trying to maintain the illusion that they are not, at all fundamental levels, already political—already the product of complex merging of long-range and short-range goals, of broader social values that are reflected in daily practice.

SOURCES FOR THE TENSION

There are many strong and diverse reasons why service work, and the substance of many social welfare issues, has been viewed as outside the broader realm of political activity. Throughout this century a range of institutional, professional, technological, and ideological developments has contributed to the widely held belief, spelled out most self-consciously by British sociologist Paul Halmos, that

. . . a seemingly simple polarization emerges. *On the one hand,* one can work for the betterment of human relations chiefly politically, that is to say by advocacy, prompting and actively effecting the authoritative allocation of resources. Acting politically means working so as to affect the very scaffolding of the rules whereby society's edifice is erected. *On the other hand,* one can work for the betterment of human relations on an individual level, working as a "personal service professional" or paraprofessional or voluntary worker. Here one's own personality, as well as one's knowledge and skills, are made to serve other single individuals or families so they can review their own ways of conducting themselves in human relationships.[1]

The support for assumptions such as Halmos' come from the left as well as the right, from professional associates, individuals, and client groups. The justifications vary, and are even contradictory, but the implications converge into a powerful consensus: service work and political activity should be viewed as separate; the individual service worker's role is to help individuals or groups or even agencies to achieve desired changes through the application of technical skills which do not reflect explicit political values; except for broad policy mandates, even most specific social welfare policies are best developed by professional experts, not by an open political process.

There are three major forms of justification for such a split conception of politics and social services. The first has multiple roots in the specific history of the development of the American social welfare profession and welfare state programs. The second stems from the way in which social welfare and social service work has been viewed by critics in the field. And the third has roots in the special development of the American left.

The Social Work Profession and the American Welfare State. The way in which the social work profession and the American welfare state developed during the twentieth century has created and reinforced patterns of separation between politics and daily service work. Interestingly enough, at least some of this pattern developed as a reaction to what was viewed by early professionals as an overly moralistic and "political" approach to services in the mid-nineteenth century. Early services, few of which were public, were administered as a direct means of moral uplift or punishment as well as of material relief. Aligned with middle-class religious and Victorian principles, many of the first untrained, and usually unpaid, social workers saw each service encounter as a chance to teach moral lessons and to set a spiritual and material example. Histories of social welfare abound with examples of the socially motivated, cloying condescension and religiosity of much early philanthropic activity.[2]

Although it is easy to criticize these early efforts, it is important not to react in an ahistorical manner. After all, the widespread contemporary cultural norms were moralistic and sentimental, as we shall see when we examine early feminist services in chapter 2. What is important for our purposes is that the shift in cultural expectations and the rise of demands for a more "scientific age" help to explain why early public administrators and social workers attempted to reject old patterns and to develop a more "professional approach."

As we shall see in chapter 5, by the late nineteenth century a number of factors converged to create widespread attempts aimed toward developing a "science" of philanthropy. The increase in immigration and the human costs of rapid industrialization created large-scale urban social needs which had not existed before and which simply could not be met by individual efforts at personal service and salvation. The growth of a comfortable, but not wealthy, middle class meant that there were more individuals, especially women, who were seeking genteel, self-supporting employment and a sense of social usefulness. Finally, the ideological "search for order" began to replace rampant entrepreneurialism as a goal for the upper and middle classes. It led to a call for public regulation and control over irresponsibly wealthy individuals and the whole working class as well as the creation of a new level of management of social behavior through social programs.[3]

In practice, these large-scale changes allowed Charity Organization Societies (COS) to begin to provide a more coherent and organized approach to social welfare at local and state levels. In doing so, the COS leaders presented themselves as systematic, serious purveyors of services who were concerned with responding appropriately—not generously—to social need, but in a manner which was "realistic" about the behavioral needs of the lower classes. They had no wish to be judgmental and utopian like their salvation-oriented predecessors. The COS developed models for practice and statistical record keeping which attempted to control the dangerous classes, eliminating overly generous duplicated services, and creating a thorough approach to families in need. Although we can view their work as intensely political in its intent to preserve social order, the early professionals strove valiantly to present their work as a scientific and systematic response to social conditions, with little room for the politics of salvation or socialism, or even social reform.[4]

As early leaders of social welfare sought to build a system of services—based on private, local, and marginal state funding—they also attempted to build a professional, not a political, identity for themselves. Although many were aligned with progressive calls for good government and public responsibility for the regulation of health and basic services, most adopted this role based upon their professional "expertise" in human affairs, not on overt political allegiances to party or ideology. Although many of the social reformers who developed settlement houses were important exceptions here, most early social work leaders chose to build their professional and institutional identity on professional skills and knowledge, not on ideological commitment, even to social reform politics. Although the professional leaders did often testify for reform legislation, and engage in numerous important studies of social issues, their own class background and the way in which they couched their requests—not as demands for social justice but instead as scientific arguments for efficient social intervention—have led most commentators to see them as "professional altruists" who sought to define the goals and practice of social welfare in a fundamentally apolitical way.[5]

This dominant style of professional identity was firmly established by the 1920s when the settlement house movement declined and Freudianism was ensconced as the scientific methodology underlying most social service activity. In the late nineteenth century COS officials had disparagingly compared the settlement house workers to the "man who found a drunkard lying in the gutter and said to him, 'I can't help you, my friend, but I will sit down in the gutter beside you.' "[6] By the mid-1920s the social work professionals and established social work agencies were saying in an almost unified voice, "We can help you, dear client, if you will just allow us to diagnose your social condition, intervene in a scientific way, and not expect that we will do anything rash about the broader misfortunes which befall you."

A word of caution here. The social work leadership did not perceive itself to be retreating from an important role in the political process through the development of professionalism and a scientific base for social work practice. On the contrary. What was created was one early version of the choice described earlier. Social work administrators and educators saw themselves as playing their appropriate professional role in defining policy priorities and advocating for the development and promotion of public services. While their approach was apolitical in that it was not based on alliances with other groups seeking power nor was it defined in explicitly ideological terms, the social work establishment at least saw themselves as committed and involved in issues of social betterment. It was the content of the services and the activity of the direct service workers which were to become totally removed from the fray. As the 1920s went on the model developed clarity. Distributing relief, or counseling, or other case-work services, was conceived to be an activity totally removed from the arena of politics. Workers were to help others cope with and transcend their social situations, not to interpret their activity in ideological terms or to become involved in direct political activity that would jeopardize their objectivity. The professional leadership would engage in whatever "political" activity was deemed appropriate, based on its professional expertise.[7]

Although elitist, this model still retained the potential for the development of political identity for social workers and for activist leaders to push for the development of social welfare programs as an explicit part of reform politics. Over time, however, the majority of the professional leadership in the field of social work became less concerned with social reform—even that based on their "expertise"—and more concerned either with the progress of the social work profession or with the expansion of funding for social welfare agencies. Although there were always individual leaders who worked to expand the social agendas of the two major parties, as well as a few socialists, most of the professional leadership settled into their role of administering the established system of services. More and more, social work became defined as a technology that was designed to implement policy decisions that were made elsewhere as part of a political process far removed from the activity of most social workers, even social work leaders.[8]

During the 1930s there was revived political awareness among certain sectors of the top leadership and from below in a grassroots social work movement, but this small rebirth of activism mainly served to point out how separated most social workers, professional leaders, and service agencies were from the political fray.[9] As the public and private bureaucracies grew, the apolitical characterization of social welfare programs and the social work profession was reinforced from two different sides. On the one hand, the growth of public programs, from the WPA to federally reimbursed state relief programs, led to increasing bureaucratization and the hiring of social workers, both as administrators and workers, who did not have professional training and identities. The constraints of bureaucratic and civil service rules and the general dependence on public funding kept many public social workers and administrators from developing a political identity separate from their agencies. While there are important exceptions among public bureaucrats who fought publicly for client benefits or expanded services, the major result of the growth of public programs was that social work and service workers were seen, and saw themselves, as part of the system, not as natural advocates for better programs or alternative methods of delivery. Often, as nonprofessionals, they were not even claimed, much less led, by professionals who might have suggested a more political understanding of their work.[10]

In the meantime accredited social workers, with professional training in the psychological and social dimensions of individual problems, remained predominately in the prestigious, less rowdy, and institutionalized private agencies. These agencies, relieved from any burden they had only reluctantly assumed for dealing with the poor, became increasingly psychological in their approach. Private, therapeutically and medically oriented social workers became increasingly identified as the most important part of the profession while public sector workers were seen as second-rate social workers.[11] Thus, neither the growing numbers of civil servants nor the increasingly elitist therapists provided a role likely to suggest political activism, so the image and practice of social work as divorced from social change was further solidified.

The 1940s and 1950s witnessed steady expansion, without fanfare, in public and private social welfare programs and a further entrenchment of the understanding that social work professionals were not actively involved in social action, even of the reform type. The professional literature was overwhelmingly concerned with the image of the profession and with the development of differing technical treatment modalities. The affluence of the postwar period was seen as creating a climate for new innovations but not as justifying a large-scale professional effort to educate the public about opportunities for enhanced social opportunities. Instead, changes were praised exactly because they allowed for more sophisticated administrative inventions, as can be seen in this glowing report in a 1959 publication:

. . . the American social welfare system has attained a scope and complexity which would strain the credibility of bygone humanitarians. New services constantly emerge and existing agencies combine and expand. Aid and succor once available only from kin, friend, or neighbor are now routinely "administered" according to "policies and procedures" as part of a "coordinated plan."[12]

Slowly professionals were accepting roles in the expanding public systems. In 1962, they adopted the full challenge, and opportunity, to bring social work services to the public sector. A select group wrote a report—significantly entitled "Having the Power, We Have the Duty"—which called for expanded public funding of social services and a stronger partnership between public and private agencies. With the 1962 social service amendments, and with the 1965 passage of Medicaid, the American welfare state was extended to provide not only income supports (as it had since the Social Security Act of 1935) but also medical and social assistance to the poor. And, after further amendments in 1967, private social welfare services could easily be purchased by public agencies.[13] So a triumphant, and profitable, marriage of both sections of social work with the emerging welfare state was complete.

However, it was a professional, bureaucratic victory, not a tellingly political one, to be widely celebrated as the achievement of a long-awaited social agenda. Nothing exemplifies this so clearly as the attitude toward social work taken by the Poverty Program. The leaders of these explicitly change-oriented service and organizing programs saw little to help them in social work theory, method, or individual expertise. Indeed, Sargent Shriver, first head of OEO, was opposed to hiring anyone with social work background. Although he was not radical by any means, he did view social programs as part of a broader political strategy, and therefore he opposed social workers because he saw them as apolitical professionals who were not concerned with, or were even aligned against, activist social and community change.[14]

America, therefore, developed a welfare state, but the professionals who managed it and the workers who did its business were not successful veterans of an open fight to win social advancement, to create a more just and humane society. Rather, they most often presented themselves as faceless bureaucrats, dispensing welfare without a social vision, services without a constant demand for more, and as exhibiting more interest in referral networks than passion for justice or compassion for the pain of others around them.

Small wonder that workers, poor people, and social activists have come to feel that the "achievement of the welfare state" was not their victory nor its keepers their natural allies in the struggle for basic social change.

Critics and Supporters of Social Services. It was not only the material development of the welfare state and the "professional preciousness" of social workers that contributed to a stubbornly apolitical conception of social services.[15] In addition, the arguments and ideas of both the critics and the supporters of services led to the same results, although not always as directly.

As many commentators have noted, the dominant populist, individualistic ideology of American capitalism has led to an easy public opposition to almost all forms of public and private social welfare services.[16] This is not the place to go into a full description of this ideology except to note that it still forms the core of conservative values today and serves as an almost unconscious source of the resistance to a public defense of social welfare programs. Not only conservatives, but many others who think of themselves as liberal or even radical still believe that individual dependence on anyone else, much less on the state, is unequivocally bad, that government authorities should "meddle" as little as possible in citizens' private lives, that the social ideal is for people to "take care of themselves" without outside assistance, and that any time such help is offered it is a sign of social failure not success. We cannot underestimate how much what Wilensky and Lebeaux call these "residual" values affected the willingness of proponents of services to engage in public debates.[17] As one contemporary advocate noted:

I want to argue publicly for more public responsibility to help people in need and to help people see that they have a right to expect better benefits for their taxes, but it's not easy. Whenever you say such things in a public debate all sorts of people—not just reactionaries—come back at you with flag-waving statements about undermining individual initiative and devaluing the worth ethic and family responsibilities. It's hard to have a serious discussion about what people need and have a right to.

It makes you feel like all you can do is work behind the scenes to get programs which you never talk about because if you did you could never get them through.

I don't like to feel like this, but it gets discouraging to encounter such attitudes in the 1980s, when times are so bad.[18]

Given such a general social climate, it is understandable that the early social work leaders sought to protect themselves with professional expertise when arguing for their programs and policies. A political approach would have meant that they had to engage in direct ideological debate, armed with ideological arguments and forced to seek allies among groups whose class position would have meant a lot of compromise and very little natural trust. However, hard as it may have been, I argue that the results of retreating from the political arena, of "working behind the scenes," finally served only to reinforce the popular antiwelfare ideology. In the end, because those most concerned with social welfare services were afraid, or too elitist, to engage in open political struggle over basic values and goals, their accomplishments were undervalued and the dominant American ideology was not challenged. Hard as this may have been, we are paying the price now as a militant New Right uses the dominant ideology to oppose all the programs which have been so carefully, yet so quietly, established.

Looking backward again, however, we can see how the very nature of the opposition to early social services made it especially hard for progressive people, who might have been most likely to provide an open political defense of public programs, to do so. Although there was early opposition to child labor laws and to the development of various public service programs from the capitalist class, this opposition was not uniform. Often, instead, very wealthy individuals were the backbone of philanthropic efforts and even of campaigns to provide certain public benefits.[19] Of course, Marxists can argue forcefully that such support only proves the contradictory nature of social welfare programs under capitalism—that they serve the interests of the dominant class to maintain social control while they also can represent advances of workers in wresting greater social security from the capitalists. But the support of such well-known rich people for many early service programs *did* complicate the position of anyone who wished to make the support of social service programs a progressive political issue.[20]

Furthermore, and partially due to this support of services by capitalists and middle-class people, much of the early opposition to public and private welfare programs came from the voices of labor, who often viewed social workers as people who came "peeking in your windows, seeing how you live and what you are; called to see what your wife was doing and knew her business maybe better than you did."[21]

Early labor leaders like Samuel Gompers went beyond this general criticism, some of which did, after all, reflect an opposition to moralism which the new profession itself also tried to overcome. His argument was drawn from a strong sense of working-class independence and involved a more fundamental skepticism regarding the uses of social welfare:

Doing for people what they can and ought to do for themselves is a dangerous experiment. In the last analysis the welfare of the workers depends on their own initiative. Whatever is done under the guise of philanthropy or social morality which in any way lessens initiative is the greatest crime that can be committed against toilers. Let social busybodies and professional "public morals experts" reflect upon the perils they rashly invite under this pretense of social welfare.[22]

Although perhaps expressed more strongly than the opinions of other trade unionists, Gompers' view was dominant in the American Federation of Labor and other labor groups until the trauma of the Depression forced some shift in the acceptance of human services. Up until this time, though, the predominant labor position was that social welfare workers were from the "employing classes" and that their work somehow meant prying into workers' private lives and making them feel worse rather than really helping them.

The implications of Gompers' criticism were double-edged, however. On the one hand, it could be, and was, interpreted as a general criticism of social welfare and social services because they undermined individualism and reflected upper-class judgments of working people. Contemporary progressive supporters of social services could only respond by providing services as unobtrusively as possible. Surely Gompers and his allies would object less to social workers who tried to be objective, scientific, and nonjudgmental than to those who engaged in those inevitably condescending (in Gompers' view) "social reform" efforts. Thus labor's objections could be, and were, used as one more way to discourage service workers from trying to bring any political or social dimensions to their work.[23]

On the other hand, Gompers' criticism might also have been viewed as a class-conscious critique of what can happen when the upper classes offer services to workers. He himself recognized the importance of workers helping "their weaker brothers and sisters."[24] Other unions went further, as we will see later, and developed their own mutual aid services as more desirable alternatives to established programs. These programs flourished, when given union support, and suggest that some unionists recognized that social services could be a desired part of a labor movement strategy for social change, so long as they were not tainted with the presence of noblesse oblige. Indeed, in Britain, it was within exactly such worker services that Richard Titmuss found roots for all that is best in social welfare, because it expressed "the amateur's compassionate answer to the challenge of the economic and psychological insecurities of the economic industrialism and individualism. It expressed also the ordinary man's revulsion from a class-conscious, discriminating charity and a ruthless discriminating poor law."[25]

It would be an exaggeration to argue that labor opposition "caused" the development of an apolitical approach to services—the roots of that were far more complex, as I have suggested. However, the fact that early progressive service workers would have been forced not only to oppose the professional colleagues but also the dominant voices in the labor (and left) movements of the day did inhibit the groups who might have been most likely to push for a more positive political evaluation of service work. Indeed, labor and left opposition to services as well as the power of upper-class people in relation to private social programs may have served to keep people who already saw themselves as political out of the welfare field altogether, especially since the positive potential of worker-provided services was not a well-known alternative.[26]

During the 1930s and 1950s those who would openly push for the expansion of social programs or would argue forcefully for the benefits of services faced a different type of opposition—similar to what we face now. Then, ideological conservatives fought New Deal programs as "socialism" and implied also that those who worked in them or supported them must be socialists.[27] Here it was the more conservative professionals who were immobilized. Many had justified their activity exactly because it was supportive of the dominant order and now they found themselves accused of being socialists. During the 1930s their major response to such accusations was an even further retreat into professionalism, Freudianism, and individual treatment models. During the McCarthy period public and private agencies reacted by policing themselves so as to avoid a dangerous association between socialism and social work.[28] In short, the mainstream of the profession could not openly take up the conservative challenge by responding that yes, it did have a long-range political agenda which might be viewed as socialism but which was based on a set of political values which it was willing to defend. In the fifties such a response would have been literally dangerous and have called for great bravery. Even in the thirties it would have meant claiming an explicit ideology which was, at best, never acknowledged, and probably did not represent the majority of social work professionals.

Instead, what developed as the dominant social work response to conservative political attacks was an argument—which grew in sophistication over the years—that conservatives did not understand the true functions of social welfare services, including both income maintenance and social service programs. The argument, briefly stated, was that modern industrialized society called for new "social inventions" to replace functions which an earlier, more rural society had accomplished through the family and the church.[29] In the thirties, the crisis of the Depression was used to justify the need for such programs—although most social welfare leaders did acknowledge that social security and other social programs were long overdue in the United States, having been a part of modern European society since the beginning of the century. By the fifties and sixties a number of social welfare thinkers—most notably Harold Wilensky and Charles Lebeaux and Alfred Kahn—had developed the argument which served as a full, apolitical response to attacks from the right.[30] Social programs were explicitly *not* political tactics to be used by one political movement and ideology. They were no more harbingers of socialism than they were simplistic defenders of capitalism. Instead, they were natural, good, social developments of a complex industrial society which enhanced the quality of life and lessened some social inequalities, to be sure, but which were as necessary under capitalism as under socialism. So conservatives were wrong in seeing them as "political," instead they were just "institutional" responses to the needs of any modern, industrial society.[31]

Kahn perhaps best represents the dominant opinion, although he draws substantially on the earlier work of Wilensky and Lebeaux and is more sanguine about the benefits of services than some of his professional colleagues. For him, social services are "the social inventions which seek to meet the needs of modern man in his interrelationships and roles, much as technological innovation is a response to the physical requirements of modern living. . . . The majority of social services deal with basic and continuous social processes."[32]

Kahn did, of course, value social services and social welfare programs, but much in the same way as one might value the benefits of technology, not as one savors a political victory: "social services reflect societal achievement, not failure."[33] He argued for universal services which would be seen as "social utilities" for everyone in society: "a universal social services strategy means public social services good enough for every American. This is the irresistable direction for any industrial, urban, democratic society."[34]

To be fair, Kahn, and his predecessors and colleagues, were not arguing with me. For them the critical task was one of convincing conservative and more middle-of-the-road critics that social welfare programs did not represent social failure, because then a healthy society would have no need for social services. These thinkers, most effectively Wilensky and Lebeaux, tried to show that modern industrial life is complex, that it puts new and powerful strains on induviduals and families, and that we can no more turn back from providing them than we can stop providing public sewerage systems. However, in making their argument, such supporters of services reaffirmed the view that services were not political, nor really a proper subject of political passion. The inference came across clearly that, although the unenlightened might fear the socialist implications, services were, instead, a value-free technology that must be used by any effective industrial society, regardless of its ideological approach.

Within the profession this apolitical approach came under attack in recent years, but in ways which are still somewhat problematic from our perspective. During the early 1970s many critics at all levels of the social welfare field began to see the political importance of all types of service programs, in large part because black and poor people were organizing against the negative political effects of such programs. The dominant argument of the period was that the "services approach," most strongly represented by the Poverty Programs, was not political enough, that it did not represent a fundamental enough attack on basic social problems.[35] While this position was important in that it suggested that service workers should have a political perspective and act on it, it was limited in that it, finally, also viewed social services as irrelevant to basic political change—which meant only ecomonic redistribution. For those of us who want to argue that all forms of social supports, not just economic ones, have the capacity to embody broader political goals, the way the issue became framed was unfortunate. It meant that service workers still could not consider their work as having any political value, indeed, it implied that their activity was part of a ruse which covered up the truly serious political, economic issues.

Similarly, Frances Piven and Richard Cloward, in their seminal work, *Regulating the Poor,* provided a critical attack on the rosy notion that services are a simple, beneficial social invention. Here they argued that most, if not all, social welfare programs were weapons used by the ruling elites to pacify, control, and punish the rebellious working classes.[36] Although recently Piven and Cloward have acknowledged that there can be progressive potential for social services, the book served at the time as a necessity corrective to the dominant apolitical view of services.[37] In regard to our debate, however, *Regulating the Poor* offered little hope for service work as a political tactic; indeed it implied that all social workers were inevitably, and unforgivably, agents of a hostile state. It is not surprising that faced with such an option, many workers would choose to think of their work as apolitical; better to be irrelevant or a simple social technician than an enemy of the people.

Left Perspectives. The left movement in the United States has only sporadically been a true mass movement. Left organizations have most often been small, rent by internal debates and characterized by bitter struggles with their closest ideological rivals. At their strongest, left movements never achieved the systematic influence over large aspects of the society enjoyed by many left and labor parties in Europe. Yet there is a left tradition, which exhibits some coherence and exerted considerable influence during key points in this century. Individuals seeking radical change have consistently looked to the left for arguments and leadership, even if they did not join organizations. Left spokesmen (and they were mainly men) have had limited, but significant access to the intellectual media and to the "life of the mind" in America. During critical times leftists, organized and unorganized, have created a powerful presence within labor unions and on the electoral process.[38] In short, when individuals, clients, professionals, or leadership sought, or avoided, connections between social services and social change they were necessarily influenced by the ideas and practices of the American left, disparate and disorganized as that left might have been at any given moment.

Although there is not space here to develop a full discussion of the left's impact on a conception of the political potential for social services, it is possible to briefly review the major ways in which the left has influenced the issue. During the course of the book we will return to many of these arguments in more detail as we attempt to show that, in spite of left skepticism, there is room for services on a left agenda.

Perhaps the most important effect of left analysis on issues of social services stemmed from the American left's consistent ambivalence regarding reform. Here the United States diverged sharply from the British and European experience, where, early in the century, left-identified reform parties were created which pushed for public social reforms, especially for a wide range of social welfare programs. More militant left organizations could still demand more, but a link was established early on associating social welfare programs with a left social agenda. In this country such national reform parties never developed for many reasons: the ethnically divided working class, the strength of the two-party system, and the sheer size of the national electorate, among others. Reform, therefore, meant alliance with bourgeois parties and was highly problematic. In such an environment, reform became not a selective tactic within an array of left options, but a deadly elixir, alluring with its promise of long-sought relevance, but deadly because once partaken American radicals felt powerless to withdraw again to a more critical stance.

Thus, some critics have found the fatal weakness of the American left its willingness to engage in reform activity: "All [major left movements] have fallen into the belief that fighting for immediate interests, for reforms, would naturally lead people to overthrow capitalism."[39] Others have seen its downfall as directly related to the left's failure to engage in reform:

. . . the failure of the socialist movement in the U.S. is rooted in its inability to resolve a basic dilemma of ethics and politics. The socialist movement, by its very statement of goal and its rejection of the capitalist order as a whole could not relate itself to the specific problems of social actions in the here-and-now, give-and-take, political world. . . . It could never resolve but only straddle the basic issue of either accepting capitalist society and seeking to transform it from within, as the labor movement did, or becoming a sworn enemy of that society.[40]

Regardless of the political judgments, the impact of the ambivalence was that few left organizations or individuals devised a sophisticated agenda of social programs which they then demanded of capitalist society, and which then became the object of constant demands for expansion and improvement. In Europe social services were on such a left agenda and became one rallying point around which the left and right could struggle in defining a social vision. In the United States (until the 1930s certainly, and then generally thereafter also), social services and welfare benefit programs were viewed by most leftists as only products of liberal capitalism, representing the interests of one sector of the upper class's need for social integration. The labor movement despised or was indifferent to them. Leftists criticized their patronizing class bias without seeing their social potential. Some insisted that they were mere palliatives which keep people from militancy.[41] Again, it is no wonder that left-thinking individuals who worked in social services would respond to such analysis by merely trying to avoid the negative, condescending, social control aspects of their work, but would come away with little sense that the social services could have a more positive role to play as part of a progressive political strategy.

Similarly, left criticism of the role of the capitalist state allowed social workers little room to view their work as political. Except for the influence of the early Socialist party, populist and anarchist ideas rendered the American left particularly skeptical of the role of capitalist government, even before the growth of the welfare state. Often the state was seen as simply a tool of the ruling class, never to be depended upon for anything progressive. Although the left–New Deal alliances broke this down for a time, by the 1960s it returned as a dominant theme in New Left analysis. Only very recently, under strong British influence and with the work of American radical economists, has the American left begun to reopen the question of what progressive demands can be met by the capitalist state. It is only within the context of such discussions that a case can be made for public social services as one aspect of a socialist program.[42]

Whether it be a populist dichotomy between the rich and the poor or a more Marxist class analysis, the class critique of social welfare systems and professional establishment naturally led to left hostility. Not only labor leaders like Gompers, but also the IWW and other early left organizations recognized and were critical of the noblesse oblige reflected in early social services. As social work schools and their professional students continued to retain an elitist, middle-class identity over the century, they did not redeem themselves with the left. Indeed, if there is any one emotional source for the open hostility toward social services from the left, as opposed to a source of analytical criticism, it is the self-satisfied way in which social work professionals have intentionally kept themselves "above" the people they serve. (I have been in meetings where activists, newly aware of the contradictions of the capitalist state and ready to consider coalitions with social workers, have immediately become hostile because of the superior, professional, class-bound manner exhibited by "sympathetic" leaders of the social work profession.)

The increase in less professional, community-based service workers since the 1960s has changed this image somewhat, but many leftists are still skeptical of the radical potential of a field which remains dominated by individuals from middle-class backgrounds and who consistently seek class allies from among the upper classes rather than the working class. Again, such an analysis has often given social workers few options, except perhaps the hope that as capitalism develops their work will become proletarianized and that they can organize a union.[43]

Finally, there are some fundamental biases within the traditional left approach, which militate against support for social services. From anarchist to socialist, militant to reformer, a touchstone of left ideology has been that collective, communal, group concerns are primary, that too much individual isolation and individual self-assertion are socially irresponsible. While all left visions would create a society where individual needs are met, all would see the means of achieving such a society in collective struggle, in the denial of idiosyncratic individual preferences often falsely induced by capitalism. Such an approach, while not fully discrediting efforts to help individuals— who, after all, need to be strong enough to engage in collective work— does create a natural bias against the personalist, individually oriented, rehabilitative approach central to the method of professional social work.[44]

Recent years have seen some rapprochment between Freudians and Marxists, and it is important not to overemphasize a split between a left analysis and efforts to help individuals.[45] However, it is also important to keep in mind that the personal styles of many who become leftists bolster what is an underlying critique of social services. Leftists want to "make history," in Richard Flack's words. For whatever personal reasons they are usually people with a sense of social mission which goes beyond the everyday "making of a life."[46] This means that even when leftists do break down and become involved with service work they can be unreliable, almost instinctively putting the achievement of a broader social goal ahead of the individual caring act. It is this fundamental tendency that has kept social workers sympathetic to left aims, such as Halmos, still shy about joining the left's intensity with ends to the social service worker's mandatory concern for means. In defense of the everyday necessity, then, such sympathizers have concluded that, for the sake of good service, social work must remain separate from political goal seeking.[47]

While I argue that both the left and the service suffer from such a division, the concern is a serious one which cannot be taken lightly by those who care for the continuation of a legitimate left vision as well as for those who desire a society which genuinely responds to individuals in need.

Some Feminist Considerations. A final influence on the urge to split services from politics may arise from our patriarchal society's need to segregate all that is "male" from all that is "female." Here I am speculating more than usual, but it seems that we cannot ignore the fact that services are a nurturing activity, a sphere which above all others has been seen as women's work. Politics, social change, is aggressive, dangerous, and demanding, "naturally" the work for men.[48] We see the split in the emerging social work profession. Women were the apolitical caretakers whose job was naturally to help people, not to fight for a better society as part of their help. The leaders of the profession, predominantly men, were, if anyone, to be the planners, the agitators, the ones who kept what political activity there was for social work.[49] Similarly, when left movements did become involved in service work, as we shall see later, it was the women who did the caring while the men spoke from the platforms, wrote the position papers, and led the charge. Indeed, even within the early women's movement, women were criticized for continuing to perform service roles rather than take up the political, tough activities which led to their "full emancipation."[50] The point is further complicated by the fact that the recipients of many human services are themselves most often women and children who are, therefore, undervalued in a sexist society.

So I am suggesting that beyond all the ideological, historical, and material reasons for splitting service work off from efforts to achieve broader social change may lie a deeper rationale, which is most effective because it is unspoken. As long as, in feminist terms, the "personal" is separated from the "political" by the dominant society as well as by the left, we may find a fundamental barrier to making links between services and social change. This division, like so many other sex-based separators, will continue to result in frustrations on both sides and the failure of both poles to reach their more fully human potential.[51]

EFFECTS OF THE SPLIT

The entire set of tensions and pressures described above has had profound effects on the way in which this society views its social programs, how service workers perform, how recipients relate to the services available to them, and how left movements operate. Here we will briefly review the most significant of these effects, remembering that the remainder of this book is concerned with a more full elaboration of them as one step in creating an end to the split itself.

Political Context of Social Welfare. Although, as Piven and Cloward have so effectively argued, many social welfare programs did arise out of a ruling class response to social unrest, this dynamic was seldom acknowledged, either by the working class or by the upper class.[52] Therefore, the American welfare state developed without a self-conscious sense of political struggle, leaving the apolitical planners and administrators as well as the workers within the public and private system with a confusion regarding their basic goals and direction. Except for times of economic or social crisis, well-meaning middle-class professionals were left with few guideposts to a system which was simply supposed to "grow in response to need." Whose need? For what?

Neither the professional leadership nor the political process provided clarity in the absence of explicit political demands. So, year after year, social welfare professionals held meetings extolling their progress measured in terms of increasing dollars spent on jobs for social workers, or in grand rhetoric about social advancement. It is not surprising, then, that more time was spent on the development of individual treatment techniques, where there was at least some definition of the problem and the goals, as well as an ability to measure whether anything had been attained beyond the mere delivery of the service.

A more political context—where a range of social programs and social services are specifically demanded by the working class and progressive groups and openly opposed by representatives of capital, for example—could create a more clear-cut constituency for social services. An acceptance of the idea that services of all types are rights which can be demanded from the state could provide all levels of service employees with a different sense of purpose. Even if workers could not provide what was demanded, they could at least know better what was wanted, and engage in political struggle to provide it. Such scenarios did happen during the early Depression relief riots and during the late 1960s and early 1970s. Even for people who did not sympathize with the demands made upon them, at least their work during this time began to make more sense. A conservative Boston welfare worker remembers those days in a way which points to the fundamental confusion present in an apolitical system:

Back when I first started working for the Department it was scary. Everything was crazy. More and more people were applying for welfare. You never knew when twenty women would come in with your client yelling at you and demanding their rights. Even if you weren't sympathetic you quickly learned to provide everything the law allowed and your supervisors supported you just to keep the peace.

They wanted everything, special diets, bedroom furniture, travel expenses, baby-sitting. It was crazy but at least you knew what to do, you knew what people wanted. Now they come in and take what you give them sulkily. Nobody demands much but nobody is happy either and it's never clear what we should do about it. Are we supposed to make them happy? But we can't within the rules. And nobody else seems to care what we do as long as we don't make an error.[53]

As much as professional leaders might talk at their conventions about planning, the lack of a political agenda made the goals of social welfare planning rather pathetic shadows of the dreaded "social planning" so feared by the conservatives. In fact, there have seldom been official, clear, political statements of the programs, politics, rights, and benefits which would reflect an acceptable social welfare goal for any administration. When planning was done it was for midrange issues like expanding or reducing the workforce, changing eligibility requirements, or coordinating services.[54] Without an atmosphere of struggle almost all social welfare professionals, even the most eloquent, seemed unable to dream, to plan, to have expansive visions. Again, we can see the roots of this in the passive notion of services as "responses to need." Without a political process for defining need, social agency directors were on the periphery, always asking for what they thought they would get from the agency, local, state, or federal budget without causing too big a stir. (Or, sometimes the debates were "political," but the whole constituency was not represented, as with the heavy battles over the passage of Medicare.)[55]

In such a context it is not surprising that service agencies are accused of coopting community advocates. Once concerned people begin to work in such an environment their political vision can easily atrophy. Without demands on them they can accrue power over people's lives they do not want. In short, they can lose touch with a community which does not itself know what it wants from an agency.

Ian Gough, a British critic of the welfare state, has seen the form and substance of British social services as emerging from a political process that consistently sharpened the working-class notion of what it wanted from the state and the ruling-class sense of what it was willing to provide:

It is the threat of a powerful working class movement which galvanizes the ruling class to think more cohesively and strategically and to restructure the state apparatus to this end. Those countries which have experienced strong centralized challenges to the power of the capitalist class are those which have developed a unified state apparatus to counter those challenges.[56]

We may conclude then, in Marxist terms, that in America the dialectic has been weak. Because workers, recipients, and the left have not consistently seen social welfare as a primary arena for political struggle, and because the professionals who created the system could not or would not do so, the rules of the whole game were blurred, contradictory, and distorted. Programs developed here because one constituency happened to assert itself. Another program ended because its defining methodology had gone out of style. Except for brief periods, including perhaps our immediate era, the contradictions have not been sharp, the material interests have been fuzzy. Granted, there was surely some broad economic constraint on the whole endeavor, but this seldom was apparent. The overwhelming reality was one of lack of purpose, confused loyalties, and shifting priorities, providing a sense that the very serious game was, for some unknown reason, being played underwater.

Implications for Individual Practice. The political confusion is especially painful in its effects on the individual service provider, whose role has been clearly limited to that of implementing policy, helping individuals, and delivering services (requested or not) to a limited constituency. The literature on social service workers and my own research shows that most workers are profoundly confused as to what they should do. They alternate between guilt for not solving their clients' overwhelming problems to confusion over which of their impossible tasks are most important and back to an enormous sense of isolation from other workers and their clients.[57] Such problems are not new. Quotes from *Social Work Today*, a magazine of the late 1930s, echo the words heard today. People describe the "incredible frustration" of not being able to do impossible jobs. Bertha Reynolds spoke of the guilt and the sense of responsibility and the "Jehovah Complex" which saddled workers in her time.

It would not be fair to ascribe all these difficulties to the separation of service work from a political vision. Surely even with the greatest harmony between one's social vision and one's social work there would be frustration, confusion, and pain over the complexity and tragedy of human life, over our inability to actually help each other. Yet, as I will argue in chapter 4, there is reason to believe that much of the personal sense of frustration and confusion experienced by human service workers is related to their isolation, their inability to perceive their problems in a broader context, and to act on that awareness.

A recent study of elementary school teacher "burnout" in Massachusetts concludes that teachers are not nearly as burned out, tired, or uninterested in their work as they appear to be. Instead, they are angry at the conditions in their schools, angry at unclear social expectations, and angry because they are not able to communicate with anyone about their work. Because this anger cannot be expressed they feel tired and unable to cope. The author of the study concludes: "While it wouldn't solve all of teachers' problems to be able to talk, to understand their situation in more political terms and to act together to improve their situation, it would surely help. It would be better than stress management workshops, at least, because it wouldn't put all the burden on them."[58]

Paul Halmos, in arguing against the dangers of politicizing social work, was concerned whether "an individual can play alternatively a personalized and a political role without exposing himself to a psychological stress which will prevent him from doing either?"[59] I would argue, with Bertha Reynolds, that the greatest danger of psychological stress comes exactly when the service worker does *not* have a broader political perspective: "A Marxist outlook finally relieved us of the 'Jehovah Complex' which had always plagued our profession. It was not we, a handful of social workers, against a sea of human misery. It was humanity itself building a dike and we were helping in our own peculiarly useful way."[60]

Effects on Recipients. As we have seen, many members of the organized working class have not looked favorably on these social services which grew so organically in response to their "need." Without acknowledged, organized efforts to attain the services that workers decided they wanted, social work professionals were forced, at best, to determine what they considered the appropriate response to unspoken need, and, at worst, were free to use services to discipline, control, and "resocialize" working-class people. A sense of rights never developed, so when people did have to use services they were often confused and unable to sort out their reactions. If the service was helpful, should they feel personally grateful to the social worker? Or should they just assume the worker was doing her job? If the service was demeaning or not helpful, should they blame the worker or the agency? And how did they know if they really needed the service anyway?[61]

In short, the apolitical way in which social services have developed has fundamentally confused recipients as well as workers. Had they seen services as a hard-won benefit that was theirs by right, clients might have made different demands on the system of service delivery and had more respect for it. Had services been delivered in a way more truly responsive to the self-conscious demands of working-class people, there might have been more hope for providers and recipients to make alliances. The broader social realities of life under a capitalist system would still have impinged, but recent history suggests that the results might have been different.

Since the mid-sixties some public services have been provided in a more openly political way, in response to organized demands from women, the handicapped, minority communities, and the elderly. All of these services (in Massachusetts, at least) have been characterized by far better relations between workers and recipients and have been fought for together by both groups when cutbacks were proposed. There are still tensions, and it is not clear how such relationships will fare over time, but even such a limited example suggests the opportunity which service workers and social movements have missed by their isolation from each other all these years.

Impact on Left Movements. It is not only workers and recipients who can look at the years of apolitical practice with a sense of lost chances; it should also be committed members of left movements. Indeed, I suggest that one reason most radical movements are currently so weak stems from their long-standing inability to convince masses of people that the left understands and is working to change some of the intense problems associated with daily life in this country. Importantly, it is the women's movement that remains most alive and is the one movement surviving from the 1960s that has given time and thought to the pain people feel in their personal lives. (Critics on the New Right have seen this same approach as the source of its appeal.)[62]

The point here is not to play "what if." Instead we need to recognize that the quality of daily life, the material and emotional needs of the family, the quality of work are all noneconomic issues which draw spirited passions today. Social services can be used to intervene in daily life in a negative, controlling way. They can also be one resource which people may demand to help improve their daily lives. In the past the left has not consistently offered an analysis and a parctice which showed that people have a right to egalitarian, caring, and appropriate services. There may be another chance, like the one missed throughout this century, for the left to define the agenda, to include good social services on its list of demands, and to work with people and committed service workers to see that those services are provided. Ralph Turner has written, "A significant social movement becomes possible when there is a revision in the manner in which a substantial group of people look at some misfortune, seeing it as no longer a misfortune warranting charitable consideration but as a injustice which is intolerable in society."[63]

We may be entering a period when a lonely, sick old age is seen as an injustice not a misfortune, when the lack of mental health services and day care are seen as injustices. If this is true, the left may have just one more chance to take up the debate it has missed, and misled, for so long.

2

HISTORICAL PATTERNS OF OVERLAP: SOCIAL MOVEMENT SERVICES

Despite all the pressures against them, many individuals within activist political groups have attempted to combine their quest for a radically changed world with efforts to care for people every day. Because of the varied forces working against them, these activities were usually undertaken without fanfare, sometimes even apologetically, by activists who feared the disrespect of their more disciplined peers as well as identification with more conservative services. But, somehow, committed feminists did offer services, as did black activists, the unpredictable Wobblies, and Communist Party militants. Many failed to understand the value of their service work. Most were not forthcoming in arguing for its worth as one part of a comprehensive movement strategy. But a few came to view service activity as a means to give depth and breadth to their political vision as well as to provide a base for their efforts, which was not so easily achieved by more angry militant actions.

For our purposes, these efforts to provide overtly political services are richly suggestive. They begin to help us understand the potential congruence between personal political ideology and the desire to help others. Also such early, less self-conscious, attempts to provide politicized services suggest the types of service activity which are most harmonious with political goals. Finally, they also begin to help us understand the inherent dangers that can arise when ideology and services are combined but not taken seriously as part of an overall political strategy.

Before we describe the efforts of social activists to provide services, however, it is important to note an impressive general congruence of historical activity. When we look at the history of the last one hundred years, we see that the same periods that spawned great energy for social movements also witnessed important developments in established social services. The late nineteenth and early twentieth centuries saw the spread of professionally provided social services into many areas of life as well as an unprecedented flurry of social upheaval and uprising. Similarly, the 1930s and the 1960s were periods of much activity and development for social services as well as for social movements. And the periods of decline or quietude (the 1920s, 1950s and the 1970s) were also overlapping.[1]

This could be used by those who see service work as antithetical to political activity only as historical proof that the ruling class developed services as a sop to the socially distressed: in times of social upheaval, those in power offered services, instead of structural change, to the demanding masses. Certainly there is plenty of evidence that services have been used for just such social control purposes.[2] A more charitable view might see the process as unconscious. Middle-class professionals, having no basic disagreement with the system, might naturally have thought of services as a legitimate response to the movement demands—"they want socialism; give them job counseling."

However, whatever the occasional uses of such analysis, there may be another way to look at the convergence. If we see both social activism and social services as outgrowths of similar human desires— the desire for a more just society where people are secure and well cared for—then it is understandable that they should occur together. For multiple reasons, certain epochs have called forth more demands for social justice than other periods. During those times certain people organized to achieve change at the broadest level, others sought to provide better treatment on a day-to-day basis to those around them. The impulses are similar; what Titmuss calls the "gift relationship" echoes what Fried sees as the essence of socialism: "The conviction that each person's obligation to society is a brotherhood

. . . that the individual derives his fulfillment from his solidarity with others . . . regarding the opposition of self and society as a false one."[3]

But we have seen that most people were faced with clear choices, that little merging of tactics for making change was allowed. Only a few individuals were strong enough to insist that their service work should explicitly embody their political values and that politics should foster the expansion of a more radical conception of services. This chapter and the next will briefly review the struggles of such people. I will argue that their work, as reinforced by the historical parallels of activity, supports the contention that social services and social activism are intrinsically linked. Indeed, a major task of this book is to argue that they are *necessarily* linked, that a healthy social vision must be grounded in the types of activity and concerns that create social services. Furthermore, I suggest that social services can, ultimately, only be provided with dignity and success when they are part of an acknowledged, progressive, social agenda.

But I move ahead of myself. The purpose of this chapter is not to make general historical pronouncements but to review specific examples of explicitly radical attempts to provide services and to see what came of them.

THE HISTORY OF MOVEMENT SERVICES: 1880–1960

Any effort to consider the influence of explicitly radical services must be made within a context of understanding the development of radical American social movements of the past century.[4] Despite a real—and often buried—history of militance, much of the activity of social movements in the United States has been defined by what some have called American "exceptionalism" from the intense class antagonisms of Europe and by the all-too-real isolation of most movements from the mainstream of American life, culture, and political activity. Much as most activists—including this author—may not like it, a reality of political life has existed in this country which has been identified by Roberta Ash: "Any radical movement in America must begin with the fact that American central institutions are strong, that they are not (and never have been) likely to break down in the near future".[5]

Therefore, when radicals in the United States have sought to provide services it has been as part of a struggle to create meaningful alternatives to American social patterns, not as part of a full-scale revolutionary movement, nor even as part of a recognized, accepted "left minority." Perhaps had this been the case, as was mentioned in the previous chapter, American activists would have had a different approach to their own service activities, as well as to the social programs of a strong capitalist state. Instead, just as U.S. radicals avoided a full consideration of the welfare state, so too were they able to pay scant attention to the important role which service activity played in their own development. Yet by examining those services radicals did provide, we can see some of the common successes and problems that characterize their efforts and draw some conclusions which help suggest what it means when less well-organized radicals attempt to combine service activity with broader social change goals.

Woman Movement Services. From the mid-1800s until the passage of women's suffrage in 1919, the Woman Movement (as it was called) incorporated many organizations which worked for many aspects of women's rights.[6] More than other movements of the time, these organizations were involved in providing services. Especially during the 1890s and early 1900s, many organizations provided services to women in the name of feminism and even more women's service organizations were staffed by feminist women. A guide to Massachusetts women's organizations in the 1890s, for example, lists more than forty-five women's service organizations, among them the Women's Educational and Industrial Union, the Female Guardian Society, the Ladies' Benevolent Society, the Penitent Female's Refuge, the New England Female Reform Society, the Association for the Relief of Aged Indigent Women, the Boston Society for the Care of Girls, the Female Home Society, and many more.[7] The bias of such organizations is evident in the names and membership, but they maintained strong links with the larger, more general feminist movement. Their founders are among the most well-known Massachusetts feminists. The tracts describing their programs reflect feminist thinking, although often of the more conservative side of the movement.[8]

The most important service-providing organization was also the most broadly based feminist organization, the Women's Christian Temperance Union (WCTU). Under the leadership of Frances Willard, who died in 1898, it led the fight for temperance as well as other women's causes: "Let us not be disconcerted, but stand by that blessed trinity of movements, Prohibition, Women's Liberation, and Labor's uplift."[9]

The WCTU is important not because it was typical (in fact, its volume and range of concerns supported far more services than any other organization) but because it reflected the fullest extension of the Woman Movement into services. Since most other organizations tried to do service on a smaller scale, we might see the WCTU's work as the model, as what many feminists would have wanted to do had they had the resources. A brief look at the WCTU services, then, will allow some generalizations about the nature of services provided by the Woman Movement itself.

Under Willard's "Do Everything" policy, the WCTU set up a national "Department of Mercy," which helped to promote as well as oversee many social services for women. In various cities "Women's Missions" were established as day centers for women. Such centers served as places for women to meet, get assistance for their problems, find jobs, and other service assistance, in addition to serving as recreation centers. Other departments oversaw the establishment of nursery schools and family aides. Each local chapter had, at least, someone responsible for services referral and support. The bigger cities had centers with larger-scale services. Many of the WCTU's members were well-to-do and most were unemployed, so their services were usually funded by donations and volunteer time.[10]

The rationale for service came largely out of the analysis of women's problems and their relation to alcohol and the family. Willard and others in the organization saw men's drinking as destructive to the family and to women, who were dependent on men for support. Besides trying to abolish the drinking and sale of alcohol, the organization also tried to strengthen women, through services and education, to help them care for themselves and their families if they could not stop their husbands or fathers from drinking. There was only limited focus on women's drinking, the assumption being that women were usually the innocent victims of masculine Demon Rum. Women's task was to use their superior virtue in fighting for prohibition while caring better for themselves and their families.

There were always factions within the organization who argued against services and the more radical approach to social reform advocated by Willard. But during her lifetime, she managed to keep the focus away from simple, single-issue temperance agitation. Willard argued: "A one-sided movement makes one-sided advocates. . . . An all round movement can only be carried forward by all round advocates; a scientific age requires the study of every subject in its correlatives."[11] Only after her death did the movement stop providing services and advocating broad reform; by 1910, it was narrowly focused on temperance. The result was the Twentieth Amendment and the decline of the movement.

Other feminist service providers were the Women's Trade Union League (WTUL) and the National Consumers League (NCL).[12] The WTUL was a coalition of middle-class feminists and women trade unionists whose primary purpose was to build women's trade unionism and better the conditions of working-class women. The WTUL's service bureau was crucial in organizing strike relief during most major strikes of the period and also in establishing permanent relief agencies in working-class areas. It conducted adult education classes for women workers in English, homemaking, and union skills. It also served as a referral and advocacy source for women workers.

The NCL was primarily a lobbying organization, but did provide basic referral and advocacy services out of each chapter office.[13] It ran consumer education classes and offered strike and emergency relief. Less organizationally involved with direct service provision, nevertheless the NCL was a vocal proponent of public services. Often the NCL was instrumental in getting badly needed public services into an area, at a time when other activist groups were unconcerned about public programs.

The political implications of such feminist services are complex. Surely the early feminists established important links between efforts to change women's daily lives and to transform the broader society. They also understood and did not denigrate the fact that many women might be drawn to feminism through participation in services. Important ideological connections were made between the problems of a male-dominated society and the troubles women faced in their own lives. Services were explicitly proposed as one way to offer direct assistance and to develop the political consciousness of women. But somehow the model lacks appeal—especially, perhaps, because such feminist "caring" was so little different from the institutionalized services being offered by the established agencies at the time. Except for the all-women environment, little was different; most services were for poor women provided by richer ones; most had a moralistic religious flavor; and most stressed the need for feminine purity.

On the whole, however, there was a basic lack of reciprocity. Most feminist services seemed to define the needs of the receivers by the perceptions and the needs of the movement providers. Furthermore, it is not clear how services helped feminists reach broad social change goals because they so often emphasized the weakness and the dependence of women, not their strengths (except women's rather ineffable "purity"). Services also did not help the movement overcome its limiting class attitudes; in fact, the needs seen by service providers often seemed to reinforce such attitudes. And few organizations had a large working-class following, despite the amount of services delivered to poorer women.

It was not until another women's movement would arise in the 1960s that a new breed of feminists would pick up and learn from these lessons. They then would create the most expansive model yet for combining service delivery and political activity.

Black Movement Services. Like the Woman Movement, the black movement for social justice has a long history of providing services.[14] Black abolitionists were involved in the establishment of services for runaways and ex-slaves. With the onset of the massive Southern black migration to northern cities at the turn of the century, more organized movement and more systematic services developed. But these two developments hinged on an internal paradox: from the movement's start black activists had both the energy to provide services and ideological arguments *against* providing such services.

The elements of this paradox could be seen in radical resistance to Booker T. Washington's slogans of self help and racial solidarity. Many of the black leaders of the early movement were consciously in opposition to Washington and the most radical of these formed the Niagra Movement, which in turn sometimes worked with white "racial reformers" in the National Association for the Advancement of Colored People (NAACP). The Niagra Movement's and the NAACP's program was protest, with an explicitly *non*-self help orientation. At the same time other leaders helped to form the National Urban League (NUL) in an attempt to use economic improvement, education, and social services as a means to better status for blacks.[15] Often more radical black leaders criticized the NUL as too timid and too close to Booker T. Washington in outlook. Blacks in the Urban League vigorously countered that, on the contrary, it was not abandoning struggle, rather the League did not trust the white system enough to lobby for power within it until blacks held a stronger position in the society.

Despite such limitations and internal disputes over strategy, there was usually cooperation between the two groups.[16] Over time an agreed-upon division of labor evolved, with the Urban League's primary task that of raising money and "seeking employment opportunities for blacks and providing social services to ease the process of urbanization."[17]

By 1918 the Urban League had spread beyond its New York City origins to other northern cities and continued to grow slowly. Its primary thrust was to open up economic opportunities for black people in any city, as well as to push for better housing. Its social services department was not originally intended to provide direct services, but rather to consult with community agencies around special concerns of blacks and to help place and train black social workers. However, as Weiss points out, although "the Urban League had envisioned itself as a 'promotion and coordinating agency rather than a direct service agency,' the needs of urban blacks brought it actively into direct service as well."[18] Services ranged from counseling to recreation programs to day care to adult education. These were conducted primarily by black social workers, although there was a conscious "integrated" policy that included whites. The method of delivering services was very much within the standard social services norms of the day, with an emphasis on "quality" services.

The continuing historical split between integrationist and nationalist forces can be seen in black movement services.[19] The Urban League provided services toward a goal of integration, in order to convince black and white people that they were equal and that blacks deserved equal opportunities. Instead, the Universal Negro Improvement Association (under Marcus Garvey), in the 1920s, and the Black Muslims (under Elijah Mohammed), since the 1930s, provided services for blacks with the goal of strengthening their cultural and national identity and capacity, with little or no desire to promote integration, or "equality."

The Universal Negro Improvement Association (UNIA) launched numerous service projects "to reclaim the fallen of the race, to administer to and assist the needy."[20] Confused and often mismanaged, the organization still signaled the first success of the black movement in rallying the black masses. Branches operated out of most major cities, especially in the Northeast. Although evidence is sketchy about the actual services offered, each charter stated the purpose "to promote and practice the principles of benevolence."[21] There were "Black Cross nurses" who worked with the needy as well as employment training and education programs.

The Black Muslims followed where the Garveyites left off in attracting working-class black people to an all-encompassing organization. Founded in 1930 in Detroit, the Muslims aimed for total black self-sufficiency.[22] Similar to other less organized nationalist groups, they attempted to build total group solidarity through black businesses and services. The Muslims ran schools, clinics, support services, recreation services—the whole gamut of alternative services. Little is known by outsiders of the nature and scope of these services except that they are, in accordance with Muslim beliefs, hierarchical, disciplined, and oriented around building black consciousness and independence.[23]

Given the wide diversity in the black movement and the vastly different reasons for which services have been provided, it is difficult to know how to assess political implications. We can see that in response to the incredible economic and social difficulties created by American racism, blacks of all political persuasions have seen the need for services as naturally tied to their broader social goals. The middle-class integrationists saw services as both a means to reach the majority of black people as well as important short-run strategy for improving the lot of all blacks. While the services they provided must be seen as contributing to the improvement in living conditions for black people, they were not successful in attracting large numbers to the movement. Perhaps the very split deemed necessary by activists—that between activists and service providers—contributed to this. The Urban League, despite its "movement" identification, seems to have actually done little *except* provide services. It did not seriously couple services with activism or even a strongly stated activist ideology, thereby finding people to serve but none to lead. The NAACP, on the other hand, abandoned all day-to-day services altogether so its pressure groups and legal agitation took place at a level far removed from most people's lives, except as actions and agitation received media attention.

The nationalists, however, seem to have been able to use services to help convince members that they truly cared about the masses of black people. Both the UNIA and the Muslims commanded large followings of people who used their services and believed their ideology. While this is probably most connected to the inherent appeal of the content of the ideology, we could argue that the importance of services to both groups helped to convince people of the sincerity of that content.

Despite their problems, both branches of the black movement, like the early feminists, created examples that could be followed later. The assumption that black liberation meant changing society *and* changing individual lives was established. The legitimacy of mutual aid was granted. When compared to the more ambivalent attitudes of white left and labor organizations, blacks were far advanced in creating a movement and a political philosophy that strove to serve the twin goals of changing society and of meeting people's daily needs.

Labor Movement Services. As we have seen, there has been no natural link between services and the labor movement.[24] Unlike black people and women, most American trade unionists have not seen their membership, or potential membership, as "needy." Thus services have largely been provided unconsciously with little formal recognition either that they were being provided or that workers needed them.

There were exceptions to this, however. Although workmen's associations in the United States were neither so numerous nor so successful as they were in Europe, a few did emerge as politically important.[25] The Workmen's Circle (primarily a German Jewish workmen's association), for example, has lasted from 1892 until the present and offers a prime example of this type of labor movement service organization. The delightful historian of the Workmen's Circle, Maximillian Hurwitz, explained why it was not founded by union leaders:

These leaders, as we know, were splendid men. Many of them, to their everlasting glory be it said, had sacrificed promising careers in order to throw in their lot with the labouring men and together with them to build a fairer and juster world, a world based on the freedom, equality, and the brotherhood of men. But so busy were they with dreaming of the future that they forgot the needs of the present.[26]

Hurwitz goes on to show, however, that "what the intellectual dreamer is apt to overlook, the workingman, who is closer to everyday life, cannot, dare not, ignore." The Circle was thus established to provide: (a) mutual aid in sickness and death, (b) furtherment of education, and (c) the establishment of cooperative enterprises. Membership was limited to "only progressive workers and intellectuals—those, that is, who were opposed to the capitalist system," but not just to those of any one left group.[27]

By 1920, the Circle was becoming known as the "Red Cross of Labor" because it provided, in addition to life and burial insurance, aid to influenza victims, the unemployed and stricken, as well as numerous camps and workers' schools. By 1925 there were 84,000 members. Its interests broadened from insurance, health, and relief into full social services. "From its inception," notes Hurwitz, "the Workmen's Circle extended various kinds of social services to its members. Whenever a member was in need of aid or advice in an emergency, he came to the General Office," but there was no formal "Service Department" until 1925. Hurwitz sees the reason for being slow to formalize social services in the "universal prejudice in radical labor circles of anything that savored of charity."[28]

No stranger to internal difficulties, during the late twenties and early thirties the Workmen's Circle underwent severe struggles between socialists and communists. Although the organization continued as a service organization, it lost all traces of being an activist movement organization by the late thirties. Still, no other American labor movement organization ever came close to the Workmen's Circle in the self-conscious provision of services as a political strategy for building worker solidarity.

The more radical parts of the early labor movement did provide some services, however. The International Workers of the World (IWW) shared the common labor apprisal of traditional services, but still opposed Gompers' limited notions of self-reliance. The Wobblies provided numerous services to their members and seemed to accept, in principle, the importance of "mutual aid." Their idea of "One Big Union" meant that the Union would "make us strong" and, therefore, naturally help people care for each other.

During the celebrated Lawrence (Massachusetts) and Paterson (New Jersey) strikes, the IWW organized, with aid from middle-class supporters, efficient relief committees which not only provided food, clothing, and emergency relief, but which also helped strikers with more general problems in the community. As strikes ended, resolutions were made to continue the committees, but somehow organizers moved on, interests waned, and no one was quite sure whose responsibility it was anyway. Even this ragtag effort was criticized by some Wobblies, as no less than "an elaborate system of begging" rather than a "fighting strategy" to take over the industries.[29]

Yet the Wobblies were most successful when they were able to combine talk and planning for the destruction of capitalism with more concrete tasks, as in the western timber fields. James Weinstein describes the situation:

The seasonal nature of the work provided the opportunity for providing periods of contact with the workers during the winter, when they gathered in the cities with little to do. Most cities in the Northwest provided no social services. In their place, IWW halls became social centers, served as libraries and in other ways serviced the temporarily unemployed lumber workers. It was away from the place of work, in these various headquarters, that scores of workers heard and discussed IWW lecturers . . . and came to absorb the union's revolutionary ideal.[30]

The Wobblies' decline brought an end to any service efforts, all of which had been crisis-related and loosely structured. The IWW did, however, establish the tradition that industrial unionism is broadly defined unionism, that the labor movement is not incompatible with mutual aid.

With the Depression and the birth of the Congress of Industrial Organizations (CIO), industrial unionism and the labor movement regained vitality. The CIO organizing drives and strikes provided new opportunity for unions to think about services. Also, the development of a CIO union of social workers forged a new link between labor and social work which led to a rethinking of earlier negative attitudes on the part of labor. Both of these events led to an upsurge in the 1930s and 1940s of labor movement attempts to provide services for members.

During the famous CIO sit-down strikes, the unions reached new levels of formal involvement with services. Witness the Flint (Michigan) strike, as Stone and Kahn reported:

The Welfare Committee stood out for efficient and autonomous operation. Before the strike was a week old, a welfare office to meet the needs of union families, either directly or indirectly unemployed because of the strike, was organized under Walter Reed, local auto worker. This committee not only helped people with applications but also worked with the County Relief Office to help certify applicants, even occasionally going on home calls to check eligibility.[31]

The union committee also represented members in adjustment of grievances with the Welfare Department, eventually broadening their services to represent WPA and direct relief clients. In general, the whole process was accomplished efficiently and in a manner beneficial to the unemployed unionists. Stone and Kahn saw the entire event as significant and went on to note:

In organizing aid for the men on strike the union had shown amazing ingenuity and skill. Men and women who had practically no organizational experience learned through the pressure of events to discharge functions which are usually entrusted to those with professional training and experience. It furnishes one more example of workers' ability to adjust themselves rapidly to new situations and to organize for their own welfare.[32]

While the United Auto Workers (UAW) was in the forefront of developing organized services which often continued beyond a strike, other unions were slowly becoming involved. More and more unions set up welfare departments. In New York City, a Union Health Council was set up which involved most city unions in mutual health planning. The United Electrical Workers and the Furriers became interested in getting counseling training for the staff, another indication that some unions at least were beginning to acknowledge the day-to-day "service work" that had always been the work of the organization.[33]

Much of this newborn interest in services can be attributed to the energy of the newest member of the labor movement, radical social workers. Reflected in numerous articles in the journal of this nascent movement, *Social Work Today*, the new unionists brought with them a new definition of social work and a new sense of the proper relationship between social services and the labor movement. Bertha Reynolds, a leader of the union effort, argued most powerfully that "in the history of unionization in social work it is impossible to separate the two notions of protecting one's own condition as a worker and safeguarding the right to treat clients ethically."[34] In almost every major city during the late 1930s and early 1940s some effort was made by unionized social workers to work with local labor councils or at least friendly unions. Unionism, and social workers, had come a long way from Samuel Gompers when no less than John L. Lewis could write in *Social Work Today* that "organized labor, growing up out of the daily needs of the people, is the most powerful ally of those professionally committed to a humane public welfare and social services program."[35]

The efforts of unionized social workers to provide services to fellow workers finally jelled with labor movement interests when World War II erupted. Labor's last reservation against receiving "charity" could be withdrawn now that the services could be delivered not to the "needy" but "to aid the war effort." The largest service endeavor was sponsored by the National Maritime Union using Bertha Reynolds and other unionized social workers.

The NMU's Personal Service Department (later expanded and known as the United Seamen's Service) operated directly out of the union hiring halls. The main job was proper distribution of union relief funds, putting the men and their families in touch with other agencies, being an advocate for them with the service system and, often, unofficially counseling and supplying other support services. All the service workers were unionists who still had to become adjusted to providing services with a whole new set of parameteres. Reynolds noted some of the changed circumstances from traditional services provision:

We had to give up the idea that we, offering benefits, decide who shall have them . . . we must serve all or none with all the resources we had . . . we had never before served clients who had an organized means of expressing the "self-determination of the client" about which we theorized . . . the sense that each applicant had of belonging (without having to face acceptance or regulation at the door) eliminated much of the resistance which social agencies expect to find.[36]

Finally, we see how a changed view of client need affected not only the merchant seamen but also the service provider:

Serving an employed group of urgently needed men carries different implications from ministering to people more or less detached, by sickness or other trouble, from contributing to society. . . . It was not a remedial service for disability and failure so much as one geared to responsibility . . . what could a man do, not just for himself but in realtion to others in a common task?[37]

Similar efforts occurred on a smaller scale all over the country during the war, largely growing out of offers by social work unions to the newer unions. In Detroit, for example, the UAW expanded its already large health programs into a social service referral and counseling service. In Cleveland, a similar referral service was set up in the city's Union Council building. The Social Service Employees Union in Chicago (SSEU) worked with the House and Electrical Workers Union to provide referral services as well as teaching basic counseling skills to union officers. And in Willow Run, Michigan, the union supported a family counseling service in a union housing project.[38]

With the end of the war almost all such efforts were halted. The labor movement returned to a cautiously circumscribed trade unionism with a corresponding narrowing of vision as to what was "appropriate." The purging of most leftists meant that many of the people most involved in supporting and providing these service efforts were no longer available. Finally, the services, which had always been linked to the "demands of the War" and never to a more general rationale for service, ended with it.

By the 1950s and the merger of the AFL and CIO, almost all unions, with the notable exceptions of the UAW, the Mineworkers, and both garment worker unions, had opted to participate in United Fund local services rather than supply their own. Here was another paradox: while this represented a kind of advance over the old union position of total isolation from any services, it was also a definite retreat from the earlier situation where many had seen themselves as best able to oversee or provide services to their own members.[39]

The political implications of labor movement services were generally favorable. When unions tried to be militant representatives of workers, services proved useful. But services remained an unacknowledged stepchild, probably due as much to time pressures of union organizing as to ideological contradictions connected to their purpose. Even during the war, when they were provided on a fairly large scale, most unionists, except the social workers, could not really investigate and assert their political meaning.[40]

For the first time, however, we begin to see some conscious rethinking of the nature of service delivery. Because within unions the reasons for services were more differentiated from standard "welfare" services, and because the service providers were trained as traditional social workers and, therefore, more aware of the comparisons, movement services started to become something *qualitatively* different from regularly provided services. And it is from this advance, especially as articulated by Bertha Reynolds, that we can today find useful implications in our attempts to create more truly egalitarian and radical human services.

Left Movement Services. As we have seen, the American left has always been strong on ideology and weak in structure. Lacking immediate hope of gaining power, it has spent much of its energies arguing over the reasons for this condition and the proper strategies for changing it. Movement organizations themselves have usually been small, loosely structured, and ideologically torn.[41] This may explain why those left services that have been provided have all been either for committed party members, as part of coalition efforts with other groups, or offered by leftists working in unions.

However, many leftists were consciously and openly involved in providing services. Left supporters of all the other movements were heavily involved in service efforts. It was almost as if services were naturally suggested by a personal socialist ideology but are too difficult to defend as a "pure strategy." So, again and again we see leftists, in their periodicals and autobiographies, apologizing for all the service work they, seemingly unaccountably, found themselves doing.

Early nineteenth-century socialists were involved in setting up many of the immigrant aid societies that sought to help specialized ethnic groups adjust to their new lives. The German socialists were especially active in this area.[42] Save for certain Wobblies and individual socialists in the settlement houses, however, the early leftists were usually too concerned with either electoral politics (as Socialist party members), or sectarian splits (as members of a variety of communist groups), to have much time for services. Members of the more radical organizations labeled any service efforts "reform," arguing always for "direct action" to "crush the system."

Things changed briefly as the 1930s found millions of people out of work with only a fast-sinking private system and marginal public welfare programs to care for them. All major cities had "armies" of unemployed in whose interests each left group tried to speak. The Communists, the Trotskyists, and the independent leftists organized groups of the unemployed. None of these groups was directly a "party organization," but their leadership and financial support came almost exclusively from the left.[43] In addition to organizing demonstrations and mass marches, the Unemployed councils and leagues responded to the immedate needs of the unemployed by setting up service centers in neighborhoods. These centers were staffed primarily by other unemployed workers and provided a wide range of "direct" services, from assistance with finding housing and food, to giving counsel to a mother whose husband had left, to lobbying with Relief over needed materials. Out of these centers, block organizations were developed to help fight evictions, often moving someone back into an apartment immediately after an eviction.[44]

In many cities members of councils fought for better relief facilities or visited with men who were unemployed to get them health or other welfare benefits. A liberal commentator described the work of these councils with praise, noting that they were effective in increasing relief benefits: "In the cities I visited the economic status of the unemployed workers, amount of relief, etc. was directly proportional to the strength of the unemployed council."[45]

The Communist party was very involved with planning the strategy for the Unemployed councils. Party newspapers of the time often berated members for "failure to merge . . . with the masses through solid personal contact." A major goal of the neighborhood communities was seen as ". . . exposing the inadequacy of the charity relief given out . . . and for (committee) control over the income and expenditures of the charity organizers and control in the preparation and distribution of food, clothing, soup, etc. by representatives of the unemployed."[46]

In retrospect we can judge the councils as active and relatively successful; Charles Boyers surmised that "until the advent of the CIO, it [the Unemployed council] was probably the most vital and necessary of all American left organizations."[47] Even if larger goals could not always be met, this acceptance of the political value in direct service was an important legacy for future leftists.

As the Unemployed councils faded the CIO began to grow and many leftists shifted from one group to the other. Although some leftists in the CIO opposed any attempt at service work, most supported the efforts.[48] The social work unions were heavily influenced by the Communists and much of the energy toward reaching out to other unions came from leftist social workers. Again, however, little of this was done in the name of the left. Partly this state of affairs seemed due to "Popular Front" line, but even more it seems to result from the curious uncomfortableness that leftists felt about taking up what they denegratingly referred to as "reforms" in the name of the movement.

Similarly, Communists did not consider their own International Workers Order (IWO) to be an aspect of direct political activity. Established to meet the needs of party members for insurance, adult education, recreation, and other services, the order provided a useful service to party members. But those who worked in it—often the wives of loyal Party functionaries—were not credited with important party work. Although party members remember the IWO as an important part of their lives, the organization once again missed the chance to explicitly link its service work with its political ideology or the development of its membership.[49]

In general, then, socialist activists were unable to directly and publicly involve themselves in services, except around the most explicit case of human need, the Depression. Had they been able to take more credit for the services they *did* provide people, then leftists might have better withstood the attacks of McCarthyism. As Roberta Ash recognized, the more the Communists, for instance, "worked among rank and file, the more loyal the rank and file remained to Communism in the years of the fifties."[50] Services could have been a way to maintain that involvement and the legitimacy of other ideological elements of its program, but the chance was missed because "serious" political activity lay elsewhere in less concrete tasks.

HISTORICAL LESSONS

The early history of movement services presented here offers a contradictory brief for merging politics and service activity. Flawed and limited as these efforts were, they are highly suggestive, both as cautions against simplistic linkages and as reinforcements for continued attempts.

On the negative side is the scant attention most movement leaders paid to the service activity of so many of their adherents. Except for Frances Willard and certain union leaders, like Walter Reuther, few seemed willing to consider the broader implications of the work, much less to seek ways to expand it or demand its public equivalent. As we suggested in chapter 1, most of the movements under consideration were not strong advocates for public human services nor for political strategies which demanded improved services as major tactics. Thus, these movements managed to participate in burying the political and social implications of much of their own service work.

Perhaps some of this failure stems from the limited thinking that most activists brought to the services provided by their movements. Almost all the services were for the relief of situations which activists (especially those *not* engaged in the work) might assume would not exist should their political goals be achieved: female and black equality was to end dependence on men or whites, just as revolution or labor's power would free workers from want. Radicals could thereby excuse themselves from thinking comprehensively about the range of human needs and the best ways to respond systematically to them in a humane society. They avoided (for economic reasons, also) services that addressed more basic human misfortunes—retardation, physical handicaps—that would have suggested an analysis of life problems as unresponsive to direct political restructuring. Thus, by only looking at one level of pain, many radicals were little pressured to develop long-range plans and demands for how to provide for human needs, which appeared to them as mere products of oppression, not as basic human conditions. As we have seen, most radical groups were also too ambivalent about the capitalist state either to make strong demands for large-scale public programs or to effectively criticize those programs that did develop. In short, the low level of social thinking which characterized most movements calling for basic change seriously limited the political context within which they could offer services.

Movement leaders also tended to neglect even the minimal support required for the maintenance of their service efforts. At key points during the strikes, support services would be forgotten. The discovery of another "priority for struggle" could mean the immedate abandonment of an Unemployed council's service work. Frances Willard was constantly opposed in her program to seeing services as a valued part of "The Work." Such disregard obviously undercut the service work of activists, but even more important, it showed that movements were not seriously concerned with quality of service. For our case here, such a limitation is critical. We cannot argue that services only reflect the ideology and embody the goals of progressive politics; we must also be able to show that such services in themselves can be better than apolitical, professionalized endeavors. Otherwise, as Paul Halmos feared, we risk the unacceptable situation where our "ardent concern for the welfare of mankind is accompanied by a protestation of indifference about the individual man."[51] Except for the WCTU's services, the Workmen's Circle, and certain left services in the unions, we must admit that the early historical support for our position is not overwhelmingly strong.

Finally, movement services were viewed by leadership as primarily a means to broader ends, as ways to recruit people, to build trust, or to strengthen adherents for the really important struggles. While such an approach does not, in itself, discredit the services provided, it falls far short of broader political hopes for service work. To be truly progressive, caring services must be valued for themselves also, for the help which they offer people in need, and for the models of social relations which they embody. Except for the work of Bertha Reynolds, few of the movements or individual activists considered here seemed to appreciate the fundamental meaning of what they were doing when they were combining their politics with service work.

On the other hand, however, there are several important positive lessons to be drawn from all this activity. The most important is simply the recognition that the desire to provide services seems virtually impossible for many activists to suppress. No matter what their professed attitudes toward services, people found irresistible the urge to help people survive against the very forces the movement wants to change. Radicals gave in; they helped others. As we have seen, some people engaged in helping more consciously than others, or with more or less identification with the recipients of service. No matter, the fact remains that large numbers of members of every major movement in this century made the effort. The women's and black movements found this helping action more compatible because of their unobstructed view that women and blacks were victims of an unjust society. The labor movement and particularly the left found activity of this sort more in contradiction with their premise that workers, or the working class, were the unrecognized (but objective, nonetheless) source of all power in the society, certainly not its victims. But they too provided services in specific situations because certain material needs simply could not be ignored.

Second, the history gives us hope that services can creatively reflect and advance a progressive analysis. Sometimes service work can even point to weaknesses in political ideology. Both feminist and integrationist services, for example, pointed up contradictions in their respective ideologies. Both groups could more easily provide services because of the premise that women and blacks were victims of a discriminatory society, but the actual delivery of services only threw into relief the striking lack of a fully alternative vision of society in either movement. If women and black people were to lead society to a new order, services that only mirrored those already provided offered no great assistance. When we compare them to the self-conscious attempt to create harmony between radical ideology and human service practice, embodied by Bertha Reynolds and the United Seamen's Service, we can see how helpful services can be in developing and embodying a grounded, and yet visionary, political ideology.

The history also suggests that services may help outsiders become more responsive to progressive ideas and may also allow activists to better understand the implications of their politics. Autobiographies of activists often mention that the first encounter with a movement was through some form of service—an English language class for immigrants or a soup kitchen. Such encounters can build trust in the movement and help, as the Workmen's Circle was especially aware, bring politics to the real concerns of people. Movement members, too, are often strengthened in their commitment to political goals by the work of service delivery. Early feminists began to better understand the meaning of feminism as they worked with women in the slums and workhouses of New York. Communists became more aware of why workers didn't immediately rise up and throw off their chains. Over and over again, from Frances Willard to Bertha Reynolds, activists commented on the many ways in which their political vision expanded, and became less rigid, as they participated in helping people cope with the strains imposed by daily life in America.

Such a mixed record might seem less a base for political service work, were it not for the upsurge in movement service activity in the 1960s and early 1970s. Suddenly the old mixture of services and politics was revived with new energy and a more self-conscious awareness of the linkages between personal and political concerns. When we examine this more modern period we see a repeat of much of the most hopeful aspects of movement service activity as well as challenges to some of the more negative sides. Taken together, the older and more recent historical records offer a strong justification for our hopes of a healthy merger of political and service goals.

3

LEGACY OF THE 1960s: JOINING THE PERSONAL AND THE POLITICAL

T HE 1960s were a time of intensity, of changing perceptions and re-evaluations. They witnessed the alteration of many expectations, from the disappointments of a privileged elite to the new hopes of rural and urban black people. The civil rights movement, the black power movement, the student movement, the antiwar and women's movements relfected deep shifts in the society as well as themselves wrought profound changes. Almost twenty years later, the 1960s have come to symbolize social turmoil, excitement, involvement, and expectations that people can make changes which affect their lives and the society at large.

For our purposes, the period offers some especially useful models. From a variety of directions, new rationales and new examples emerged that suggest the power of combining social service activity with an explicitly political analysis and strategy. Although largely unaware of the experiences reviewed in the last chapter, many activists engaged in work that assumed and strengthened the links between human service activity and the goals of progressive social movements. In the Poverty Program and the Black Panther Party, in the women's movement and the United Farm Workers Union, dedicated "change agents" laid the groundwork for a politicization of social welfare that had not occurred in seventy years of professional "development." It is exactly this experience, added on to that of earlier activists, which serves as a base for suggesting that human service workers can bring greater political content to their work and that social welfare programs can be embraced less ambivalently as part of a progressive agenda.

SOURCES FOR THE SHIFT

The best way to understand the new model is by examining the specific examples of how services came to be conceived more politically. But there are some general characteristics, if not causes, of the shift which need to be acknowledged briefly.

Unlike the diverse political groups examined in the last chapter, many sixties activists self-consciously shared critical ideological and strategic approaches to similar goals. Indeed, by the end of the decade many white leftists, feminists, and black activists would see their efforts as part of one "movement."[1]

Ideologically, all three groupings shared, at least initially, an approach which was encapsulated in Lawrence Ferlinghetti's phrase "a rebirth of wonder."[2] Each was relatively free of restrictive prior movement models. The older black movement was strongest, but dispersed. The labor and left movements were politically moribund and the women's movement seemed like a forgotten antiquated joke. So when people, especially young people, in the early sixties felt a need to seek fundamental change, they had few appealing organizations to join. There was only a weak or nonexistent radical orthodoxy to define proper or "correct" behavior for those who wanted change. While this may have created confusion, and much "reinventing of the wheel," it also seems to have allowed for a shared sense of power and hope.

A range of intellectual sources did, however, provide some common traits and values which served to link the movements of the sixties. Most were consciously committed to "going beyond," if not rejecting, the movements of the past.[3] To varying degrees, all stressed activity and decentralized democracy over formal organizations and hierarchical discipline. There was a general emphasis upon the psychological aspects of oppression and liberation. Personal life was seen as *necessarily* embodying political values. The new worlds desired by each involved more than simple structural shifts in the economic or social order. The calls for a new understanding of human potentiality were common. A basic value or posture shared by all was social experimentation; each agreed upon the fact that the old rules lacked humane usefulness and only varied and continuous practice could hope to establish better ones.[4]

Hence, if there was any description which fit all three movements of the sixties (especially in their early periods) it was "eclectic," perhaps richly so. The highest value in all groups was upon intellectual and practical experimentation. Newsletters, position papers, public speeches, and even militant tactics all claimed ignorance of any old models; all called for the creation of new forms of analysis and activity. From feminists to black power advocates, all shared this free-wheeling approach until the intensity of the late sixties began to create a need for more certainty. By then, the violence and the growing awareness of the strength of the opposition began to make activists more cautious, more prone to in-fighting over the correct position and less willing to risk. Except for the women's movement and the newly strong United Farm Workers Union, the 1970s signaled the beginning of retreat. But the seeds of a new vision were planted and often grew in the decentralized, "laid-back" seventies, even as more overt political militance declined.

Yet what remains most striking, even in their later phases, is the logical compatibility of these movements with the idea of services. All shared a need to define their political goals broadly in terms of changing a wide range of the experience of human lives, not just a small part. Civil rights activists and black nationalists, student militants and feminists were explicitly unhappy with their particular education, their housing, even their social relations, in ways which earlier movements were not. They saw the oppressive aspects of racism, sexism, or "the system" as far more than economic inequality or narrow discrimination. Such ideologies were much more likely to see a place for serrvices as one way to meet that wider range of human needs.

Further, all of the movements served to reinforce each other in this wide-ranging ideology. Since it was not just one group, but many who argued, in essence, that "the personal is political," the idea took hold in all movements. Far more than in any earlier movements, the style of one's life became part of one's politics. Blacks pondered the meaning of African dress and of having sexual relations with whites. New Leftists worried about wearing ties and about the process of participatory democracy. Women questioned their footwear, style of relationships, personal mannerisms, and physical fitness. Certainly, such introspection and strict personal standards were hard for everyone and sometimes reached extremes—Peggy Hopper, for example, would finally cry out, "I don't want to change my life-style, I want to change my life."[5] But for movement adherents, such pressures forced consideration of exactly those individual issues most related to services.

Structurally, the lack of tightly controlled movement organizations was important. It meant that service efforts could arise out of immediately felt needs without having to gain "approval" from slower moving bureaucracies. The degree of individual initiative possible in all the movements also allowed room for what seems one natural response to an awareness of injustice—the immediate helping hand.

There were some obvious drawbacks to services delivery, too. One was the sheer intensity of so much movement activity. The fever pitch, the spirit of Armageddon, real or imagined, did not easily foster the study, calmer atmosphere required for most services. Another was the absolute chronological youth of many movement members, which meant that most were missing some skills needed for certain services. The lack of organized structure, while allowing some freedom, also increased instability. Projects might easily fail and disappear overnight. Collectives might disband and regroup. Service delivery, by contrast, requires a certain stability. It is not spontaneous work nor can it long sustain itself in a totally crisis atmosphere. Also, the very desire to be a movement, to be "radical," to be moving to broader goals sometimes worked against the less militant tactic of service delivery.

On the whole, however, these problems seem to relate to the difficulty of delivering services, not to the logic of providing them at all. Each of the movements of the 1960s had at least as many reasons for providing services as it had against doing so. When they also encountered a broader social milieu which was itself expanding the notion of services through a "War on Poverty" and an expanded notion of "self help," the basis was laid for a new congruence of political vision and service activity.

As we briefly examine the experience of these newly politicized services we find significant support for the argument that service work may be viewed as political work. Further, we begin to realize how the activists of the 1960s may help their present-day counterparts to see the personal and ideological benefits of combining a concern for everyday needs with broader efforts to change the whole society. The economic and social climate of the 1980s may not often support the development of autonomous, alternative, political services. However, as today's activists struggle to combine politics with service work in more traditional settings they may draw both lessons and hope from the activity of a generation of radicals who were perhaps less contained by economic and social "realities."

STUDENTS IN THE COMMUNITY

In 1963, the Students for a Democratic Society (SDS) decided to institute an Economic Research and Action Project (ERAP) which would place young leftists into poor communities to organize around community issues, especially around unemployment and welfare. For the next two and a half years ERAP functioned as the community organizing branch of the New Left—a way, as Tom Hayden said, for SDS

to be *relevant*, . . . to leave all the academic crap behind it . . . to break out of intellectuality into contact with the grass roots of the nation. ERAP, by getting off the campuses and into the ghettos would get to the grass roots, get to where the *people* are. There we can listen to them, learn from them, organize them.[6]

Whatever the romanticism and arrogance involved in such a concept, the ERAP projects gave young New Leftists an opportunity to link their developing political analysis with the actual needs of nonstudents, with the victims of American society. In doing this they served as a model to many who did not actually participate in the projects. And the nature of their work forced them, somewhat unwittingly, into the middle of the debate over the relationship between services and political activity that is central to the concerns here.

In many ways the young radicals reacted to the issue just as nervously as had their predecessors in the Communist Party and the CIO. They posed a distinction between political work and "social work" and vowed to use services only for "political" ends. Although, finally, ERAP organizers were to continue the old split between politics and services, they at least were aware of the tensions, as evidenced in one workshop listed in the schedule for the first ERAP training conference:

The Role and Function of Service: How can service be used to mobilize the community around economic, political, and social issues? Should "service" in fact be used this way, as a means of establishing a base in the community? What kinds of service programs do we consider of the greatest importance?[7]

At its height, during the summer of 1964, ERAP involved about two hundred young leftists, working in nine communities, and its progress was followed by many more back on campuses. The general goals of each project were vague, but all tried to "transform America" by organizing the people to develop "indigenous leadership" that would make radical demands and build a militant movement to change the local power structure. The movement was to be interracial and to challenge the economic and social system through democratic and cooperative local organizations. Initially the focus was Jobs or Income Now (JOIN), which led to leafleting and organizing at unemployment offices and at local welfare offices. Although this activity often led to individual advocacy, such activity was not the goal. Rather, it was to "radicalize" the unemployed and welfare recipients by community meetings, demonstrations, and confrontations at local agencies. Considerable time was spent working with individuals needing personal assistance in all offices, however. At first this activity was done with little seriousness, but over time the importance of services came to be more accepted. This report from the Chicago chapter indicates the common base of activity:

Office work always means talking to people who come into the office. . . . It is usual for at least one person to come into the office with a problem or a complaint against the compensation office that he wants JOIN to take action on. Sometimes we can help—it took two phone calls to get groceries and the promise of a check from public aid for a man who was unemployed, ineligible for compensation, out of money and food—a man with a wife and small child. Other times it is necessary to phone or visit the compensation office . . . Clearly we need to be attacking the roots of the problem—the red tape and inefficient operations of the unemployment offices—and not merely helping people cope with them. But, just as clearly, we are too small at present to attempt anything so ambitious.[8]

So the project, especially its women staff, continued doing service work, even training themselves to do it better. But, always, project leadership would discuss this activity—which amounted to much of the collective work—with criticism about its "social work conception" and with cautions about the dangers of "not seeing any other functions than helping people with their problems."[9]

Other ERAP projects developed a model which involved organizing around a wider set of community issues than only jobs or income. These settings—most notably Cleveland, Ohio, and Chester, Pennsylvania—took up issues of health and safety, sanitation, day care, or housing. Dubbed the GROIN approach—Garbage Removal or Income Now—the strategy led to a more flexible integration of services into political work, as seen in Cleveland ERAP reports:

The service function . . . is necessary both to give people immediate tasks and to provide the potential for short-run successes which might serve to bind the group together. Unlike Chicago JOIN, service is not seen as something we will provide as a means of recruitment as much as means of immediately involving at least a core group. . . . In terms of service, the need for help with technical problems was pointed out. Also various types of programs to aid in the economy and to break down the welfare routine were seen as desirable, e.g., service planning, day care for kids.[10]

Yet here too such service work was still differentiated from "action programs" which would "relate to the fundamental problems of people on welfare." All reports continually raised questions as to "the 'radicalness' of the issue, i.e., how directly does it seem to confront the other problems of the society?" Indeed, some project staff began to apologize for their service work—especially if it involved women: "Am I too wound up with these women?—damn it, they *need* a day care center—I don't think it would harm them to get one."[11]

ERAP, then, finally chose the approach toward services which had characterized older left organizations, but it did so after an explicit struggle. Services were always provided, by all projects, and usually by the women staffers. But they were, in the end, not valued because no argument was raised for their intrinsic political worthiness against criticisms like those made by the Trenton project:

In short we feel that although the service program could, if it had been more efficiently organized, have become more productive, any time spent on service could have been spent in some other way. A service program does not help alleviate or solve basic problems. It does not lead the people toward political organization.[12]

What makes the ERAP experience interesting to us, and a harbinger of things to come, is that it engaged in open debate about the role of services, a debate which would be resolved differently by other movements of the 1960s. Later activists would not only continue the practice of providing services but would also, in practice, come to accept the minority position expressed best at the time by Aronowitz:

[We need people] . . . skilled in service operations such as dealing with relief, unemployment compensation, and other agencies. This is more than a "come on" for more serious organization. . . . The poor just are not going to put their fortunes in the hands of people who can't help solve immediate needs while battling for long-term solutions.[13]

THE POVERTY PROGRAMS

At the same time that New Leftists were trying to radicalize the poor through ERAP, the government was launching its own organizing project, the Poverty Program. Rapidly, in the cities where both existed—especially in Chicago, Newark, and Baltimore—a critical dynamic developed. ERAP projects staked out positions to the left of the government-sponsored attack on poverty, and thereby pushed themselves to develop a clearer analysis of what a "radical" counterproposal would be. On the other hand, the presence of outside radical organizers in the community forced Poverty Program staff to define their programs more politically than they might have without such left opposition. (A similar pressure happened on a national level also.) The net result was that the dynamic of left-liberal tension around the activity of Poverty Programs served to create a sense that community services were a desirable good, even a right, to be struggled over in a political—not a professional—process.

However, it was not only pressures from the left which politicized the local Poverty Programs. Such an approach was inherent in the nature of the Economic Opportunity Act which authorized the Community Action Programs (CAPS) in 1964. The programs unintentionally served to bring social services forever out of the realm of charity and into the arena of socially desirable goods which poor people (and, by extension, others) could demand and acquire in order to improve their quality of life.

Officials in the CAP agencies were usually liberals who initially worked hard to develop "innovative" programs, which often meant little more than "non-social work" services.[14] New types of staff were used, even those without college training. Efforts were made to have the CAPs serve as the catalyst for more comprehensive community planning. Most agencies developed a loud criticism of traditional welfare bureaucracies.[15]

Although services were the major part of the actual activity and costs, they were not seen by programs themselves as their prime emphasis. As if a liberal mirror to ERAP, CAP administrators argued that even though services were the most important activity, it was exactly their combination with community political activity that distingusihed them in the eyes of the community. Also, the fact that services were often delivered by local residents, and that other poor people were involved in the agencies that delivered the services, was seen as affecting the ways in which the services were regarded.[16]

Program staff interviewed in many studies stressed the "special nature" of their services. There was a general feeling that CAPs were effective as long as services were delivered by agencies with an activist outlook toward community activity. Indeed, the reason that poverty programs were viewed as declining during the Nixon years was that, even though expenditures for specific services actually increased, the community change orientation that had motivated programs was no longer present and highly visible.

Contemporary left and liberal critics alike opposed the Poverty Program position that services could be a means of achieving greater social change. ERAP organizers saw them as frauds and creating an illusion of radical change where none was possible. Professional critics saw CAPs as only "another variety of the standard social service agency," or as taking an approach which "reinforces and perpetuates the dependent status of the poor."[17] In other words, liberals and radicals joined in a criticism of the "service approach," both arguing the old refrain that if social change were to take place it obviously would have nothing to do with the delivery of social services.

On the other hand, we might see the Poverty Programs as important exactly because they explicitly brought services in as one tactic in a political (albeit, reformist) effort to change communities. They created services which were, undoubtedly, sought by their clients, and which later became rallying cries for local organizing that spilled over into a range of other issues.[18] In short, the Poverty Programs helped to establish a popular demand for social services as a right and suggested that services did not have to be the professionalized, hierarchical entities which good social work practice suggested.

It can even be argued that the Community Action Programs affected what people wanted from government agencies as well as changing their sense of what they could get. Both services themselves and "quality" services came to be seen as reasonable public demands. Charles L. Schultz et al. expressed this feeling in *Setting National Priorities: The 1973 Budget:*

In the 1960s . . . people began asking more of the federal government. First a variety of new programs were enacted, many of them designed to provide direct services to people. . . . Poverty was to be reduced not just by giving people cash income but by providing medical care, preschool programs, job training, legal services, compensating education and opportunities for community action. . . . Along with new activities came the gradual development of new and far more ambitious standards. . . . Administrators of education programs were asked, not just to show that money was spent for teachers' salaries or books or equipment but for evidence that children were learning more.[19]

While the Community Action Programs were clearly off the mark in asserting, or implying, that service programs could end poverty, they were crucial in promoting the general idea that good services are an important and necessary part of a decent standard of living, and thus are an appropriate focus of political debate. Sar Levitan and Robert Taggart have argued with some persuasiveness that "the benefits of the Great Society programs were more than the sum of their parts and more than their impact on immediate participants and beneficiaries."[20] The contribution of the idea that services are desirable, even a human "right," is the unintended benefit of the Community Action Programs, one which makes it more possible to argue that services, and service work, are naturally part of a progressive agenda.

BLACK MILITANCY

As we have seen, black movements have always understood that their constituency needed services but they did not always see the content and style of those services to be an issue. During the 1960s black militants in the South and the North began to be more explicit about the political meaning of services. Indeed, another reason for the Poverty Program's more political use of services may well have been its ties to black community traditions.

In the early 1960s the Student Non-Violent Coordinating Committee (SNCC) built services such as tutoring, child care, adult education, and advocacy into its rural Southern organizing. Although service work was seen as critical to building trust in SNCC, it often played the same role that such activity did in ERAP. Services were delivered by women, were seen as useful for organizing but not valuable in themselves, and were also criticized for their lack of "radical potential."[21] Indeed, even though violent attacks on SNCC—and SNCC services—allowed black militants to see their services as part of their "threat" to a racist society, they seldom went beyond a defensive strategy to evaluate how their services were, in themselves, a source of ideological and political power.

When the Black Panthers emerged in the Northern cities they made no such omission. From their roots in Oakland in 1966, they always viewed service issues as key demands in regard to white society and their own service activity as central to their political effectiveness. In doing so they suggested to a whole group of young black and white activists that such services as child care, health care, and nutrition programs were not simply safe activities or a means to recruitment, but that instead they were critical elements in a revolutionary strategy.

The original "Ten Point Program" of the Black Panther Party stressed the importance of services to the black community. Four of the ten points explicitly demanded things which are usually considered "social welfare": housing, education, clothing, and jobs. In addition, the Panthers began to attempt to follow their own admonition to "Heal the sick. Rescue the dying. Practice revolutionary humanitarianism."[22] Early programs stressed breakfasts for children as well as protection from the police, clothing exchanges as well as armed self-defense. Later they even supported health clinics, schools, and legal aid offices.

In attempting to self-consciously integrate services with a militant revolutionary strategy the Panthers came under criticism from many external commentators as well as internal critics of providing services, all of whom were answered in the inimitable style of the party newspaper:

> To the half-baked, the narrow-minded, and the avaricious fool this may seem as though the Black Panther Party endorses reform action and is no longer interested in Revolution. What these people fail to see is that by developing a blueprint that the people can use to solve their problems and by showing that it can be done our Party takes another step forward on the path of successful revolution.[23]

With comments like these, the Black Panther Party became the first radical group to loudly proclaim the importance of service activity to "building a revolution." Despite all the problems of the group, this approach was significant because it brought to explicit political culmination the long-held approach to services taken by black movements. For the first time movement leaders, such as Huey Newton, were willing to defend services:

> The original vision of the Party was to develop a lifeline to the people by serving their needs and by defending them against their oppressors, who come to the community in many forms, from armed police to capitalist exploiters. We knew that this strategy would raise the consciousness of the people and also give us their support. Then if we were driven underground by the oppressors the people would support us and defend us. . . .
>
> Many times people say our Ten Point program is reformist, but they ignore the fact that revolution is a process. We left the program open-ended so that it would develop and people could identify with it. We do not offer it to them as a conclusion; we offered it as a vehicle to move to a higher level.[24]

This rationale can also be seen in the goals for the Panther Community Information Centers, which housed such activities as breakfast programs, liberation schools, community newspapers, legal and welfare aid, and clothing exchanges:

The purpose of opening the Community Information Centers is that we realize that in order to be close to the people in the community it is necessary that we locate ourselves among the masses. The Centers will be able to reach more people and bring the Black Panther Party closer to the people.

The Community Centers are set up primarily as a base in the community for the people to identify with, work with and claim as their own.[25]

Thus the Black Panther Party provided services for four reasons. First, services would draw support, as represented by the aphorism, "Feed the youth and the youth will feed the revolution." Second, services could show the seriousness of the party and expose the false friends of the people, such as "the vacillating Black bourgeoisie" and the "civil rights organizations with their middle-class orientations" who do nothing to feed the children.[26] Third, services could point out the inadequacies of existing structures:

We understand that the capitalists in America will never provide adequate medical service, so the Black Panther Party has moved to establish another community program in which all oppressed people can be involved.[27]

And finally, the act of serving the people could help to create a new spirit and view of the world among black people:

The Black Panther Party has shouldered the task of educating the people to the realism of the oppressive nature of this decadent system. . . . We must first create an intelligent society containing people relating to altruism instead of relating to materialistic ideas perpetuated by the pig power structure.[28]

The Black Panthers also attempted to suggest that the nature of revolutionary service delivery was different, that it was more equal because it was not condescendingly professional, but was offered "from brother to brother." In this they echoed some of the earlier claims of Bertha Reynolds, regarding the powerful new dynamic of services provided by union members for union members.

Of course, the Black Panther Party could not attain its revolutionary goals. It was broken by police harassment and violence, by internal dissension, and by its own revolutionary romanticism. But for a brief period it inspired huge numbers of American progressives to believe that a militant, black organization could be aware of class, make alliances with white leftists, and build a base in the community, using services as a major tactic. For all the rhetoric and exaggeration, for all the ways in which the Panthers were used by trendy whites, they did widen our definition of what was the nature of militance in America and suggest that one way the victims of this society could mobilize themselves would be through "revolutionary humanitarianism"—a goal which is a far cry from social work practice.

REVIVING UNION SERVICES

As the Panthers developed their services they began to embody a model which assumed new, more equal relationships between Panther service workers and community recipients of services. Such dynamics were not part of the original goals of "revolutionary work."

For the United Farm Workers Union (UFW)—and even more so for the women's movement, as we will see later—services were always provided both as a means of building the movement and as a goal through which farm workers would be able to envision the elements of a better society. Thus, with the UFW we move closer toward a necessary aspect of the understanding of radical practice: an awareness that not only the *goals* of services but also the *process* by which services are delivered must embody political values.[29]

The United Farm Workers Union was one of the few parts of organized labor to retain a sense of a labor "movement" during the 1960s. It saw itself as a movement for social justice for all farm workers, especially Chicano farm workers, not just as a narrow trade union. Although, by the 1980s, success as a union may have led to some loss of "movement mentality," during the 1960s and until the late 1970s it was clearly defined as much by the broader political goals of its leadership as it was by more restricted trade union principles.

One of the major political goals of the UFW has always been that the union should serve its members and potential members in a wider range of ways than that of traditional trade unions. Cesar Chavez, the intellectual and political leader of the movement, came from a background with the Community Service Organization, an Alinsky-style group which stressed block organizing and community services. His own sense of farm worker needs led him to argue, from the beginning, that if poor, non-English-speaking migrant workers were to be organized they needed more than just the standard work-place benefits. As the UFW services director put it in 1977,

Cesar has always seen the movement as needing to be concerned with all of people's problems, not just job problems. He knows too that farm workers do not work all the time, that if the union is going to mean something to them, to be something that they will fight for, it has to touch them in all parts of their lives. It has to show that it understands, and can help all of their problems.[30]

The result of this approach was that UFW offices always did a combination of traditional organizing, union business, and service work. Whenever possible a union worker was labeled a service worker with the special job of helping people with employment, welfare, housing, or medical problems. The first clinic was opened in 1970. In 1975 a special program was set up, the Martin Luther King Fund, to provide social services for union members. Sometimes, due to outside pressures, the service programs would dwindle down to small disorganized adjuncts to organizing. But they would always be revived and strengthened again after a time, because, typically, it would come to Chavez's or others' attention that services had been "shoved back into a corner" and that this was not acceptable.[31]

UFW services involve a range of activities including assistance with unemployment insurance and food stamps, medical problems, immigration problems, SSI or disability, translation problems, housing problems, and family problems. Much of this assistance involves helping people fill out forms, going with them to bureaucratic offices, explaining procedures to them, arranging for special benefits. There is also a good deal of what might be called "counseling"—listening supportively to a range of difficulties and helping people sort out priorities.

Such services are obviously provided both to help farm workers with their problems and to build the union by allowing it to be relevant to people's lives. In these purposes they are similar to other political services we have examined here. But in addition, the UFW has tried to be quite self-conscious about the way in which it offered services and to try to link its broader goals with the *process* of service delivery. So, although at times UFW services fall back and appear like any other functional activity, at other key points training sessions are held and the leaders come around to inspire service workers with a broader understanding of the special nature of work.

One such session took place in the summer of 1976 and the comments made there begin to suggest some important aspects of how the UFW viewed "radical practice" in social services.

The keystone to a healthy UFW services program, as seen by the leadership, is not just the "content" of the service delivered, but the nature of the relationship developed between the union and the person needing service by the process, explained by the service director: "It is the union's job to understand the problems of farm workers and to *help* them solve them. . . . We must involve people in the process and stress preventive educational services."[32] While many seem to agree with those goals, Chavez and others state them more forcefully, and it is worthwhile to examine their positions in some detail. As Cesar Chavez stated it:

> We came to the Union with some definite ideas—if the worker didn't carry his own weight, forget it. That is what built the Union. . . .
>
> The Union was built with house meetings and the Service Center. It's like the Church in China—they gave out rice to Christians. The minute there was no rice, there were no Christians. The goal is to help people help themselves. You don't do it because you're a nice guy—you can't expect people to appreciate your help. We're there to help our brothers, not to be appreciated. It is good to be in love with people, but it is also good not to let them use you. . . .
>
> It's bad to say "I helped you, now you help me." But to say "I helped you, now you help me *to help others*" is good. . . .
>
> People cannot be organized unless they feel responsible. Without participation, you develop a Welfare Department. . . .

Delores Huerta, another original UFW organizer, put it this way:

> For years the Service Center was shoved back in the corner. It is now time to go back to the original purpose and make the MLK Campesino Centers powerful organizing tools. Use services to organize people to help themselves and others versus the agency mentality of helping people and keeping them dependent, having set office hours, referring them on to someone else, etc. . . .
>
> Part of the "agency mentality" is paternalism. Get rid of it! You need to sort out your feelings. Watch out for feeling superior to "those illiterate farm workers" or for prejudice in reverse, feeling sorry for "the poor little farm workers." I know what I'm talking about. I used to be a schoolteacher and had to sort through my own feelings. Feeling superior or feeling sorry for the farm workers are both wrong attitudes. We have to establish equality—service for service. We're neither more nor less than farm workers, we are equal.
>
> The only way we can make changes though, is to put everything on an

equal basis—service for service. I help you, you help the Union to help someone else. Expect help for the Union in return for services. And don't overservice. Get an exchange for every little service. If you don't, you'll find you're doing a lot of little things with no return and you'll lose time that could be spent organizing. . . .

This is the opportunity we are all being given and it is our responsibility to involve others; if we don't we are depriving them of a better way of life.

And Richard Chavez, Cesar's brother and long-time organizer, shared the challenge:

You're all familiar with poverty programs and you've seen people go into the welfare department, head down, hat in hand. They feel degraded because they feel they're asking for charity. We don't want people to come to us that way. We want them to come to us for services with pride because they will be giving something back to the Union in return for what they get. Service for service.[33]

Such an approach to services is a far cry from the standard "professional practice." It requires that service workers and service recipient be comrades with an equal, if complementary, relationship. The idea of exchanging a "service for a service" was hard to maintain, even within the UFW. It was a goal which union workers often forgot, or denied because it was difficult to put in practice. But, as a basic premise for a service work which is more political, which will be seen by the broader population as something desirable, it is highly suggestive.

In defining the root principles of "political practice" at both individual and societal levels, activists have a long way to go, as we will discuss shortly. However, a key ingredient to a new conception of social welfare may be our ability to replace old ideals of altruism—which necessarily imply a certain inequality of need—with enlightened versions of reciprocity—which suggest that all people share basic needs and that we owe it to each other to provide mutual aid. There are complicated moral issues embodied in such an approach which have not been fully dealt with by UFW leaders—or by most radical service workers. But what is exciting is that, out of a desire for a stronger union and a better base for social change, UFW officials have linked service work to the forefront of their political ideology and practice—a long way from Samuel Gompers, and a model for us all.

FEMINIST SERVICES

Although UFW services offer fuller models regarding how to conceptualize politicized services, their practice in carrying out such activity leaves something to be desired. In daily operation it seems fair to say that the Campesino Centers functioned more like normal multiservice centers than like the innovative service "exchanges" put forward by UFW leadership. It would take time and constant support to develop such an approach and external pressures left the union with little of either. However, using its own, similar, evolving model, the women's movement in the 1960s and 1970s was able to develop a notion of feminist services that both paralleled and went beyond the ideas of the UFW. Thus, in many ways women have been able to put in practice many of the service goals envisioned by Cesar Chavez, Delores Huerta, and Richard Chavez.[34]

Since its origins in the mid-1960s, all branches of the women's movement were, to some extent, concerned with service and health related issues. NOW's original platform included demands for abortion rights; most early women's liberation groups included activity around rape, abortion, women's health, and mental health. Indeed, a major form of early feminist organizing, the consciousness-raising group, could almost itself be considered a form of service.[35]

As we have seen, earlier feminist also found service work highly compatible with their vision of feminist organizing. But in the 1960s the expanse of issues defined as "feminist" had changed so that the services developed by contemporary women's groups were a far cry from the predominantly staid, hierarchical services provided by our feminist predecessors. Modern feminists began work with women who had been raped and battered, usually in groups where the helpers shared similar experiences. Feminist abortion counseling and health clinics—the first feminist services of this new generation—involved different notions of sharing and support, not just "good medical care" for women by women, as was the earlier model. Feminists tried to create nonsexist child care. Women's centers and women's schools all over the country developed to sponsor support groups around a wide range of issues: lesbianism, fatness, parenting, disabilities, alcoholism, career needs, aging—to name just a few. In short, for the past fifteen years, to be a feminist has meant to engage in service work as

much as it has meant to do other things normally defined as political—to stage demonstrations, to organize general-purpose political
groups, to become involved in multilevel political activity.

There have been continued criticisms from within women's circles
regarding this "overreliance" on services as the dominant feminist
tactic. More middle-of-the-road feminists in NOW as well as some
socialist feminists have raised political criticisms of service work since
the days when such women were skeptical of the political potential
of consciousness-raising groups. More recently, criticisms have sur-
faced as service groups have become more professionalized, more
involved with the financial and procedural constraints imposed by
public bureaucracies. Many of these criticisms involve a call for balance between services and other activity; a few recall older assumptions that politics and services are different and cannot be mixed
without either a loss of political vision or the provision of inadequate
services.[36]

But few criticisms of feminist services have been as thoroughgoing
as the standard left disinterest in service work. In general most
branches of feminists have understood the links between service activity and feminist ideology, even if they have not chosen to provide
services themselves.

Nor should it be surprising that, no matter what the internal and
external criticisms, feminists consistently find themselves providing
services. If there has been any constant in the wide-ranging issues
raised by contemporary feminist theory, it has been the notion that
"the personal is political," that, for women, especially, one's daily life,
one's body, one's personal relationships are major arenas where sexual
politics are played out. Drawing on current observations and building on the work of earlier feminists, today's activists have begun to
understand how women's physical, sexual, and emotional needs have
been misdefined by male doctors and psychologists. Women's roles
in the family have come to be understood as serving patriarchical
economic and social needs. As feminist historians and theoreticians
have expanded their work since 1968, women have gained far more
data about how they have been asked to acquiesce to the physical and
emotional violence perpetrated against them, to define a highly limiting "feminine" role as natural.[37]

All such concerns have led feminists to be angry and to demand

change. But they have also led women to seek ways to develop themselves, to help each other, and to heighten a shared understanding
of the strengths and special skills that have evolved from women's
experiences. This has created a natural base for service, which cannot be ignored as women also engage in efforts to stop and change
the systems, institutions, and individual men who oppress them. This
time around feminists were not claiming to provide services to "other"
women, rather they were attempting to grow themselves, and part of
that growing involved participation in all manner of services. The
common ideological base for services has also suggested a distinctive
style of service delivery. Whether it be rape crisis, counseling, or health
services, almost all feminist services evolved a type of format which
attempted to be more informal than traditional professional services,
which involved more sharing between helper and helped, more
democratic decision making among staff, and a generally skeptical
stance toward male-identified expertise.[38] At one end of the spectrum were enthusiastic women who came together to provide services out of a general sense of common need and shared experience.
Such projects often evolved from women's discussion groups, in the
community or college women's programs. In health care, they provided health information and general advice to women. Typical
comments are:

Consciousness raising was started first by an ad in the newspaper. Several
women felt a need to get together and discuss feminism and our lives. From
a need for information and referral services, the social service part of the
center was established . . . now we are more service-oriented than planned.

or

We are a group of women vitally concerned with alternative directions for
women. Our broadest goal . . . is to provide experience and opportunities
that will enable us to activate this potential and develop new capacities as
women. . . . We desire to establish a community-oriented resource center
and source of health information.

or

[Our purpose is] to fill the need for adequate, compassionate health care for
medical problems specific to women and to make available information about
our bodies in order to know them more fully and thereby to care for them
more fully.[39]

These types of general women's services flourished in the early and mid-seventies. Many died as the complex pressures for adequate funding and appropriate organizational development were increased. But even for them there was a general sense that feminist services were egalitarian, explicit in merging a feminist analysis with service delivery, and based on assumptions that women should share together and learn together as part of the service process.

At the other end of the spectrum were feminist self-help services, especially prevalent in the mid-seventies in health care and battered women's shelters. These programs reflected the most developed and self-conscious attempt to create an alternative "feminist practice" in social or health services. Usually founded by women with more knowledge of feminism and more experience in the women's movement, such programs developed quite sophisticated political analyses of every phase of their activity—from how to resolve cultural differences in diets in a shelter to the rationale for group self-examination in pelvic exams.[40] Such groups began in the early 1970s when different women across the country began to develop common standards of feminist practice, especially in health care. In 1974 a group of Hyde Park (Illinois) Socialist Feminists circulated a position paper which described the role of counterinstitutions as part of socialist-feminist practice. Their thoughts are representative of the base from which many feminists went on to develop ideas of radical practice:

Role of Counter-Institutions

A major trend in the current women's movement is to organize counter-institutional projects to directly meet the needs of women. This work is important for the women's movement but must occur in the context of a movement which has other foci as well.

Counter-institutions can do a number of things. They can help to raise the expectations of women who use and staff the institutions as to what is possible. They can provide services which meet the needs of women now. They can demonstrate that the problems addressed are social in nature and in solution. They convey to the broad constituencies we seek to address that we have positive programs to offer for solving the problems we drew attention to, and that we are not simply negative in orientation. In contrast to consciousness-raising, such programs dispel the spectre of endless problems without apparent solutions.

For example, a feminist-sponsored health center provides a needed service that materially improves our immediate condition. It demonstrates that women acting together can change some of their circumstances. It can contribute to building an organized base of power among women ready to fight on an ongoing basis for their rights.

However, counter-institutions have some limitations. They may foster false optimism about changes by indicating that problems can be solved in the spaces between existing institutions. Such programs could take up all the time of more than all of us involved in the present movement and never meet all the needs. Such activities cannot alter the power relations if they make no demands on those in power.

We argue the importance of combining counter-institutions with direct action organizing to build on the strengths of each. Such organizing focuses demands on social institutions, thus countering the conclusion that society is unchangeable. It also counters an overoptimism about the potential of self help to change women's lives by pressing the point that significant changes can be made for all women only through far-reaching changes in power relations. The most useful role of the counter-institutional projects is providing a vision for an alternative and at the same time demonstrating the need for demanding change from those in power.[41]

Feminist health clinics and certain battered women's shelters went forward from such positions to develop models for practice, where the goal was to combine a well-defined feminist analysis of health care, or violence against women, with a self-help approach. Self help in such contexts meant women helping women, women sharing information they gained through research and group discussion, women sharing most service tasks and avoiding the use as much as possible of outside professionals. Over time it meant, especially for health clinics, more care about payments and records, and for shelters more restrictions on how to relate to outside funding agencies. In short, feminist practice meant a seriousness that was lacking in less self-conscious services, as can be seen in comparing the materials from Boston's Transition House or Los Angeles' Feminist Women's Self-Help Clinic to more general women's publications.[42]

Of course, feminist services were not without problems. Over time, some women became interested in services more for professional reasons than out of a self-conscious commitment to feminist ideology and goals. Funding pressures became intense, often forcing feminist services to collapse, or to adapt to more traditional models, at least on paper. And, perhaps most unfortunately, in many areas feminist self help services were rent with internal disputes over the proper feminist practice, or the degree of commitment to poor and third world women, or the best leadership and organizational styles. Such tensions were intense and painful. But on the other hand, they were real *political* struggles which may be a natural, and finally healthy, outgrowth of understanding the significance of service work in achieving broader goals. Difficult as such conflicts are, they reflect growth from the days when service work was just seen as supportive to important political struggles, hardly worth a comment, much less a fight.

In conclusion, with feminist services—especially self help services—a new plateau was reached in the definition of political services. Feminists came to see almost all services as political and to view a major part of their activism as bound up with organizing to demand better services. At the same time, women began to design a model of feminist practice that offered important challenges to traditional social work approaches and that asserted that the best services for women were those which are explicitly and overtly political.

THE "SELF HELP" MOVEMENT

The lessons of the feminist and UFW services are reinforced by the rise, since the 1960s, of what has been called a "self help" movement. This new surge of activity has occurred in almost every area of service delivery and also is part of new definitions of community development as well. There is now a "national self help clearing house" and a wide range of resources are available to help newcomers develop self help approaches to almost any social concern.[43] In many ways the movement reflects a growing recognition, among large numbers of people, that the issues which services address are critical to the definition of a good society and are too important to be turned over to professionals and large-scale bureaucracies.

But it is of course misleading to view self help as a strategy of recent origins. As we suggested earlier, theorists like Richard Titmuss have found the roots of a truly humane social welfare system in the self help of workers, poor people, and communities. Sociologists and anthropologists have long noted the proliferation within all societies of indigenous helping networks, what Martin J. Lowenthal has come to call the "social economy."[44] Indeed, self help has been seen as a basic American trait, a quality Ralph Waldo Emerson recognized as "self-reliance." Self-improvement books and lecturers have flourished since before the days of the Chautauqua. From Booker T. Washington to Norman Vincent Peale, from the Female Improvement Society to Alcoholics Anonymous, Americans more than most have had self help.[45] Yet the "self help" movement which is spoken of today and which is the subject of numerous books, conferences, and magazine special issues is more sharply circumscribed. It embodies an analysis and set of programs which are both diverse and bound by common characteristics. Its roots are the American populist tradition, but also more recently in the development of para-professionals, the newer psychodynamic theories, and the criticism of "establishment" systems generated by the movements, consumer consciousness, and other social developments of the sixties. Indeed, almost every social issue which might be seen as causing problems, e.g., weight, sex, neighborhood crime, dissertation writing, cigarette smoking, and childbirth, can be found to have spawned self help groups.[46]

When the resurgence of self help developed in the late sixties it was seen as part of the "counterculture." More recently self help and mutual-aid groups are coming to view themselves and be seen more and more as adjuncts or valid alternatives to the established human services system: self help groups have made major contributions toward dealing with problems which cannot be dealt with by other institutions in the society.[47]

Among other aspects, the practice of self help seems to be clearly based on an awareness that services are needed and essential to the quality of life. In fact, at its root may be the notion that services are critical social goals which must be given constant social scrutiny. Certainly what Levin calls a "self-care competent society" would be one where services were valued and a mutual social responsibility.[48] Indeed, it would seem to be one where there was not only a right to receive services, but also a duty to help provide them.

It is possible, then, to see the self help movement as contributing to the politicization of services in a more general way than does the activity of movement services. While feminist activity, the UFW, and Black Panther efforts linked services to particular ideological and material goals, the self help movement simply states that a better, more democratic society depends on the existence of services. Although some social conservatives try to clam self help in the name of capitalist individualism, many self help advocates seem to be in the tradition of "social democracy," of people who want a gradual transition to a democratic socialist society without the upheavals of violent or revolutionary activity. They see the practice of self help as an alternative to much of the hierarchy and elitism of professional practice, as one critical aspect of a political agenda. Services thus become important *political* activities, too important to be viewed as simply normal social functions of an industrialized modern society. They are rights in themselves; how they are delivered has political impact and they are a necessary aspect of social debate. This is a far distance from Mary Richmond's metaphor that social services are an individualized, "retail" activity with little impact on the broader "wholesale" concerns of the body politic.[49]

OPTIONS OPENED

. . . Without invention nothing is well spaced,
unless the mind change, unless
the stars are new measured, according
to their relative positions, the
line will not change, the necessity
will not matriculate: unless there is
a new mind there cannot be a new
line, the old will go to
repeating itself with recurring
deadliness. . . .
           WILLIAM CARLOS WILLIAMS[50]

Taken together, the experiences of radical social services, the Poverty Programs, and self help activists provide a base for developing a more political understanding of social welfare activity.

First, they give evidence to support our assertion from chapter 1 that there is a natural link between a radical vision of social change and a concern with services. Earlier movements provided services, but almost in spite of themselves. They were usually unable to directly address the issues of how services should relate to their work because they did not want to get "bogged down with daily activities." Activists of the 1960s and 1970s were more secure, more able to see the need for harmony and congruence between their daily work and their long-range goals. Feminists, the UFW, and the Black Panthers were more vocal in their demands for accountable public services and more willing to try to "serve the people" themselves. With the Poverty Program and self help activities we began to see a spectrum, from radical reformists to revolutionaries, who would argue the natural affinity between the delivery of services and the pursuit of long-range goals. In times when budget cuts and the social climate combine to make traditional service activity appear quite conservative, it is important to remember that our most radical progressive movements have recognized an affinity which may no longer be so readily apparent.

Second, the experiences suggest that our long-range visions for a better society can be enhanced by the insights coming from service work as well as from considering our eventual social programs. After revolutions—in Nicaraugua, Cuba, China, Tanzania, or wherever— a first concern has always been to set up extensive new service programs, based upon, and targeted to build, a new "revolutionary ethic." As we struggle to achieve meaningful social change in a nonrevolutionary situation, we may well need the lessons of such experiences also. Antonio Gramsci wrote movingly of the need for "prefigurative communism," for experiences where our minds and emotions could anticipate the goals and new values we hope to achieve someday.[51] The involvement in service activity from an explicitly political perspective may provide some similar insights.

Over and over, feminists in battered women's shelters explain how their understanding of patriarchy and the social effects of women's poverty are deepened by involvement in the lives of other women. The Panthers spoke of the need to maintain their roots in the black community, not just to keep a base but also to remain "grounded" in the everyday concerns of black people. Participants in self help groups mention that their commitment to democratic processes is consistently enhanced by an ongoing experience with egalitarian mutual aid. The lessons are, of course, not always pleasant or easy to take. Involvement in political service work means that activists have to face their own limitations, to deal in more personal ways with the contradictions between their political ideals and the daily realities. Such experiences may be hard, but they can serve as real sources of strength.

It may not be coincidence that the movement which survived the longest after the general climate of militance died in the early seventies was the women's movement, and that the women's movement was the most actively and unashamedly involved in service work.

Similarly, it may be that the involvement in service activity helps to build broader trust in radical goals. Chavez understood this clearly when he argued that "contracts are no substitute for the basic help we provide workers in all aspects of their lives."[52] Indeed, this vital link between the legitimacy of a political perspective and service work has been the unanswerable argument which has first involved many activists in service activity. Here the point is that the legitimacy is not just that of narrow utilitarianism—that progressives are listened to because they provide a needed service. Rather it comes from a more profound testing of the trustworthiness of radical ideas. One woman expressed it this way:

If I really believe all this feminist stuff it means that the whole way I think about my life and the whole way I act changes. I'm not going to make such a change just because somebody writes about how nice feminism is. I want to see how people who are feminists treat me and each other, I want to know if I can trust what these ideas do to people. Otherwise I've thrown away what I have and replaced it with something which may be even worse.[53]

Third, the beginnings of an awareness of the components of a political practice may be suggested by the experiences reviewed here. No full catalog is forthcoming, but common approaches do surface regarding how to link political values with service work. Such basic approaches will be discussed much more fully in later chapters. Here we will only briefly note the beginning outlines. First, all the efforts assumed that services should embody democratic interaction between service provider and service consumers. If the long-range political goal is egalitarianism, then both parties are potential allies in the same struggle. Therefore mutual respect is not just "effective treatment," instead it becomes an essential premise if both can work together for change. A feminist with experience with the courts may help someone deal with the legal system after being battered, but also, as women, they may fight together for a different judicial system. Bertha Reynolds was especially aware of the difference that membership in the same union made with labor movement services. Cesar

Chavez and Huey Newton argued that their movements were stronger because "brothers helped brothers" in resolving each other's personal problems, in fighting growers or in opposing The Man.

Such a basic approach implies the sharing of experiences between "helper" and "helped." It suggests that people be viewed "holistically," not just as a manifestation of one "presenting problem." It argues against hierarchical, professional structures and suggests that expertise be shared, not owned by professionals. Exchange of skills based on mutual needs is rewarded, not one-sided altruism, no matter how munificient. Large bureaucratic organizations seem antithetical to the approach, as does a narrow specialization among service providers.

Admittedly, all the approaches mentioned here—which will be discussed much more fully later—seem limited to small settings, where the implications can be worked through and controlled. A major task still remains unaddressed, whether it is possible to act on any of these notions of "political practice" within settings that are not self-consciously "alternative." It has been difficult enough for movement services to act consistently on these values within controlled settings. Models for transferring them to agencies where the goals and shared values may not exist still need to be invented, much less tested. But, the power of the examples on a small scale gives energy to the quest to create such new models.

Finally, the personal experiences of those involved in radical services suggest the importance of trying to combine political and service goals. Over and over, for all the movements reviewed, individuals spoke of the "personal harmony" which came when they were able to provide daily assistance that reflected their broader political goals. Despite all the frustrations of feminist health services women continually mention the "personal growth" that came from learning and sharing and helping others. A former welfare worker who went to work for the UFW spoke of the difference when her service work was done with "the union spirit." Panther militants mentioned the satisfaction which occurred when they were able to exhibit a softer, more compassionate side of themselves.

Perhaps, then, the most meaningful reason for providing political services is to avoid what Frances Willard feared as "one-sided" advocates. Those who think they only want to "help others" may become imbalanced because they lose sight of a larger vision of why this society keeps creating a need for help. They can become overwhelmed by their personal inability to make changes unless they come to see their activity as integrated into broader attempts to bring change. And activists with only that broader vision may lose touch with the everyday reasons why their vision is needed and with the parts of themselves that need a better society. Thus they become distanced from the very pain they want to alleviate; they can become brittle, unable to tolerate the reasons why "the masses" are skeptical of what seems so obvious. The "reality testing" that is involved in any honest care giving may provide a way for activists to keep working toward their vision, as well as to make their vision more accessible and more accepted by those who would benefit from it.

4

PERSONAL DIMENSIONS OF SERVICE: DEFINING POLITICAL PRACTICE

In the 1980s there are few social movements strong and diversified enough to provide services. The weak economy, the sense of international and economic rather than domestic and social crisis, and the waning of older movements leave individuals who seek social change with few options for alternative services. At the same time there are increasing reasons to link service activity with political concerns. Even antinuclear activists demand cuts in military spending so that we can "fund human needs."[1] Conservative budget priorities have led organizers to defend many types of human service programs against cutbacks.

So, whether one is an individual with explicitly left perspective who is attempting to do meaningful work or a committed service worker politicized by fighting for one's job, there continue to be important reasons to be concerned about the links between service activity and a broader social vision. All such people face the problem of creating a way of acting and thinking which is responsive to both their personal and political needs.

The purpose of this chapter is to examine the ways in which individuals can continue to link—in these times that are so different from the 1960s—their political values and goals with their service work.[2] Its beginning premise is that "the personal is political" and that socially committed service workers, wherever they may be, will need to achieve harmony among their politics, their work, and their personal lives. Not to accomplish this is to court personal disaster and the danger of performing harmful work. Success may mean an increase in personal effectiveness as well as the development of a model for healthier services and a more inclusive social vision. Given the options, then, we might as well try.

SHARED DREAMS

Deep in my heart, I do believe
We shall overcome some day.

Individuals who become radicals and individuals who become social workers are often described as at opposite ends of a spectrum. The radical seeks truth and pure justice, while the social worker wants love and immediate caring. Yet, as we have argued earlier, there may be more similarities between the expectations and goals of service workers and radicals than has been acknowledged.

First, the ability to hope for and to believe in change is at the root of the desire to provide services or to engage in political organizing. Indeed, without a dream that individuals can change, or at least that their suffering can be helped, even the most conservative social worker would be without a role. And social movements build their ideology and activities around a sense that change can come—through the historic logic of material forces, perhaps, but with the necessary help of human actors. Mary Richmond believed, with what Halmos called "the faith of the counselors," that well-conducted casework could help individuals change their circumstances. Karl Marx reminded followers that the presence of dialectic forces in history still demanded that people act together to accomplish the new world.

It is, however, the specifics of this shared belief in the possibility for change that have been seen as separating service workers from movement adherents. Services were only to address individual changes, while movements were to concern themselves with the large-scale societal arrangements. Outsiders consistently criticized radical service efforts because they were bound to be "serving other purposes," (i.e., social change goals) instead of the pure, individualized changes desired by service workers. As we have seen, both movement theorists and professional social workers wanted to stress the differences, rather than the underlying similarities.

Yet the common theme cannot be ignored. Over and over movement service providers expressed the same sentiments about the connections between their service work and their politics, as those mentioned by a young feminist health worker:

> I want the world to be better for me and for other women, that's why I'm a feminist. I do health work because it connects up to something personal— our bodies, our sense of our selves. If we can help each other take care of ourselves better then maybe we also can make the world change.[3]

And service workers, without a self-consciously political perspective, often mentioned a desire for change as at the core of their work; as one family worker explained:

> I worry about the children and what kind of world they'll face if nobody helps their parents treat them better. So I'm a family service worker to try to do what little I can to help some children have a better future. It sounds corny, but that's part of it, anyway.[4]

The unity comes, then, from a belief in change and often follows with a sense that, somehow, there is a link between individual change and broader social development. For leftists, the links between social goals and personal changes are essential. Without a sense that services are a means to a broader end, that improvements in immediate situations (or at least public demands for improvement) strengthen people and make them more able to build a better world, there would be little radical support for services. For service workers the demands may come more gradually. As helping with one problem only reveals another, it may become evident that there are broader causes for individual woes. The possibility for this shared insight into the uses and limits of immediate or individual change is a critical support for the notion of radical social services.[5]

A second link between involvement in service and political activity can be drawn, negatively, from the common criticisms that both movement adherents and social workers act out of "personal" motives, not from pure principles, and that they personally overidentify with the victims of society. For years the standard criticism of social movement members was that they acted out of irrational, even pathological motives.[6] Even sympathetic critics spoke of alienation, status anxiety, authority problems, and overidentification with the underdog in a psychological labeling that attempted to discredit any desire for radical change or concern for society's victims. Movement members' lives were severely scrutinized and personal reasons for unhappiness used to discredit collective attempts to alleviate social unhappiness.[7]

Similarly, critics of social workers have also suspected personal motives. Here Geoffrey Pearson's analysis is telling:

When social workers do consider the motives which bring people (presumably including themselves) into social work they find a familiar pattern: just as social work has traditionally emphasized the personal and familial determinants of clients' distress and social problems (to the neglect of the determinants of social structure, class, inequality, and power) its version of what motivates social workers abstracts personal whims from the realm of moral and political discourse. Thus people are reckoned to be interested in madness because they are afraid (or intrigued) by the madness inside themselves; recruits are judged to want to care for the downtrodden in order to satisfy some inner (psychological) need; they are thought to be interested in working with neglected children in order to work through some emotional complex of their own childhood.

Pearson goes on to link this common self-criticism within the profession to a "peculiar mistrust of helping motives" and an inability to see the legitimacy of a social base for one's interests.[8] While artists or novelists, it seems, are to be praised for building on their roots and expanding on personal experiences, both standard scholarship and the popular media are quick to condemn those who—for any personal reasons—go against society's norms and identify with the needy or demand social justice.

On the other hand, we may readily acknowledge that radicals and service providers have personal experiences contributing to their actions and causing them to identify with others' troubles. Such roots may be seen as part of a natural base for building one's politics and one's work. Indeed, they may be reason for seeing reciprocity instead of altruism as a healthier goal for service activity. Personal pains are one wedge that allows middle-class people to see beyond themselves, black people to support each other, and women to identify with each other. In fact, it was the recognition and the shared elaboration of victimization upon which the women's movement was built.

Self help services and other movement services all are strengthened by an ethic of sharing of pain. And, we will argue, an essential element of political practice may well be one's ability to identify with service users and to link one's own experiences with theirs.

Further, one especially beneficial aspect of bringing service work and political aspirations together may be to allow service workers greater opportunity to acknowledge and develop the personal dimensions of their work. Middle-class radicals, especially men, have often shared, in Paul Potter's words, "a deep inner conviction that *our* grievances were not legitimate . . . and therefore our concern with social change would only be authentic if told to people whose struggle was legitimate—people who were getting creamed."[9] An understanding of politics and service activity which is based, at least in part, on an understanding of shared personal experiences may make people feel more whole, more able, in Flacks' words, to combine "making history" with "making a life," as we suggested in chapter 1.

A third shared expectation of service workers and radicals is a common assumption that one has a personal responsibility to do something about problems. Again, this common tendency has often been a source of criticism for both service workers and radicals: "do-gooders," "busybodies," and "meddlers" have been common terms applied to both. And, we must admit, that in their worst moments service workers and socialists can be experienced as difficult, demanding people. Both *can* share the intense sense of emergency which Starobin observed in radicals who are "more driven than others by the hope that somehow the movement which engages them will achieve something more lasting than any individual can."[10]

Paul Halmos sees great differences between the politcal approach to change and what he calls the "personalist" approach. But even he acknowledged that both "are motivated by the belief that they can improve the condition of their fellow men" and are "recognized (if not liked) for similar roles as 'moralists' in society."[11] This tendency seems to be a natural corollary to the shared desire for change. It can even show up when popular "personality tests" are given to groups of service workers.[12] At its worst, it can lead to romantic self-importance and overly grand, individualistic plans. In better form, it can be the driving force of leadership and courageous confrontations with unjust authority. The goal is to harness the energy and to direct it toward desired outcomes and not toward infighting and jockeying for the one, correct way to fight injustice.

The desire for solidarity with others and for community is a fourth commonly recognized attribute of both radicals and service workers. Social services had some of their roots in "friendly societies" which, as Richard Titmuss notes, were "aptly and significantly named, [and] during a century of unbridled competition, they were *the* humanistic activity for the artisan and his family."[13] Others have noted the ability to achieve nurturing relationships with people as one of the expected and desired benefits of service work.[14]

For radicals, the desire for solidarity can be seen as a central goal, indeed often as a driving personal motivation. Feminists acknowledge "sisterhood" as a critical goal and guiding principle for action. Indeed, the generalized quest for collectivity and for new and better forms of human relationships have been consistent aspects of left social movements throughout this century.

Individual activists consistently spoke of service work as appealing exactly because it allowed for sharing, closeness, and community. Health groups that tried to provide more "hard" services found themselves offering discussion groups and consciousness-raising sessions instead because "women wanted to talk." Even the men in ERAP did acknowledge that the sharing and closeness which came from services work was "personally rewarding"—it was just not "serious political work."

Here the congruence of concerns seems clear and its implications obvious. All writers who attempt to define a radical practice stress the importance of collective solutions, of equal, honest relationships with clients, and of "bringing people together around common problems." Some service workers may wonder what this means, and many seek their satisfaction in a series of individual caring relationships instead, but the link is clear: many service workers and radicals share a desire to be connected with others through their work, to "work with people," a phrase every career counselor knows.

The final trait which activists and service workers seem to share is not as well documented as the others, but is one which has become obvious in this research. Whether they were movement activists, professional social workers, or paraprofessionals, my respondents all supported Halmos' observation that "the Counsellor needs to see himself [sic] as useful to feel worthy."[15]

This desire to be useful was an important motivating force for one Boston service worker and perhaps exposes why many service workers tolerate their work longer than outsiders can comprehend: "When there is a disaster, I'm wonderful. I can work very hard, putting the organization back together, helping co-workers and clients because I feel so useful. The bigger the mess, the more I feel needed."[16]

Her comment may also suggest one source of the paternalism that has led to the long-standing criticism of social movements and social workers. Is it possible that, in our desire to feel useful, we may create definitions of "need" that require our intervention?

All of these shared attitudes, dreams, and aspirations suggest—and our brief discussion is only meant to be suggestive—an important personal basis for combining a radical vision with service work. Rather than bending ourselves out of shape to provide services, the work could come as a relief as, perhaps, one of the few places where one has the potential to express political goals and to meet personal "human needs." The convergences may also suggest ways, without arrogance, to "raise the consciousness" of fellow workers. If we begin by exploring together the personal dimensions of our work we may find more in common than we, or they, expected and a material, not rhetorical, base for political discussion.

Before moving on to the much better documented areas of stress in service work, however, we must acknowledge one worrisome observation: our list of shared characteristics looks suspiciously feminine. Women are the traditional nurturers, who identify with others, who feel responsible for relationships and caretaking, and who need to feel useful. Can it be that we have only "discovered" what has troubled feminists for a century, that—as one nineteenth-century writer put it—a woman's life is but an "opportunity for service"?[17]

Here our only answer can be a strong "yes, but." Yes, the traits identified are associated with women, both with stereotypes about women and with new research on women's values and psychology.[18] This should not be surprising, since so many service workers are women and it was often women who did radical service work. But, precisely because of a growing feminist appreciation for women's skill in playing their roles, and of the social values of these roles, we may be advocating more than we realized. In arguing for the congruence of service work and radical vision, and for both the left and the male-led social welfare profession to appreciate the value of direct services, we may be calling for the "feminization" of social welfare, and of socialism. If either were to occur, its significance might rival that of the newly discovered "feminization of poverty."

We will return to this discussion later, but we cannot resist closing with a portentous quote from the frontispiece of the 1880 Memorial Volume of the American Female Guardian Society, *Life Among the Lowly:*

'Tis Women's Work to guard and save,
And rescue from the moral grave.[19]

SHARED PRESSURES

Service workers with a political perspective share problems with other workers, no matter what the setting. These workplace pressures form a common environment and serve as a source of unity between radicals and other workers. Since the problems facing human service workers have been so well documented in the social work literature, here we will only offer a brief review and discussion of how a left analysis may help workers to understand their situation.[20] We have probably omitted some problems here, in overcompensation for the ever-present danger of getting bogged down in a cataloging of all the forces which conspire to make effective human service work seem impossible, but enough is enough.

For the past few years, "worker burnout" has become a fashionable topic. Organizational consultants can be hired (at stiff fees) to help workers "cope with stress" and to help management to prevent worker burnout.[21] While it is easy to make fun of such organized, pseudoscientific efforts, they do reflect an increasing awareness of the difficulties of human service work, no matter what one's perspective or organizational setting. While burnout workshops tend to blame the worker for her or his stress, rather than the organization or the broader society, they are sought by many service workers who feel frustrated, unable to cope, tired of their jobs, and stuck in thankless tasks. One role for radicals may be to respond to such pressures by suggesting different ways of acting and alternative means of understanding the pressures facing human service workers.

We can see three broad categories of pressures on the human service worker. First, there are those stemming from the nature of the human and social problems to which service workers respond. Second, there are the difficulties arising from the way the service delivery system is structured and delivery is organized. Third, there are those resulting from the seeming contradictions between the needs of service workers as individuals and those of their clients, co-workers, bosses, and the broader society. All three sets of problems have been widely discussed and each can be understood better with a political analysis, although radical solutions are less quickly forthcoming.

Service workers face the human result of all the contradictions and inefficiencies of a capitalist, racist, sexist society as well as the sheer pain and suffering that is part of life. They see, to return to Turner's phrase, much that is "unjust" but also much that is "misfortune." Because services are so heavily aimed at the poor and outcast of this society it is possible to convince oneself that all social problems would go away with an end to poverty, racism, and sexism. Maybe. However, much of what gives social work its special poignancy is the recognition that comes from experience, that human life also includes its own intrinsic suffering and that some of the pressures come from dealing with, for example, the diseases which kill young children, the irredeemable losses which come from untimely deaths, the mental illness which takes over some lives, and the myriad ways in which life can be so cruel—disfiguring diseases, birth defects, human weakness.

The overwhelming need resulting from such misfortune, and the even more frustrating (because ultimately preventable) needs caused by injustice, confront most service workers every day. But always, they cannot *solve* the problems which come to them. In every instance their best hope is to respond to one part of the pain. Even when there can be individual success—one woman leaves a battering household or an elderly man receives enough services to remain at home (for how long?)—there is always the gnawing reality that the problems never go away and that workers can never do enough. The classic metaphor is the locked file cabinet in *The Case Worker* by Konrad, from which "closed cases" begin to talk back to the worker.[22]

None of this is new. If anything, it is the goal of "training" to help workers deal with such problems more effectively. One learns, in self-defense, to "set limits" on responsibility and to develop "distance" from the problems. It would be naive to argue that workers abandon such defenses totally, surely they are the only ways which anyone—including needy people themselves—copes on a daily basis. But the grinding reality does break through, especially in times when already inadequate resources shrink and when public assaults leave workers feeling alone with the responsibility.

Traditional analysis of social problems has tended to "blame the victim" or to create "systems analyses" which try to explain away the problem as natural, evolving social conditions.[23] Left analyses can be more helpful because they acknowledge the injustices and are more explicit about the underlying logic of the system. But we cannot fool ourselves that a progressive analysis can take away all the stress, even if it could explain misfortune as well as injustice. Even with the best of analyses, human service workers are placed in impossible jobs. They are to "help" (often assumed to mean "cure") problems which are fundamental. They see the worst and they have pitifully few resources for responding. It is no wonder they experience profound distress, and no wonder that most of the time even radical service workers "deal with it"—like the couple with the monster in their living room in the *New Yorker* cartoon—"by not talking about it."[24]

Human service workers can, and do, talk more easily about the other two areas of stress in their work—problems with bureaucracies and personal complexities. Conservative and radical critics develop analyses of the problems with social welfare policies, programs, and bureaucratic agencies. The conflicting and contradictory policy mandates are analyzed, the inadequacies of conflicting goals and bureaucratic double binds are exposed.

Every level of this society's structured response to social problems creates stress for the worker, whether it be conflicting, punitive national policy or bureaucratic work design which makes rational response impossible. As Michael Lipsky notes in his careful analysis of the "street-level bureaucrat," the "structure of work" is responsible for much of the biases, frustrations, and undesirable performance of the service worker. His conclusion is apt:

> To deliver street-level policy through a bureaucracy is to embrace a contradiction. On the one hand service is delivered by people to people involving a model of human interaction, caring, and responsibility. On the other hand, service is delivered through a bureaucracy, involving a model of detached

and equal treatment, under conditions of resource limitation and constraint, making care and responsibility conditional.[25]

Finally, the individual worker faces daily stresses that go beyond organizational design and the contradictions of job functions. Class, cultural, and racial differences with clients add to stresses, even where the client is voluntarily seeking service, as one day care center worker noted:

We're a good program, people like us and me. But I still worry that I'm not able to do the right thing for kids from a different culture and still wonder if the parents take me seriously since I'm young and don't have children of my own.[26]

The frustrations in clients' lives create pressures on workers, even when their agency is not responsible. Indeed, workers in sympathetic community agencies often report that clients put stronger demands on them than they do on state bureaucrats because they seem more responsive and concerned. Even when a worker can intellectually understand the dynamics, and discuss it with a client, the pressures are still great. Also, the rational lack of trust which many clients have learned to exhibit toward *all* service workers can create defensive reactions in many workers: "I know other people have treated them badly but why should they take it out on me?" is a common complaint. Finally, it is very hard to fight the sense of personal superiority which is so enmeshed in the "helper" role. One mental health worker summed up the problem well:

I keep trying to remember "there, but for the grace of God, go I." But it is so easy to look at other people's troubles and feel superior, and to think "I wouldn't ever do anything so stupid." You have to fight these feelings all the time because if you give in to them you're just like all the others around here who go around so smug because at least they're not mental patients.[27]

Service work is often isolating, with the criteria for success unclear, even in supportive agencies. Here the experience of movement services becomes relevant again. Even without controlling bureaucracies, or social control intentions, movement service workers often felt discontented about the quality of their own work. They worried about not doing the right thing, about hurting people with their lack of knowledge, about insulting or disrespecting people out of ignorance. They found it hard to accept the lack of expertise which Piven and Cloward see as an underpinning for radical practice:

> The professional dedicated to serving people will understand that his or her most distinguishing attribute ought to be humility. The doctrine that "we know best" must be exorcised; there is simply no basis for the belief that we who have Master of Social Work degrees or other similar university credentials are better able to discern our clients' problems than they are, and better able to decide how to deal with these problems.[28]

Similar stresses arose with co-workers, even in alternative settings. Differences in approach were threatening: was it all right that one person was more formal than another, or more didactic? Insecurities could develop if a certain worker seemed more "popular" with service users than another. All differences among workers—even committed, political workers—could serve as sources of tension, because definitions of competence were unknown.

Human service work, then, is necessarily fraught with tensions, some of which can be opposed in the short run, and some of which seem inherent in the process, at least without massive social changes. The task facing any caring worker, whether self-consciously political or not, is to try to gain some fulfillment out of the work, to render services that are as respectful and helpful as possible, and to avoid activities that are self-destructive or destructive of others. As we will see in chapter 6, the structure of most social welfare bureaucracies invests this task alone with radical potential, because the systems are so rigid that they cannot allow even such limited practice goals. Similarly, as we will explore in chapter 5, the standard definitions of "professionalism" also serve to undermine the ability of a human service worker to achieve even these modest ambitions.

A self-consciously political practice, however, can both increase the obligations of being a caring worker and, ultimately, make the task easier. Combining a political analysis with one's service work can effect one's self-conception of the job at hand as well as one's sense of long- and short-range social goals. At its best, a more political understanding of service activity may allow workers to better comprehend why they cannot "succeed" and to identify collective, rather than individual strategies for change. Finally, a political analysis and practice may be the only real hope for fighting burnout and for retaining the potential to serve socially useful—rather than unequivocally social control—roles in this society.

ELEMENTS OF A POLITICAL PRACTICE

The idea that socially committed workers in the human services should act differently than other service workers is not new. It may go back as far as the settlement house workers who carefully presented themselves as different from the traditional Charity Organization workers. Surely it was a concern of the radical social workers of the 1930s and of the writers in *Social Work Today*. In 1935, Bertha Reynolds laid out the five "simple principles" of what was called "the Rank and File Movement":

1. Social work exists to serve people in need. If it serves other classes who have other purposes it becomes too dishonest to be capable of either theoretical or practical development.
2. Social work exists to help people help themselves and therefore should not be alarmed when they do so by organized means, such as client or tenant or labor groups.
3. Social work operates by communication, listening, and sharing experiences.
4. Social work has to find its place among other movements for human betterment.
5. Social workers as citizens cannot consider themselves superior to their clients as if they do not have the same problems.[29]

Such principles are not very different from the arguments laid out today by today's radical workers.[30] Indeed, all of us, this author included, are still trying to accomplish the goal which Bertha Reynolds recalled in a 1975 interview, when she was ninety years old:

We were trying to create a place for social work with the other movements of the day—the workers' movements, the others. We were social workers and thought we had something to contribute but it meant we had to go back and take a hard look at how social work had been practiced. Many people did not trust social workers and we had to show them, and ourselves, that it could be different.[31]

Many of today's social service workers still strive to build alliances with other movements—with blacks, women, the left. A need continues to exist for social services to be viewed as one part of a progressive agenda. This will only happen if the goals of services, at least, reflect a set of values that project the kind of relationships we would want in a better society. What is presented here is the beginning of an attempt to draw from the experience of movement services, and from that of today's service workers, the elements of a practice reflecting radical and humanist values and applicable to the jobs of today's service workers. This chapter stresses the personal dimensions. Later chapters will suggest analyses of professionalism, bureaucracy, and the welfare state which will be incorporated into a final set of suggestions for combining social service and social change goals. In this form, the suggestions are presented as options, which must be evaluated for particular contexts and under collective scrutiny. The purpose is to help us think and plan together, not to lay down any ossified model to be applied without interaction and criticism.

Special Problems Facing Radicals. Self-identified radicals share the problems of other human service workers. In addition they face some special tensions which they must understand if they are to identify and pursue options to traditional practice. They may be surprised by the barriers that are erected against them, or that emerge within themselves and hinder their own ability to act.

First, once radicals declare their political goals they must be prepared to face hostility, no matter whether they call themselves activists, progressives, socialists, radicals, or whatever in order to differentiate themselves from mainstream traditions. They are likely to encounter everything from nervousness to open hostility from co-workers, clients, and administrators. There is a deep historical distrust of radicalism that runs deep in this society and has filled many people with fears about any type of overt politicization of one's activity.[32]

The question to ask, then, is why identify oneself? Why not let one's practice "speak for itself"? The answer is complex. Of course, it makes no sense to walk up to perfect strangers, with no context, and announce one's political persuasion. But it *is* important that co-workers understand the importance of one's political identity and that, when appropriate, one's clients know. If co-workers and clients are informed, radicals will not have to tell administrators; they will figure it out.

Exactly because feelings against socialism in the country are so strong, there is a great tendency to censor oneself. One wants to be judged on the merits of what one does and says and not be labeled. But, on the other hand, anticommunism stays so strong in this country partially because many people don't know any avowed radicals who take the time to explain differences among left groups or to compare goals of an American socialism with those of other countries. By not identifying themselves, activists may continue the cultural ignorance about socialism. The people who are already identified as leftists are then hurt and isolated. In addition, good work largely results from political values and analysis. If radicals do not acknowledge this, they defeat themselves and may foster the individualistic myths imbedded in this society.

Of course, identifying oneself is easier if one is in a political caucus. It requires that one must think carefully about how to describe one's politics. An adolescent chip-on-the-shoulder attitude, "I'm a socialist, and what of it?" is not the way to proceed. Radicals discuss their politics not to isolate themselves but to make honest connections with co-workers and clients. So a serious, careful description of one's politics is necessary. Finally, there may be exceptions to this approach. Some settings and perhaps even some communities may literally be dangerous for a self-acknowledged radical. I am not advocating suicide, but I am suggesting that radical work is seriously undermined if its political content is unacknowledged, so the choice to stay in the political "closet" should not be made lightly. Indeed, one might begin to question whether possibilities exist for effective political work in a place where one is afraid to be politically open.

Second, as people do political work in a workplace they should attempt to establish some kind of caucus, or work group. Such collectives are essential for mutual support and effectiveness. They need to be as open as possible and identify themselves in relation to workplace issues, not abstract political formulations ("client-oriented caucus" was the title of an effective Boston social workers' union group in the 1960s). But no matter what one does, the very fact of forming a group may be viewed as threatening or exclusionary by some co-workers who are grounded in individualistic ideologies. The idea of "strategy"—that a group of people with similar politics anticipates changes and plans alternatives—is upsetting to some workers (and to management, for different reasons) because it brings to light the political nature of interactions at the workplace. Some co-workers still want to believe, all evidence to the contrary, that decisions are made rationally on the basis of information and policy. Radicals are seen as "breaking the rules" and "polarizing issues" just because they suggest a different analysis.

Such problems cannot be totally avoided. When one identifies oneself politically and acts collectively some people are frightened. Activists must avoid taking pleasure in this—it is possible to become the political equivalent of a high school gang, full of swagger and bravado—but they cannot stop it altogether. After all, such political structures scare some co-workers exactly because they *do* side with management. Caucuses also may serve to attract people to our positions exactly because radicals in them may appear more powerful and effective.

A third problem stems from the difficulty of reconciling one's critique of social welfare programs under capitalism with the need to give oneself, and one's co-workers, a sense of daily hope for meaningful work. As we saw in chapter 1, radical service workers are on the cusp of a contradiction. They are trying to promote the helping potential of social services while admitting that they also provide a social control function. When co-workers hear activists explain the social control purposes for their work they may feel attacked, unable to understand the usefulness of such an "undermining" of their everyday work. Especially when a radical analysis leads activists to "side with clients," less politicized co-workers may feel betrayed. All of this is especially difficult exactly because a self-awareness of the societal functions of their work can make radicals especially sensitive to how little trust can also be expected from clients. Here again, radicals need allies. Trying to work alone in the face of such pressures is probably impossible.

Finally, activists need to be very aware of current shifts in political climate. The rise of the New Right has already begun to suggest that institutions will be far less tolerant of token radicals. Co-workers may be fearful of association with radicals and overt efforts may be made to isolate activists as "troublemakers," "unrepresentative," or, again, as people who "polarize issues." But we have not fallen back into McCarthyism yet, and the best defense against such attacks, especially in their early stages, may be to expose them, publicly. If possible, assertions or innuendos should be challenged openly. The alternative is self-censorship, which is self-defeating.

The purpose of all these warnings is not to frighten people away from developing a political practice. Rather, it is to emphasize that political practice is serious, it is not a game one plays to be "smart." One needs to take the development of a political practice seriously and to take one's opponents seriously. Some people, especially those who were good, middle-class students, may arrive at the human service workplace full of experiences where they challenged the teachers and got away with it; where they were the "enfants terribles" in their first jobs. Such experiences were born of privilege and were permissible because the stakes were not clear. Now is not the time for romantic revolutionary play. It may be the time for, in Rudi Deutscher's words, "the long march through the institutions." That means being careful, being serious about one's strengths and weaknesses, doing all one's homework, and being as clear as possible about what one is trying to accomplish and why.

Getting Ready. Radical practice begins with the recognition that we must honestly assess ourselves, and do what Jeffrey Galper calls "paying attention to ourselves":

> If we are to be responsible in undertaking any sort of action in the world we must inevitably consider our own preparedness, ability, needs, commitment, and level of energy as we make the decision to act. This is as it should be. We will not be successful and we will be limited in our ability to sustain our efforts if we feel consistently overextended, if we act without the internal and external supports we need, and if we simply do not have the personal skill to do the job.[33]

Activists need to begin by asking a number of political questions about themselves. Such questions are most useful if discussed with politically trusted co-workers. Of course, such opportunities are not always available, so one must engage in some self-analysis. However, as work groups are formed, members should review such questions together as a way of building trust.

First, activists must explore the motives and expectations for their work. Is this job part of a long-term "career" commitment or is it interim? How much interest does one have in the problems addressed by the agency? Does one expect to be a real militant, standing up as a leader, or to be more in the background? What are the political goals for one's workplace: bringing in more clients, of a different background; changing the style of the agency in terms of how it relates to clients; organizing a union; involving oneself and the whole agency in the community; exposing the agency to the media? Or, do we see the workplace only as a setting for individual work with clients in more liberating ways? What risks is one to take? After all, Piven and Cloward have warned:

Anyone who undertakes to fight for clients' interests must be prepared to be discredited. . . . At best if we seriously resist in behalf of the poor and the victims we are not likely to be rewarded with professional esteem and we will probably not advance rapidly in the bureaucracies.[34]

Such warnings remind us of the need to look at private life in relationship to our work. How much money does one need to keep working effectively? Are there other commitments that may limit activism? What about prior experiences: what has been learned about one's style as a service worker; is one quiet or noisy; how does one respond to conflict and tensions? Finally, workers need to acknowledge the personal rewards they derive from work and consider what makes us happy on the job.

Such questions may seem obvious, or too much like the latest pop psychology—a kind of left-wing *What Color Is Your Parachute?*[35] But their purpose is not frivolous or merely aimed at self-fulfillment. Instead, they form the personal base from which we can begin to answer questions about our political legitimacy. It is a standard tenet of political organizing that one must know the sources and limits of one's legitimacy in order to be effective. For human service workers—with necessarily contradictory roles and real potential to be agents of social control—such questions are especially critical. The political goal is not to foster liberal guilt but rather to fight such guilt, on the one hand, and at the same time to defeat the unknowing arrogance which can also accompany political work, on the other.

A second step in establishing personal legitimacy in human service work is to conduct an ideological/material analysis of the work setting. This activity can also serve as a way to build a workplace caucus. Study groups may be less threatening as a first stage of organizing and can allow people to learn to trust each other in a less-pressured setting. With any workplace, large or small, one needs to know its organizational power structure, how it fits with other agencies and the community, its sources of money. A class analysis of the workplace is required: what types of people work there; how do they compare in class, race, and sexual dimensions to the clients? The different jobs performed within the agency should be considered in regard to their potential for social control purposes and as bases for change activities. The types of "problems" addressed by the agency and the nature of the agency constituency must be analyzed. In short, such questions serve two purposes. They allow activists to know important information about the workplace and to develop a political analysis about the social meaning of the work.

In hostile bureaucracies such study can in itself help workers cope with our alienating situation. It can offer important insights into the workings of the agency which can be of help to other co-workers and to clients. Although study can be seductive, because it is sometimes easier to study a hostile environment than to change it, it can also give the courage to act. In smaller programs, or in agencies which seem less socially negative, study can serve similar functions. Women's health centers and ERAP groups often engaged in helpful self-analysis to see how they related to the rest of the community and to look at their own work processes. In short, a major political obligations is to understand the power, class, sex, and social relationships in our environment. The process of learning about such things collectively can be the first step in building a radical presence in our agencies.

Study and self-analysis give radical service workers a base for examining their own personal power within the workplace. Discretion, for example, is something that all human service workers seem to demand in their work. It, as Lipsky notes, allows workers "to intervene on behalf of clients" but also "to discriminate against them." Activists must be clear about how much discretion they have and how they can use it for the good of clients. However, they must remain heedful of the inherent danger in discretion, as recognized by Lipsky:

Street-level discretion promotes workers' self-regard and encourages clients to believe that workers hold the key to their well-being. For both workers and clients, maintenance of discretion contributes to the legitimacy of the welfare state.[36]

Power may also come from our access to information that can be useful to co-workers and clients. Although one must think tactically about how to share specific pieces of information, in general activists should share all information which will affect workers' or clients' lives as quickly as possible. It is strange that professionalism has usually meant tight lips over any changes in budget or staffing, but water-cooler chitchat about the details of clients' lives.

Power may also come from sources outside one's organizational role, however, and then it is always more problematic. One may have power because class and education have provided a language and a tone of personal entitlement. One's status as a white man may give power. A young "attractive" woman may think she has power to get what she wants from administrators, co-workers, or clients. These types of power can be used only for ill purposes. Progressives should never contribute to existing social bias by playing upon the prejudices of others—because to do so betrays all those without that option. Often certain "acceptable" workers may be singled out by management during times of workplace stress. One should never allow oneself to be used this way. At the very least, such an "acceptable" worker should insist on group discussions and should take a backseat in negotiations. Assuming a leadership role "because I can speak their language" or because "I am less threatening to them" is a liberal tactic, which finally asserts privilege, not solidarity with others.

On the other hand, individual characteristics that push against social prejudices may be used as a source of power—with care. A black or Hispanic staff person can sometimes express demands with special force. A woman may be able to speak of women's issues. Again, the danger is of being used or of being confused and thinking one's power is due to one's personal attributes and not one's perceived status as a representative of a threatening group. But it never hurts to force white male administrators to deal with black women.

Here again, issues of one's personal power cannot really be understood alone. How one is perceived by others needs to be explored. Many of us, especially women, do not view ourselves as powerful. We feel that whatever we say or do will be ignored, or discounted, so we don't think before we speak. We need collective support to recognize that we may have more power than we think, as recognized by one worker in an alternative educational program:

I don't supervise anybody in our program, although I have worked here a long time and know everybody. One day I was angry at someone in another department and said so to people, just thinking it was my opinion. The next thing I knew the rumor was out that I was trying to get him fired. I realized then that people perceived me as having more power than I felt I had. I've learned to be more careful.[37]

Finally, one purpose of analysis and self-study is to identify potential allies and supporters. A structural analysis can suggest which administrators may be trusted and those who are helplessly compromised by the nature of their work. A sense of one's own legitimacy may encourage bravery in discussing desired changes with co-workers. Such information and awareness should help clients get what they need from the agency. Finally, it should allow workers to recognize those whose position and practice can be trusted and to be clearer about why others cannot be trusted, regardless of how "nice" they seem. Activists are short-circuited when they cannot trust anyone, but are dangerously naive if they try to trust everyone. A strong sense of the material and social relations in the workplace can help identify the limits of trust. It can free workers for honest spontaneity in many situations and help them stay on guard in others.

Building Relationships with Clients. As director of the United Seaman's Service Bertha Reynolds was acutely aware of the importance of delivering a service that belonged to its users. Some of her observations help us understand the crucial character of the relationship between the human service consumer and provider:

The sense that each applicant had of belonging (without having to face acceptance or rejection at the door) eliminated much of the resistance which social agencies expect to find. . . . Trade union members, moreover, have a rather realistic acceptance of genuine lack of resources. Their activities as a union group tend to overcome childish attitudes of asking for everything. . . . The basic fact [in a union setting] is that admission is inclusive, not exclusive, and sifting is directed to sorting requests according to service needed, and what can be given, rather than to eliminating applicants. . . .

We had to give up the idea that we, offering benefits, decide who shall have them. Serving a democratically organized group, we must serve all well or none with all the resources we had. . . . We had never before served clients who used an *organized* means of expressing the "self-determination of the client" about which we theorized.[38]

Such an experience is a far cry from the relationships with clients which Jeffrey Prottas describes in his chapter "Poof! You're a Client" in *People-Processing:*

A person is far too complex to be effectively processed by a bureaucracy. . . . Since the task of street-level bureaucrats is processing people, they must simplify and standardize those people before processing them—that is, they must make a client.

Later he goes on to explain:

An aggressive and self-assertive client is therefore much disliked. Such a client has a great capacity to dispute the street-level bureaucrat's definition of the situation . . . knowledgeable clients are also perceived as a threat by street-level bureaucrats. Just as aggression increases the predilection for making demands, knowledge increases the capacity. . . . 'Naive' clients whose information is more trustworthy and who haven't the resources to manipulate the categorization decision are preferred.[39]

When the relationship between workers and clients has the capacity to swing between such extremes is it, finally, surprising that clients are ambivalent about the whole thing?

I've been there, I've been on welfare and SSI. I've dealt with Mass. Rehab and with the Mental Health Center. I had to get day care for my kids and a nursing home for my mother. And I'll tell you, it's a trip. Some days you're so mad because they won't help you and others you're sick of them bothering you.

I want to get away, but then I have to admit I couldn't have made it without them. I had no choice. I just wish I could have felt better about it.[40]

The lesson of all this for political practice is that all interactions with clients, no matter what the setting, form a relationship. That relationship has the potential to be mature, mutual, and rewarding to all parties. It also has the potential to be unpleasant, uncomfortable, and manipulative. Some of the factors influencing these relationships are beyond our control: the purpose of the agency, the nature of client needs, the material reality of class, race, or sex differences between client and worker. But, in many cases, an important relationship can be developed if workers are willing to think strategically and humanistically about it.[41] Workers must acknowledge their power, but also attempt to break its grip on the interaction by specific acts and attitudes, as well as by sharing and self-disclosure. Especially, service workers must realize that just as they try to develop strategies for dealing with clients, so clients also—based on past experiences, and on their rational judgment of personal needs—attempt to develop a strategy for dealing with workers.

The bureaucracies have tried to convince both workers and clients that their relationship is a zero sum game: if the worker wins, the client loses. The primary job of radical service work is to break such rules. We do not have to be gladiators fighting to the death for the benefit of the spectators. Instead, our goal, and our hope, has to be that we can someday stop fighting each other and turn, together, on those spectators who think they control our fate. As Steve Burghardt has argued, less metaphorically: "Our pivotal 'insurrectionary' role can be to produce relationships between clients and worker that run counter to dominant social relationships produced elsewhere."[42]

Since workers have the power to provide resources or support that clients want—or even worse, are judged to want—it is up to them to make the first moves in changing relationships. Indeed, because of the long history of how agencies and social workers may have "processed" clients workers must often make a whole series of moves, for a long period of time before anyone trusts us at all. New workers, even workers "from the community," are often taken aback by how much they are distrusted by clients, by how hard it is to convince people that they are "different." They often feel "taken advantage of" as clients see how much they can get out of them, before the inevitable lid clamps down.

Although understandable, such reactions are based more on a moralistic desire to be liked than on a material analysis of the situation. If anything, given the history of racism, sexism, and class injustice in this country, it is a tribute to the optimism of the human spirit that links can ever be made. Again, the notion of a "long march" with a slow accumulation of positive experiences which break old molds—for workers and for clients—may help us be patient.

An important base for building new relationships is to see the people one works with as potential comrades, as people with whom it is possible to make a *political* alliance. This means identifying with clients, without ignoring differences or romanticizing problems. Workers should consider themselves as potential allies with the option for friendship or other more personal relationships.* One does not have to like potential comrades, one only has to see them as possible allies. If workers assume that clients are sizing them up as potential comrades also, it should help both develop a more materially based definition of trust.

If the workplace doesn't allow workers to see the "clients"—now the word seems hollow—as potential comrades, perhaps they should look for other work, or stop thinking they can act politically in that setting. Any other attitude toward people leads to paternalism, condescension, objectification, and other forms of manipulation in the name of political practice. When one finds oneself feeling protective of clients, doubting their abilities to determine their needs and work for change, then hope for a political practice is lost.

The notion that clients are potential, rather than automatic, comrades is important. It allows one to avoid romanticizing people and forces one, instead, to work with them and observe their practice. Undeniably some people may have destructive political attitudes or behaviors, but then the political judgment is that they have made other political choices, not as "poor souls needing help." In "nonprofessional" organizations, for example, community workers are often (but not always) far more able to spot the true hustlers than middle-class outsiders and also able to be more supportive of real bravery in the face of adversity.

Admittedly, this notion of client as potential comrade needs further development. It was at the root of what Bertha Reynolds was doing in the United Seaman's Service and at the heart of United Farm Worker and recent women's movement services. It implies mutuality and reciprocity between two potential comrades, even as they work together to get as much as possible from the system. It suggests that both have something to gain from the relationship—a potential ally.

One potential danger is that activists may fall into the same dangers as some social movements—they may be too exclusionary in identifying potential comrades. Indeed, one positive effect of this

*I am assuming that the power of sexual politics is still in play, however, and that an equal "sexual friendship" may be impossible, as long as we have power over someone's life.

approach on our political development will be that it will force us to be less judgmental of those with whom we share political affinity—hardly a drawback for the faction-torn left.

Concretely, however, workers interact with potential comrades in a particular location and around specific issues. Another step in our reconceptualization is suggested when workers examine their own expectations: who are the "good clients," the "typical clients"? By looking at their own categorizations, workers can start to see their own biases, and the ways in which they try to influence potential comrades to make the work easier, or to meet abstract ideals of "the constituency."

In movement services, where political validity was often determined by the social characteristics of its clients, the problems of expectations arise clearly. Men in ERAP complained when "only housewives" came to meetings, not the "unemployed." Feminists sought to serve working-class and third world women and often were confused when white, middle-class women (the base of the movement) came. Organizers of one clinic, in Somerville, Massachusetts, went so far as to exclude women "from the movement" who were not "community women," from receiving their services.[43] They "expected" to serve community women and were going to do so, regardless of who wanted to use their clinic.

The point here is that activists often want to make people fit their categories just as much as nonpolitical workers may want clients to meet theirs. Some co-workers may wish for sweet, docile, young white women and try to turn their clients into that. Radicals may prefer militant, minority welfare mothers. But activists must acknowledge that they can be as manipulative and controlling as anyone else. Here Galper's admonition is relevant and even offers hope:

> In fact the techniques radicals employ, even if they are most self-conscious in developing a radical practice are not inconsistent with humanitarian liberal social work techniques. . . . Radicals have no monopoly on openness or personal sharing in the helping relationship.[44]

Following from this, and accepting with gratitude the notion that radicals need not claim to invent everything anew, we can briefly suggest some general guidelines for working directly in a more political way with clients. These are still broad suggestions that need to be clarified and developed in the context of specific workplaces: working with teenage boys is different from working with welfare recipients or with the elderly. The purpose of the listing here is to consider how these suggestions help build relationships with clients that open up expectations for them, for activists, for all workers, and for the broader community. Some of these proposals may surely be "good humanitarian liberal techniques," as Galper suggests. The hope here is that, taken together, and in the context of self-awareness and the goals mentioned above, they may begin to suggest a practice which is more explicitly political and more linked to broader social goals than is possible with technocratic ideals of "good practice" which currently define the field.

1. *Do the job.* The client comes for a reason; workers are paid and expected to do certain tasks. In almost all cases the first responsibility is to avoid hurting the person by adding new goals onto the relationship before the basics have been met. Forms and records must be kept properly if they are needed for the client to get the resources she or he expects. Doing the job does not mean ignoring the person; it means forms are explained, answers explored, rationales given. But in the desire to make connections and develop political unity, workers cannot justify ignorance of procedural requirements.

This becomes complicated if one's job has a strong social control function, where information and records may be used to hurt someone. Radicals should try to avoid such jobs; they make the inherent contradictions too great. If one finds oneself in such a role, or an inevitable component of otherwise more progressive work involves such tasks, collective discussion is needed to determine acceptable options. Sometimes one can steer clients to the correct answers without committing "fraud": "You don't have any baby-sitting jobs where you get money under the table, do you?" or, "Full-time students cannot receive benefits: are you a *full-time student?*" Or one can be vague with information which would be used against the client: "difficulty adjusting to life anxieties" was a phrase one political caseworker used often to meet billing requirements without dangerous labels. A full analysis of all required information is needed, including its purpose and the potential for possible misuse. Workers should know whether clients have legal rights to refuse to provide information and still receive benefits. Always the future uses of any information should be explained so that the client can make his or her own decisions about what to disclose. In extreme situations workers may choose to re-schedule meetings and to connect clients up to an advocacy group or lawyer before taking information which could be used against them.

No matter what the reasons, however, it is never acceptable to break the rules *for* clients without their knowledge—such generosity can only get clients in trouble. Such situations point out the need for alert advocacy groups. There are some roles that workers cannot directly perform without potentially hurting the person. However, the main task in such situations should not be forgotten: it is to help clients to receive absolutely as much as they are entitled to, to inform them of all options, and to warn of all potential pitfalls with what is happening.

At the other end of the spectrum are jobs where roles are less defined: recreation counselor, mental health worker, social services coordinator. Here the task is to be very clear about the options for what the relationship can be. Workers may need to supply a written summary of what tasks they can perform so that clients have some power in choosing options. Here the "contracting" and other explicit agreement systems which have arisen in the past decades can be useful to us. Workers cannot build relationships if clients are always waiting to be told what to do.[45]

2. *Acknowledge expectations and expertise.* Workers should be clear, in writing if necessary, what they must expect from clients (because it is required) or what they hope can come from the relationship. As much as possible workers should urge clients to describe what they want and expect from the encounter. Clients may, reasonably, be very circumspect but it is the worker's job to be open and encouraging, the client's to decide what to disclose. A key aspect of credibility (as a worker and as a potential comrade) is openness about one's knowledge. As Piven and Cloward note, we "need to know intimately all the rules and regulations and the ins and outs of agency rules for clients and workers," and tell clients so that they can discover what they need to know.[46] Ideally, activists should urge agencies to publish information, or they should pass on all relevant information to informed client groups. At least, typed lists of necessary information should be available so that clients do not always have to ask for information.

3. *Share political values.* All commentators on radical practice note that political education is one essential component of radical practice. Galper says it clearly: "Every helping interaction contains components of education implicitly or explicitly and each of these components has a political dimension." Yet he also warns that political education "does not necessarily involve sharing an explicitly radical analysis with users."[47] Activists are usually pulled in two directions here. On the one hand, they want to share a general political perspective with clients, and especially a political analysis that relates to the issues at hand. If they do not do so they may feel either manipulative or apolitical. On the other hand, no one wants to lecture clients or to divert them from more immediate tasks. Most radicals feel extremely sensitive about imposing their politics on people who do not ask for such information.

There are no easy answers here. At best we would have such a sharp, sophisticated, and subtle political analysis that it could be woven into all discussions, so that values were both clear and nonimposing. One of the reasons for a work support group is to help develop such an analysis. In the meantime activists should experiment, trying to incorporate politics into explanations of expectations, actions, or options, into the decorations of desks or offices, or by aside comments. But we must beware of too much fearfulness. After all, most people discuss the dominant ideology openly all the time, they just do not recognize it as ideology. So, if activists are a little heavy-handed sometimes, it will not do too much harm. Remember, potential comrades should not be as fragile as "clients." Most likely, activists will go back and forth, from attention to the "skills" clients need to worry about the political content of our work. Such pendulum swings served to characterize most movement services and, although slightly schizophrenic, never were too destructive:

We spend a while worrying about our politics, the meaning of what we were doing for the community, for women. Then something happens, a file gets misplaced, an examining room is found dirty and then we all freak out about how *bad* our services are, how little good we can do for people if we don't know our stuff. So we all shape up, study in groups, take courses, and really work at providing good health care. Then somebody starts to complain that we don't have any *politics* any more, that we are just like the hospital, and it all starts over again.[48]

4. *Shared personal experiences.* Political practice means avoiding condescending "distance" and seeking to be open about one's private life.
Such openness is important for the sake of mutuality, but radicals
must recognize that they can abuse it and assume more trust than
yet exists. Telling personal experiences can also emphasize class, race,
or cultural differences before enough trust exists for such differences to be useful. Unlike political sharing, here it is probably best
to err on the quiet side. Short comments about one's life may be
enough. If clients want to know more, an open atmosphere can encourage questioning. At all costs experiences such as that related by
one welfare recipient are to be avoided:

I guess he was being nice to me, but the more he talked about his wife and
her problems and how they were like my worries the madder I got. Who was
he to assume anything about my life? And how could he think that his prissy
little wife with a husband and a job of her own could be anything like me?[49]

Even if workers' class, racial, and sexual differences are not so far
removed from those of clients, false assumptions of connectedness
serve no purpose. The task is to build honest relationships based on
shared experiences (around the human service interchange) and
shared values. Asserting the presence of a relationship by an overly
generous disclosure of one's life may embarrass, bore, or anger clients.

5. *Groups work best.* The overriding problem in building relationships with clients stems from realities of institutional power. Workers
are paid to work with clients, the clients either pay the agency, or the
service is "free." Clients never forget this material reality, and neither should workers. Therefore strategies for building relationships
need to be twofold. Workers should support the development of as
much power as possible within clients and abandon those aspects of
their power which can be given away. One can divest power by sharing all information about procedures and options, by sharing personal and political expectations, and by attempting to treat people as
potential comrades, as equals who can be allies. But a relationship
cannot be built on our changed actions by individual workers alone.
Clients must be able to change the way they relate to workers; they
need to feel able to make demands and to express what they like and
do not like in the relationship.

Such goals may feel utopian in the context of some agencies. If they are possible at all, they absolutely depend on the development of the collective strength of clients, in opposition to an individualist strategy. One of the foundations of a left ideology is its questioning of what Corrigan and Leonard call the "cult of individualism" that is embedded in capitalism. In their words:

In the welfare state and its services, ideology is embedded in the practice of social workers and in the organizational delivery of services. State services are, following the definition of problems, geared to individual delivery: *individuals* are assessed, their "needs" met, and their progress monitored. There is no place in dominant State definitions for practice which contributes to transforming the private problem into a class experience.[50]

If the real voice of clients is to be heard, it cannot be an individual voice. It is too much to ask one man or woman to speak all the bitterness and make all the demands which need to be made. Political practice means establishing groups of clients, not staff-led therapy groups, but "mutual aid" groups, in the best sense. Such groups can discuss common concerns and organize joint demands on workers. They can also provide support and assistance to each other. We do not live in a socialist society: we cannot organize real "mass organizations." Any efforts will be compromised and feel contrived. But the presence of such groups could help articulate client demands: they may be a safe place for sharing "bootleg" information about the agency, and they may give clients a place to do their own "power analysis" of the agency and determine for themselves whom to trust.

Such a strategy is not new and it would take different forms depending on the agency and problems faced by the clients. Often it would supplement rather than replace individual contacts. But at least it may be a start on building client power bases outside the agencies and helping to create a situation where potential comrades can become active comrades.

6. *Remember the outside world.* A few years ago any discussion of political practices would have automatically assumed that radical service workers would struggle to link their own work and their agency's work to broader community activity. Today, it is not as clear what "community activity" means. However, activists must see clients, themselves, and their agencies in connection to a broader context. Just as they must know all relevant information about agencies and benefits within their agencies they must also know about outside programs. Ways should be found to support local advocacy groups, by

giving them information, by attending their rallies, by referring clients to them. Even if mutual aid groups are created through the workplace workers cannot expect such groups to function with the freedom of an independent advocacy organization. To do work effectively, both formations are needed.

Also, we cannot forget the special effectiveness which belongs to workers in their own communities. Movement services, the paraprofessional movement, and the self help movement all understood that the more clients saw workers in their own neighborhoods and at local community events the easier it was for trust to develop. At least, activists should know about and attend community events which affect clients' lives. At best, they are able to live in the areas in which they work. The reality of urban segregation by class as well as by race may make the ideal difficult, but attempting some closeness outside of the work role is a key element of a political practice.

Building relationships with clients as potential comrades is a difficult, long-term task. It is easier in some settings than others. In fact, the pressures resulting from contradictions in the work role and the seriousness of individual problems have led some radicals to argue that radical practice with clients is impossible, that we should concentrate on our relationship with co-workers, on unionizing and consciousness raising there.[51] While I understand such frustration, I cannot agree. A political analysis helps activists see the nature of class oppression and the importance of capitalistic labeling of an "underclass" which can be excluded from the normal processes of society, in part due to its definition as the client population of the social service institutions.[52] To say that building relationships with clients is impossible and that radical practice should only focus on organizing fellow workers, who have jobs and some social status, may be the worst form of radical "creaming." It means doing what seems easiest rather than doing what must be done. Finally, it becomes another cruel choice that political service workers are asked to make in the name of expediency. It too is a choice that fragments us and asks us to deny the centrality to our politics of what we do with clients every day.

Building Relationships with Co-Workers. Developing a political practice involves seeking two groups of potential comrades. Clients can be allies but they may not trust us due to the contradictory nature of our power over them. Fellow human service workers may be allies, but due to the same contradictions in our mutual work it may not always be possible for us to trust them. The goal of a political practice is to build as wide and strong alliances with co-workers as possible and to go beyond those alliances to develop a criticism of the negative ways in which service workers are made to function in the welfare state. With the current crisis and its assault on all jobs such alliances seem especially possible.

In order to build alliances with fellow human service workers the first step is to gain a good sense of what it means to work as co-workers and not as professional colleagues. We will explore this question more in the next chapter, but here we mean that "professional" colleagues see themselves as autonomous technicians whose place in society and in the human service workplace is defined by their particular expertise. Professionals may share information, pretend to review each other, and protect each other from ignorant clients and boorish administrators, but, in the end, they work alone and make their identity alone. By definition, they cannot be trusted to work collectively—it might compromise professional ethics—or to sacrifice the "principles" of their practice for improvement in other workers' or their clients' lives.

Co-workers, on the other hand, share the same material workplace conditions and acknowledge the same pressures. They unite together to protect the shared quality of their work and their own rights. Co-workers may not be the most extraordinary experts but they struggle to do the best job possible given the pressures and constraints on their work. To view our fellow human service workers as co-workers means that we have a right to demand unity around workplace protections and a shared interest in maintaining and improving the conditions under which we labor.

The only hope for a political practice is, wherever possible, to turn professional colleagues into co-workers, to value the benefits accruing from solidarity more than the benefits available from the myth of individual autonomy. This is no easy task. The myth of professionalism has given many people a sense that they can exercise power and has also supported them in upholding standards of "quality" services against efficiency-oriented administrations. Neither of these goals is valueless, although both may have been privileges granted in times of less political turmoil. These times may mean we must give up the illusion that we had power as a professional—as one Boston planner found out during a budget crisis: "I was an information junkie. I wanted to know everything because I thought it would help me convince people of what to do. Now I realize that nobody really listens to me, no matter how good my information."[53]

Such recognitions are part of what many have called the "proletarianization" of human service workers. While a painful process for individuals to go through, this newfound awareness of the futility of individual power may help co-workers listen to political discussions in a new way and be willing to join with other workers in some common tactics.

In order for this to happen, however, activists must discard unreasonable distrust and remember that they believe in change. It is easy to define oneself as different from "them," from the bureaucrats, or professionals who are one's peers. This stems partially from good motives—from awareness of the social control side of the work and the desire to separate oneself from it. But much of it may stem from less defensible roots—from the desire to be "professional" radicals, to be individual, brave activists fighting for clients against all those stupid, neanderthal social workers. Just as one cannot work in a radical way with clients without seeing them as potential comrades, neither can one work with co-workers if they cannot be viewed as *potential* allies. Some individuals may prove harmful and need to be opposed, but an effective political practice cannot be built on an assumption that everyone else in the agency is an irredeemable agent of social control.[54]

The acceptance of co-workers as potential comrades is only the first step, however. A range of tactics for working together with co-workers must be devised so that workers can test each other out as allies. Here again collective activities are best. Lunch groups can allow discussion of workplace issues or of how best to work with clients. As noted earlier, many apolitical practitioners may be very open to discussions that help define the everyday dimensions of a political practice. Activists should always push for group supervision sessions and more staff meetings. The more staff hear each other on issues the more they may learn to trust each other.[55]

Unions, of course, can be initial means for workers to come together. Organizing a union is an especially exciting activity and allows workers to know and work with each other, despite perceived differences. The ongoing business of a union can be more disappointing, however, because it is very difficult for a busy union to go beyond narrow economic issues. As we will discuss in chapter 6, unions may have other options, but the pressure is always on them from management, from other unionists, and from some members to stick to limited issues.

Because of the limits of unions, workplace caucuses are an important form of workplace organization. A caucus can be fairly open in terms of political differences and still serve to help activists sharpen their understanding of issues and receive personal support. A weekly caucus meeting can anticipate upcoming organizational issues or can help individual members consider how to discuss racial, class, or sexual issues with other workers or with clients. Especially in times of economic stress on agencies, they can help members cope with the tensions which build up over threatened layoffs or job redesign. The major danger is that a caucus can be seen as exclusionary. As noted earlier, some of this fear is political, a ruse for people who don't like to see activists getting together. But other co-workers may simply feel left out or judged. Caucus members should be sensitive to this and should consider more open forms of meetings: in addition to the caucus there can be agency-wide discussion groups on critical issues.

In short, the goal is to build relationships among co-workers that allow people to work together politically and suggest ways to improve the collective practice of the agency and to fight management. The hope is that an effective political practice can support this unity so that troublesome issues can be worked out among workers without divisive conflict. But sometimes this cannot happen. Sometimes fellow co-workers are acting individualistically, or are taking advantage of class, race, and sex privileges in a blatant way with clients. At worst these conflicts come out into the open with client complaints against a staff member, or the problems are so outrageous that radicals feel they cannot ignore them without betraying relationships with clients or basic political values.

These are unwelcome situations that activists cannot avoid. They, in essence, force a choice between a commitment to fellow workers and a commitment to clients. We should use discussion groups, union pressure, even individual appeals to avoid such confrontations. If they do come, however, a class analysis of the welfare system should give us direction. Finally, activists have to defend the right of clients to be served in a nonoffensive, nonracist, nonsexist way over the "rights" of a co-worker who is now acting as an agent of social control. As much as possible we want to push the problem up to management; it is often unreasonable policies or insensitive job assignments which enhance conflict. But we may not be able to dodge the issue. Management may be all too willing to stand up as the defender of clients against "bad" workers. It may be our political responsibility to explain why radicals cannot support such behaviors, even from fellow workers, and make clear demands that workers be transferred or even fired.

This is not to suggest, however, that clients are always right in their criticisms of workers. Sometimes white clients do not accept third world workers, or homophobic clients cannot respect a gay staff member. Even worse, a worker may be unfairly accused due to cultural or class misunderstandings. Administrators may even "set up" troublesome staff members by placing them in difficult, vulnerable situations. All of this means that radicals need to be especially cautious in regard to workplace conflicts, never able to defend co-workers automatically nor immediately to assume the clients' side. And all of this subtlety must emerge in the midst of the most tense, heated workplace situations.

The politics of daily work, then, are even more complex and difficult than the politics of working with clients. With fellow workers one must show both loyalty and a constant skepticism regarding the legitimacy of joint roles. Many may also distrust activists who can never be totally uncritical of institutions for which all work. Radicals are constantly standing professional assumptions on their head. Good professional practice teaches distance from clients and identification with one's agency. A political practice substitutes identification with clients and distance from the institutions of a capitalist society. Such differences are the hardest part of politics; they are, indeed, what separate others who might seem to be allies. The profound political task remains to explain such positions and why, ultimately, radical goals are linked to those of all working-class people (clients and workers among them) and not just the concerns of those who work for one agency. The difficulty of doing this was why many activists felt forced to build counterinstitutions. Now with such institutions temporarily weak we may face the bitterest winter seasons of our "long march through the institutions."

Co-Existing with Management. In most human service agencies, except those where "management" is still an ally (see chapter 6), the task is not to build relationships but to coexist without undue harrassment. Sometimes workers may feel forced, or powerful enough, to challenge management directly through strikes, union drives, or other work actions. But daily practice most often involves trying to do work with the least possible harrassment and intrusion from management. Although it may sound "radical" and exciting, the toll of constant open hostility with management is very seldom conducive to effective political practice. In situations of prolonged strife the whole focus of one's work becomes management. Clients suffer. Dissention can grow among workers and the potential for liberating practice can be lost. Such struggle cannot be a constant goal, even in times like these—although it may be forced upon us. Political practice thus becomes an ongoing effort to weaken management's power, or to expose it and to keep options open for opportunities to expand workers' power or client benefits.

Again, a base for any such strategy is thorough knowledge of the agency. A full analysis is needed of where the money comes from and who the real managers are. Since some people with little power over other workers or over policy have been labeled "management," each person's role should be reviewed to see what they do and the source of their power. Quiet exposure of very wealthy backgrounds or unsavory associations can be important. In short, activists should never be surprised by management—everything there is to know about them should be part of a political analysis.

Later we will consider options for responding to management initiatives and for defining progressive change. Here, in focusing on the personal dimension of practice the constant themes should be organizational openness and democracy. The more one fights secrecy, privileged information, and narrow specialization the more options are kept open. Demands for "more involvement in decision making" are always difficult for management to refuse directly. On the other hand, workers must not become confused and, under the guise of sharing decisions, be used to do management's dirty work. If decisions about firings must be made, or other unacceptable "policy options" are contemplated, we should force the blame on management (except perhaps in rare cases where alternative strategies do exist). In these bad times some smart managers have been more willing to share the dirty work. If such unpleasant decisions must be made, which is almost always doubtful, management should do it.

Individual workers face important questions in dealing personally with managers. Here a major goal is to maintain enough distance to act with control and authority. In many agencies bosses or supervisors may try to label any radical values or actions as "immature," as obvious "authority problems." One's style here must be the opposite of the openness sought with clients. Workers must be cool, detached, full of information, and unflappable. Many radical service workers report that supervisors try to "bait" them into unproductive discussion or emotional outbursts. While one has the right to be emotional, and should not be too self-critical if one falls into it, usually too much personal intensity is disfunctional. If used to confront management, anger should be a tactic, under control.

Often anger comes from illusions about management, especially about individual people. In most human service settings everyone knows each other fairly well. If people are friendly and polite it is easy to overlook their broader roles. Well-trained professionals are particularly adept at sounding "concerned." When the ideological and material gaps between people are exposed, one can feel betrayed, shocked, and upset because one "expected more." This type of anger does not help the development of strategy and denies understanding of class power.

In small offices such detachment is unpleasant; it goes against all the other habits of mind workers are trying to develop. Supervisors and bosses can turn the tables and feel hurt because they are not trusted, as if an equal relationship ever existed. Because of the overwhelming reality of racism, people of color are often much more able to deal with such tensions than whites. White activists have a lot to learn from workers like the black woman who described her work in a small, liberal training agency:

I'm all business. I know I can't trust them but I have to work with them; it's my job. I need my job and besides I'm learning some useful skills, in spite of them. But I keep my distance. I make my criticism in memos and in controlled, public meetings. I chitchat in the office but I never share anything important.

It's not hard for me because I *know* who they are, honey, they're the enemy.[56]

Part of what makes us radical is our desire to avoid social relations such as this. But, in most situations, seriousness about ones politics means accepting the real differences that come from class position in this society. Indeed, another difficult thing to accept is that distrust of management is returned. Some people have to learn that, in the words of one surprised youth worker:

They didn't like me any more than I didn't like them. It shouldn't have been a surprise, but when I applied to be house director I thought they would hire me *even* though I was a radical because I was also good. When they hired a "safe" co-worker it hit me—they took me seriously.[57]

Sometimes, however, the system is not so straightforward. Its own contradictions or the confusions of liberal administrations mean that one is recognized and praised for hard work, even offered certain promotions. Often such new roles can be accepted; they would not be offered if they were crucial to maintaining power. Promotions should be carefully weighed with trusted co-workers though. They may offer only illusory power and can create distrust. Or new roles may involve representing agency policies in public, a classic means of controlling activists. Many administrators, supported by "professional practice," argue that workers can dissent within the agency, but that they must defend it outside. Sometimes this may be true, but often it may not. Or at least, the type of defense activists would raise will not please a public relations office. So they are caught in the classic double bind experienced by one children's worker:

They wanted me to represent the agency about our children's services. I explained that what I would say might be too critical, but they insisted "because I was such a good speaker." Well, I gave my talk all about the problems we faced and the limits of what could be done. It was quite mild. But they were very upset: "Why did you have to be so negative?"[58]

Again, we can never really be loyal enough, by definition. In liberal agencies it may even help to explain this to bosses as a "personal problem" so that managers are not upset. One woman consistently refuses to deal with rich board members by arguing, "You know how it is, I'm just not good with people like that. They make me nervous." Such a response is probably more effective than a full-blown discussion with her boss (not with co-workers or clients) about the limits of capitalist "charity."

Our political analysis should be clear: management is not our constituency. We are not trying to radicalize them; we are trying to keep them from defeating us. If we can keep this in mind it should help us to develop a more effective political practice and to avoid cooptation or being set up to play the role of "crazy, immature radical."

LIMITS OF A PERSONAL APPROACH

Times of stress and crisis like the present tend to push all human service workers to forget themselves. Both one's politics and one's awareness of immediate human needs become more intense. Activist's naturally become less patient with the process of change, more angry. As their own jobs and identity are threatened they may find themselves wanting a "correct analysis." And, in fact, the stakes are higher; radicals are faced with becoming welfare cops or with losing the opportunity to do any real service work. Yet, exactly because of the personal stress associated with such times, activists need to be *more* aware of their own and others' personal needs to build action and relationships, not abstract credos.

The guidelines suggested above are still sketchy. They could imply that effective political practice is up to us, as individuals. Before they can be fully useful, especially in times like these, they need to be informed by broader understanding of the uses of professionalism as a brake on radical practice, and the intricacies of bureaucratic arrangements and their effect on our operations. I began with the personal side, however, because of its immediacy and of the lessons from movement services. Even where radicals made up the rules and defined the organizational questions the personal definitions of political practice were not often clear. Radicals had to work hard to act in liberating ways, even when other forces were not so hostile. If anything, this experience should show that a major concern in developing a political practice must be a consideration of personal relationships with clients, co-workers, and management. To deny this aspect of human service work is to deny a major lesson of the movements of the sixties: that the personal is political.

5

THE LIMITS OF
PROFESSIONALISM

"You are what you pretend to be."
KURT VONNEGUT, *Mother Night*

PROFESSIONALISM serves as the dominant ideological alternative to the development of an explicitly political conception of social welfare and of social service work. At every step it is a barrier to political practice and radical analysis. Activists who try to discuss politics with their clients, or in agency meetings, are confronted with overt and subtle messages that such actions are "inappropriate." Those who would organize unions face endless discussions over whether professional responsibilities are jeopardized by union obligations. Even with colleagues who engage in "social action," professionalism poses a counterstrategy. Social workers often want to advocate for issues because of the perspective gained from their "expertise," to lobby as professionals. Radicals, instead, engage in such work based on their sense of the importance of collective action and the need for class struggle. And at the policy level, the goal of professional "responsibility" means that activists are always asked to reduce expectations, to pose realistic and feasible policy goals, and never to become too passionate or moralistic in their presentation of issues. Finally, the mere fact of being labeled professionals can isolate service workers from the very co-workers and clients with whom political alliances are crucial, such as this Boston alcoholism worker:

I like my job now—working with alcoholics—because I am one myself and I believe I can help people better because I've been there. It also helps me to stay sober and to understand myself better.

I would like more training because I know I could do better but I'm not sure I want to be a regular "social worker." All the social workers I know—and I've known plenty in my day—are pretty cold and uninvolved and act like they are better than you are—especially if you are an alcoholic. So how do I get the training and credentials I need without becoming like that?[1]

Ironically, social work leaders have been concerned with their own professionalism and its meaning since the field began to emerge at the beginning of this century. For social workers the continuing debate has centered around questions of defining professional identity and the implications of their professionalization or lack of it. Most recently the emphasis has been on empirical research. How many social work professionals are there compared to nonprofessionals? What do they do and where do they work? Do their attitudes and practices reflect standard sociological definitions of professionalization? As is often the case with such "objective" research, the results have been differently interpreted. Some continue to assert that social work has become increasingly professionalized; others that social work is only a semiprofession. Still others argue that it is not now and never has been a profession and that our current task is to accept its deprofessionalized status and move on. Finally, some would view social work as a profession which is becoming increasingly "proletarianized."[2]

Luckily, for our purposes, the question is not to determine the extent to which social work is professionalized—whether, according to some standard measures, it meets the criteria of professionalization. Instead, we are concerned with the political implications of the *ideology* of professionalism which has been promulgated by dominant leaders who call themselves "professionals." In this case we can agree that, as with any ideology, "What is real has less importance than what is perceived to be real."[3]

The basic theme of this chapter is that professionalism evolved as an ideology seeking to define both social welfare programs and social service work as apolitical, as removed from struggles of power, resources, and class identity. Of course, the underlying effects of this

approach were extremely political.[4] However, the very success of social work professionalism as an ideology is reflected in the difficult
struggle radicals face when they try to expose this ideology and replace it with a more explicitly political set of goals. Not only professional leaders but also many workers will cling to professionalism because it seems to give them a safe identity and a defense against social
confusion and political risk. As Pearson notes in a perceptive essay:

"Radicalism" assaults the sensibilities of the professional because it deroutin-
izes and points through routines to moral dilemmas which lie behind them.
It asks quite simply, "What are social workers really doing?" . . . Thus radicalism points to uncertainty.[5]

DEVELOPMENT OF A PROFESSIONAL APPROACH

As was discussed in chapter 1, the late nineteenth-century origins of
the social work profession help to explain the "apolitical" nature of
the professional ideal which developed. In an amazing show of historical unity, there is wide agreement about the social roots of
professionalism in this period and about the shared origins of the
"search for order" by the emerging medical, legal, engineering,
teaching, and social work professions.[6]

As postulated by Robert Weibe and developed by others, social work
emerged with the "new middle class" in the 1880s, a class of people
who were not needed as entrepreneurs nor were forced to work at
any job to earn a living. Such individuals collectively formed a class
of people "who sought to transcend island communities," to develop
a socially useful role for themselves, and who "found their rewards
more and more in the uniqueness of an occupation and in its importance to a rising scientific-industrial society."[7] They sought to become professionals, with special goals, as Larson notes:

Emerging themselves with an emergent social order the professionals first
had to create a market for their services. Next, and this was inseparable from
the first task, "they had to gain special status for their members and give
them responsibilities."[8]

For the new middle classes, professionalism served as a means to
attain status through work, instead of through inherited or earned
wealth. For the developing capitalistic economy, social workers helped

to create a more centralized, rationalized, controlled social order, in place of the chaotic, violent, unpredictable society that had allowed for rapid capital development. The new order was to be more bureaucratic, more "scientific" and "efficient." People would be more manageable if they were organized into occupations, rather than around vociferous political parties, and if they found their identities through work instead of through passionate moral and political values.

For the new social workers at the beginning of the twentieth century professionalism meant an end to the moralistic philanthropy of earlier charity efforts. It meant a "scientific approach" to poverty, the use of social scientific knowledge in dealing with need, and the development of an organized professional identity to maintain the standards of modern social work. The goal was to strive to substitute the "normal" for the "abnormal" in social relations:

Rationality and peace, decent living conditions and equal opportunity, they considered "natural"; passion and violence, slums and deprivation were "abnormal." Knowledge [the early social workers] were convinced, was power, specifically the power to guide men into the future.[9]

Thus the new profession began to organize itself to better provide efficient service and to better define its own role as the natural leader in "scientific philanthropy." Social work schools were organized, professional associations were formed, and journals were established as part of what Larson has called the "professional project"—the goal of achieving secure status as a profession.

Such tasks were easiest for members of established charity agencies, which evolved into public relief agencies. Their work was already somewhat bureaucratized by the beginning of the twentieth century and their few paid staff had never held strong moral-political goals for their work—only the volunteers needed to be purged of "unscientific attitudes," or just purged to make way for paid professionals.[10] But for the settlement house workers, the transition was more difficult and more complex. Although their class backgrounds were similar to other new professionals, their intimate involvement with the urban poor had begun as moral acts and often had grown into a passionate struggle for political change. They were not attracted to the bureaucratic, apolitical model of efficient professionalism which already was defining charity organizations. Instead, social reform was their progressive cry, nothing less.[11]

Indeed, some settlement workers never identified as social work professionals because of such tensions. They opted, by the third decade of the century, to become socialists, a few even became labor organizers. But most forged a new role for themselves, one which collapsed the demands of professionalism and their concerns for change: they became professional reformers and proponents of social activism *within* the social work profession. Most settlement workers had never supported the idea of class conflict; their goal had been Christian brotherhood and social responsibility. As the service ethic of professionalism developed it allowed them to consider "scientific reform" as the answer to the difficulties they saw in the slums, to urge—based on their scientific study of social problems—changes as part of their new role as social "experts." In addition, settlement houses gradually developed into complex organizations, calling for "efficient procedures and expert management." So one-time reformers could easily allow their urge for local reform to evolve into a call for responsible "social administration."[12]

It would be unfair to be too harsh on individual social workers here. Professionalism was a rampant new ideology that offered them the opportunity to substitute "expertise for moral superiority" and to keep the "ideal of personal contact and influence" while avoiding "the fiction that such contact was one of friends and peers."[13] It allowed them to continue their struggle for social reform and find themselves new allies as their "progressivism became tamer, smoothed into a tractable corporate liberalism."[14] As *professional* reformers they could "speak the same language" as certain liberal politicians and capitalists, a language which was foreign to real allies of the poor or—even worse—to socialists.

In addition, as we noted in the first chapter, it was not clear that options for a more political practice were available to early social workers. As we have seen, most trade unionists were suspicious of them and their capacity to be of service to working people. While some local socialist parties did take positions in favor of stronger social welfare measures, most of the energy of socialists, too, was not channeled into such "reform" concerns. And the more radical parties took even harsher positions about the inherently repressive nature of service work. While it may have been true, as Dykema argues, that the development of professional "social services may have preempted demands a more effective socialist movement might have made," the fact is that no socialist movement that was around wanted to make such demands.[15]

So the origins of our choice began. Either one defined oneself as a radical and was forced to sneak desires to provide services in on the margins of one's political work or one defined oneself as a professional and tried to find some ways to covertly express one's politics in one's practice. Over time the choice, being denied, became less obvious. By the 1920s it could not really be construed by most social workers as a conscious choice. Social work professionalism had begun to express itself in a variety of techniques, none of which would be explicitly political although some remained concerned with "social reform." And the American left had become engaged in a series of internicene battles which left any development of a radical social welfare strategy far from anyone's agenda.

Instead of an arena for ongoing political debate, then, the practice of social welfare in both its individual and social dimensions became a "function" of liberal capitalism, with a developing technology and an explicit ideology of apolitical expertise.

Professional Options. As a process of its institutionalization, and its ongoing "professional project," social work began to subdivide into a range of subspecialties, several of which were engaged in constant battles with each other over which one represented the "true profession." The heat of these internal debates—especially those who argued against casework in defense of "social policy" or "community work" or "social reform"—can be confusing. It often appears as if only casework is "professional" and all other forms of social work have waged important struggles for a more "political" practice. However, a look behind the smoke of rhetoric shows that each branch of the field asserted for itself the accoutrements of expertise, the responsible community of peers, the service ethic, and the "objective" standards of practice that are required for professional status.[16] A brief look at the elements of professionalism embodied in each option provides a more unified sense of what is meant by social work professionalism.

Casework was the dominant area of social work practice and theory. From the second decade of this century its principles of practice were developed and elaborated, and it developed something akin to the defined, discrete "body of knowledge" so sought after by professional experts. Indeed, Wilensky and Lebeaux, no staunch advocates of casework supremacy, could remark, in the 1950s, that casework "is so dominant that it is doubtful that there would be any such identifiable entity as professional social work without it."[17]

It was the influence of casework, with its focus on the individual and the intervention strategies necessary to support individual change, which has most angered activist social workers, as well as other types of social work practitioners. Especially with the advent of Freudian theories during the 1920s, casework became the symbol for the escape of social work from its "social" responsibilities. Upper-level academics, administrators, and policy makers (predominantly men) decried the therapeutic approach, even as the largest numbers of students in social work schools continued to concentrate in casework methods.[18]

For socialists, it is easy to join in with the ideological criticisms of casework. It does focus on the individual as the source of social problems, and thereby reinforces the capitalist emphasis on individual, rather than social, responsibility for societal problems. Society with its exploitative patterns is taken as a given. It does tend to isolate both client and worker from the broader social networks of support and to reinforce the primacy of the professional as the only one who can adequately help the powerless client.[19] We will return to such criticisms later. For now, however, it is important to acknowledge that the original conception of casework was somewhat more broadly framed than the critique would indicate and to speculate again that the professional criticisms of casework may reflect deeper, less desirable, prejudices.

Casework was originally defined by Mary Richmond in two critical books, *Social Diagnosis* (1917) and *What Is Social Casework?* (1922). As framed by Richmond and developed by others, even after the increased influence of Freud, the role of casework was to help assess individual needs and to provide assistance in meeting them, "based upon thorough investigation of their social environment and social relationships."[20] Richmond herself and most subsequent defenders of casework never stated that they felt that casework was the single solution to social problems: in *Social Diagnosis* she stated clearly, "Mass betterment and individual betterment are independent . . . social reform and social betterment of necessity progressing together."[21]

So why do liberal social work professionals, who also want social adjustments to capitalism, sound so vitriolic? One reason could be because the professional turf distribution is askew, that casework attracts so many students that other areas are left begging. Another may be that we are back onto another dimension of our original forced choice: casework represents daily ongoing nurturance and caretaking; it cannot be important in the "serious" business of creating a social welfare system. Could it be that it is the social policy experts or the community organization professionals, not the caseworkers, who cannot imagine combining broader social concerns with attempts to help individuals? Especially when the majority of all MSW social work students are caseworkers and 60 percent of these are women, we begin to wonder.[22]

Community organization presents a different aspect of social work professionalism. With roots in settlement house activism and community agency organizing, its practitioners (a greater number of males than in any other branch of social work) have often presented themselves as the "radicals" of the profession. They focused on collective activity, on change in communities and agencies. Since the 1920s when settlement house organizers tried to build "social units" in the neighborhood, "CO" people have presented their approach as the natural heir to progressive reformers and have attempted to develop a "scientific practice" of community organizing. As community organization developed, especially in the late 1940s, it was most often linked with "social planning" for agency aggrandizement and for the development of hegemony for dominant social agencies in a community.[23]

Perhaps most telling here is the fact that community organizing professionals still attempt to define themselves as professionals, to argue for students, for the legitimacy of their "knowledge base," and to steadfastly refuse to identify primarily as activists. From our perspective, such an approach means that they are clearly part of the shared social work ideology of professionalism and serve an important function within the profession, by allowing it to claim a reform wing when it is criticized for conservatism.[24]

Social reform and social policy are other areas of social work professionalism that are used to combat arguments for a more political approach. As we have seen, social work leaders have engaged in efforts to shape social legislation and social policies; this cannot be denied. Professional groups have researched issues and made recommendations, and social work leaders have lobbied for desired policies. Such activities fulfilled a critical part of the developing professional role in the "transpolitical state," as Larson explains:

> . . . [the new class was] arising and asserting itself in intimate connection with the central institutions of the new social order . . . [they] defined the form that institutions, policies or services were to take, reserving for themselves, at least in principle, the role at the helm.[25]

Over time, however, the rationale for attempting to influence government policy shifted. Early reformers engaged in such work out of an explicit awareness of their "Progressive" political goals. While they did not pose radical goals, there was a sense among early leaders that their activity was a part of their political identity, it linked them to other "good government" reformers in a variety of areas. Gradually this elite, but self-consciously political, "social activism" became something else. Social policy professionals increasingly based their demands for influence not on political values and allegiances to a reform movement but, instead, on the legitimacy of their "expertise" as a base of policy making and implementation.[26]

Ironically, the way in which social work professionalism replaced early capitalist reformism as the base for activity in the area of social work policy served to weaken the scope of power for social work professionals. Increasingly, throughout the century, the claim to influence came from the value of one's professional expertise, not one's political identity. Naturally, such an approach meant deference to existing economic and social realities that were outside the realm of expertise. It led leaders in the field of social work policy to argue, in essence, that all that social welfare policy professionals could do was to make recommendations regarding the implementation of policies which were forged in political arenas beyond their rightful concern and control. So, in assuming the mantle of "scientific expertise," not of political advocacy, social work professionals ultimately lost credibility to deal with the very political questions which, finally, were most powerful in determining basic policy direction. They set themselves up to become technicians with limited influence.

At the individual level, social administration and social planning have similar effects on the professional identity of social workers. The professional responsibility of the social worker, at all times in all settings, is to "be guided by his sense of professional competence."[27] Thus the worker's political values and allegiances are deemed irrelevant and "unprofessional."

Good professionals have been tricked by their own ideology into thinking that their expertise and practice is not political and can best be guided by technological criteria for success with results that can be measured and counted. Our muddled professional policy experts thus become like the drunk who seeks his lost money under the streetlight, where "the light is better," rather than in the dark down the street where he lost it.[28] Our task as activists may be to force all of those concerned with social welfare into the dark, but real, arena of political struggle over basic social priorities and out of the false light of professional policy analysis, which ultimately can reveal nothing because it asks the wrong questions, based on inadequate assumptions.

Finally, the fate of group work as it was adopted by social work professionalism during the 1930s gives a good, brief indication of the political effects of an apolitical professionalism. As Reid describes in his history of group work, the origins of the field were outside of social work, in education, recreation, and youth work. Group work was originally presented as explicitly political in its goals—either as providing a microcosm for developing egalitarian interactions or as "training the lower classes to habits of industry and initiative." Much of the profession had kept its early activist approach for combining direct service with political struggles against social conditions that fostered problems. As they joined the social work profession during the 1930s, economic pressures of the Depression and the perceived need for a "professional identity" brought changes in the accepted norms of group workers and their agencies. There was an increase in theoretical labeling and a "decrease in emphasis that group work-

ers placed on social action," according to Reid.[29] Thus the depoliti-
cizing effect of social work professionalism occurs across the range
of areas of professional practice. The essence of an effective political
practice, then, lies in better understanding and challenging professionalism in all its forms.

CHALLENGES OF THE THIRTIES AND SIXTIES

As we have already seen, the 1930s and 1960s were times of development and energy for radical services. They were also times of
pressure and change for the profession of social work. A brief review of the professional reactions during these times may give us some
insights into the possibility of transforming professional into political
practice.

During the 1930s the social work profession was buffeted in many
directions. Harry Hopkins, Frances Perkins, and the Abbott sisters
were among the many social workers who rose to prominence. Ow-
ing to intense economic pressure many Progressive-era social policy
dreams were achieved, including social security and a federal welfare system. But as a historian of the period remembers, the social
work leadership was not united in a sense of political victory.[30] An
activist faction, the Rank and File Movement, arose which became
noisy and even "unprofessional." The group adopted its name from

. . . its frequent use by opposition groups in labor unions to identify themselves when challenging the leadership. It implied that the challengers were
representatives of the foot soldiers in the ranks, of the membership of a larger
union of the powerless silent majority . . . [they saw parallels between the
labor establishment] and the Establishment in social work, not corrupt or
bought out to be sure but faint-hearted, at times pusillanimous, deferential
to the conservative views of the businessmen who provided the lay leadership in social work, and committed to the preservation of the status quo.[31]

Through their newspaper, *Social Work Today*, the Rank and Filers
offered the option of a more political identity for social workers. The
group's focus was on organizing and political education within the
profession and in building alliances with the trade union movement.
In some cities its members seemed to serve almost as a left caucus
within social work agencies and organizations, exerting a constant

pressure for more social responsiveness. It also was responsible for making the first positive connection between trade unions and social workers. As we have seen, these new alliances allowed some radical service workers to provide services within union settings.

The Rank and File Movement suggests strongly that it is worthwhile for service workers to organize around a range of political issues and that, through their efforts, other workers may be politicized and a constant left pressure kept up on the profession—which often shows itself to be vulnerable to political pressure.

Other developments of the 1930s are less positive, however. At the same time that radicals were applying pressure, the profession was also reaching new stages of growth. The number of social work schools increased greatly, as the welfare state established itself as a perpetual job market, and the number of social workers doubled.[32] And it was during the 1930s that Freudian psychology established itself as the dominant theoretical approach in the prestigious private agencies. Indeed, during this period a gap widened between the private sector and the public sector of the profession.

Finally, it is perhaps a sign of the limitation of the old left that even among social service radicals there was little discussion of the political content of casework. Leslie Alexander and Phyllis Lichtenberg conducted a survey of the "Casework Notebook" which ran in *Social Work Today* throughout the journal's lifetime. They found that, in spite of the fact that "it was professional caseworkers who both spearheaded and formed the largest professional contingent among the social work unionists," there was still an ambivalence about making casework itself more political. In the great majority of the columns "casework was considered to be separated from political action" and little criticism was made of the substance of casework practice. The columns did not suggest a critique of the individualistic function of casework, nor did they explore how workers should respond to unjust authority settings. They did not question the professional distance that social work demanded. Although the importance of "craftsmanlike pride" in helping work was stressed as well as the need to understand how workers and clients were buffeted by the Depression, the insights shared were far less radical than those reported by Bertha Reynolds from her union service work.[33] It was as if leftists were still bound by old divisions and old unwillingness to combine their radical political insights with anything that approached personal relationships.

The 1960s posed different—perhaps more fundamental, if less direct—challenges to social work professionalism. The Poverty Programs, the welfare rights movement, the black movement, the widespread upsurge of social activism threatened to render social work professionals irrelevant. As we have seen, little of the activity was done in the name of social work, and much of it embodied a distinctly antiprofessional bias. The New Careers movement of the late sixties served to bring new workers into systems, workers who were collectively conscious about their distrust of old methods.[34] And black professionals and community activists hit social workers squarely in their liberal guilt when they began to launch a frontal assault on the paternalism and racism of much social work practice.[35]

But the power of professionals to adjust to changing developments while still holding their ground is remarkable. The social work journals began debates on "social action." The early social reformers were remembered and their calls to battle unearthed. Although not the center of student unrest by any means, social work schools did undergo their own "relevancy crisis" and moved toward a more advocacy-oriented curriculum.[36] And a study by Jorgansen indicates a pronounced shift in political values in the journal *Social Work* from 1957 to 1973. During this time all categories of authors became more sympathetic to values of "clientism, social treatmentism, and self-determination" and less supportive of "professional autonomy, clinicalism, and paternalism."[37]

Brief as they are, these sketches of two decades suggest that social work professionalism as an ideology is somewhat subject to pressure. Exactly because the daily activity of most social workers lends itself as much to a radical analysis as to professional explanations, activist service workers may be more able to organize and posit different models of practice than their counterparts in medicine or law, for example. Maybe instead of a semiprofession it is a "soft" profession which is vulnerable to serious political organizing from below and outside. And, in times such as the 1980s when all service workers and the professional elite are so rejected by the groups holding state power, we may find many people beginning to wonder about the benefits of such an ineffective professionalism.

THE CONTEMPORARY STATE OF SOCIAL WORK PROFESSIONALISM

Reaganism, cutbacks, the economic crisis, even the current popular "culture of narcissism" combine to pose critical questions to social work professionalism, even without pressure from the left. More important than particular cutbacks, devastating as they are, is the assault on basic—if contradictory—social commitments. The New Right is using Reaganism to challenge social arrangements in place since the New Deal—arrangements by which the capitalist state agreed to guarantee certain protections to the victims of the political economy. Such an assault symbolizes an overwhelming defeat for the "professional project" of social work. The ascendent Right has made it patently clear that neither the elite of the social work profession, nor the average social worker, is to be trusted with power. Even though most programs still exist the message is direct—any benefits remaining are *not* due to efforts of the social work leadership.

Such an overt setback in professional advance can be deeply unsettling to an already insecure profession. Recent social work conferences have been pathetic, as "leaders" tried to figure out what were their remaining vestments of power when actual power was so obviously lacking. In such a climate, honest reassessment may even be possible—at least for those not totally invested in continuing to search for someone to whom to sell out.

Individual service workers also are feeling the stress of job insecurity. Especially hard hit are those who had long ago traded any illusion of professional autonomy for the "security" of civil service protection as a street-level bureaucrat. When daily fears for one's job are added to the inevitably self-defeating ongoing pressure of bureaucratic work, there may be room for change.

Some highly trained social workers are attempting to move out of vulnerability into the "control" offered by private practice. Licensing laws and the availability of third-party payments made this option more viable. There was a steady increase in privately practicing social workers from 1978 to 1982. Such service workers usually move into isolating jobs, but they are at least able to retain their "professional" status. What they are doing is retreating to an older, preorganizational form of professionalism (which was never really experienced by social work). However, the demand for such private services may not keep up with the rapidly increasing supply, so what we see may be only a small advance before another big loss.[38] And who will know to protest when, one by one, private practitioners must take down their shingles because of lack of demand?

In spite of such major crisis in the milieu that supports social work professionalism, we can assume that there will be resistance to change. There is already a "this too will pass" school of experts who are waiting for the "pendulum to swing back." Social work schools are still recruiting, although with less success, especially for the expensive private schools. There is even an increase in bachelors level programs. Social work journals are still calling for better "knowledge for practice." One new human services journal has even become recognized for its persistent attempt to develop a scientific approach to implementing cutbacks.[39] One can be sure that before any radical departures occur in social work professionalism there will be a rash of "new techniques" meant to allow social workers to handle their problems in the tried and true, apolitical, technocratic ways: stress management, burnout workshops, and midlife career planning are but a few of the possibilities.

On the other hand, internal weaknesses may provide the necessary motivation for change. First is the weakness of the leadership. Professional coherence depends on a dominant ruling elite who will define the ideology, interpret the appropriate technology, and suggest further directions. For internal solidarity this elite needs to be perceived as having power and influence. The weakened state of the social work leadership suggests that new leaders may emerge without the standard controls over whose voices can be heard. The classic "vacuum in power" may be at hand.

Second, alienation from bureaucratic agencies may put pressure on an "organizational profession" like social work. Studies have shown that social workers affiliate themselves more with their agencies than do other professionals. Their very professional and personal identity has often been determined by the nature of their bureaucracies.[40] Workers who remain in jobs may find themselves increasingly alienated from their agencies, increasingly unable to deny the social control functions of their work, and thereby may become open to a more political identity.

Finally, an increasing feminist consciousness of women in social work may force an internal reappraisal.[41] Just eight years ago a contributor to a major British anthology on the "new social work" could draw a profile of the social work activist as "in general such a worker is male *(or a female with masculine traits)* of middle class origins."[42] Today many women in the field, whether activists or not, may be able to see such "masculine personality traits" as part of the problem for social work and may be willing to push for some basic changes in approach.

These three internal pressures, therefore, mean that the profession may be especially vulnerable to the range of criticisms which are launched against it.

CHALLENGES TO PROFESSIONALISM

The social work profession has long characterized itself as divided between those with an orientation toward individual change and those with a more "social" orientation. As Clarke Chambers notes, these two differing perspectives on the direction of social work professionalism have historically been at odds, and during "times of rapid social change or of economic crisis it has often seemed as if the two components were mutually exclusive or even opposed."[43]

Another persistent internal critique of social work professionalism is that it has forgotten the poor, or even served to make their plight worse. This is an important structural critique and one which bolsters a left analysis of capitalist social welfare. When it is made from within the profession, however, the answer that is often accepted serves to reinforce old patterns. Many leaders acknowledge the truth of the allegation but then explain that the profession was never intended to deal with poverty:

Social work is criticized today for having adapted its service structure in recent years to a middle-class clientele. Yet if poverty is interpreted as a problem of income redistribution requiring substantial changes in the institutions and power relationships of American society, social work has never identified with the poor.[44]

It is perhaps another sign of how soft a profession social work is that it can honor a historian like Lubove, quoted above, and turn his criticisms of the profession into simple "facts of life" about the "reality" of professional possibilities.

The most significant recent internal criticism of social work was made by Willard Richan and Allan Mendelsohn in *Social Work: The Unloved Profession* (1973).[45] In this strange book, the authors present an impassioned account of the personal and social failures of professionalism. Finally, however, what keeps this criticism internal is that the solution proposed is still a professional one. For all their negativity, the authors only complain because the profession has missed its chance to allow social workers to operate like a true professional elite:

Social work reveals itself today as a "might have been" profession: a profession whose dynamic potential has been channeled into so many paths that it makes little impact. . .

A professional group that can carry the message inside the system, locate the weak spots in the castle wall and use the system's resources against itself becomes especially strategic. Given a different brand of professionalism, the social worker can run interference for the client—reach a key decision maker while the client gets put off at the reception desk.[46]

Internal critiques such as these suggest that we need to be quite careful in selecting allies for a new approach to service work. The very confusion of social work professionalism may mean that some are, indeed, casting around for new models—but for new models of professionalism, of new ways to protect their privilege, not for radical change. There is no reason to help them in this effort.

Human Services vs Social Work. Another current challenge to social work professionalism has come from the growth of human services as a broader concept and field of activity that does not claim "social work" as its professional parent. As Betty Reid Mandell has pointed out, the increase in community services in the 1960s and 1970s brought a whole influx of new workers into service work.[47] Now many of those workers seek training and recognition but often still remain skeptical of social work professionalism. Many attend "alternative" undergraduate and graduate programs to receive "skills training," without professional socialization. In short, if they are able to stay in the job market, such human service workers pose a real threat to the professional hegemony of social work.

Admittedly, a few years ago the challenge from this new human service workforce seemed greater. The current cuts have affected both the jobs and the schools for such workers. And in the search for leadership in the current crisis, social work professionals may be able to reassert themselves. But, even with these setbacks, there still remain thousands of workers like the alcoholism counselor quoted earlier, workers who feel committed to service work but who have rejected professional elitism, class bias, and neutral approach to social services.

Human services is not only a term that has been used to cover direct services. It has also been a catchword, since the Nixon administration, for an approach to services which stressed a management, "coordination," and a systems approach. As Mandell also argues, this new breed of human service managers was explicitly critical of social workers because they were too specialized and did not understand "generic approaches to case management." It is hard to classify this trend. It grew up in response to federal grant initiatives and federal attempts to create integrated and coordinated services which were sometimes exciting service innovations and sometimes technological cover-ups for service cutbacks.[48]

The effects of this new development are unclear. On the one hand, in some quarters it already has pushed some social work schools to consider programs in "human service management" and has led to career-upgrading seminars in management techniques. So the profession may try to swerve in this direction by adopting yet another new technology—perhaps one that can finally overtake casework methods in popularity—and a further abandonment of service ideals. On the other hand, the incompatibility of such efforts with parts of the professional tradition—and perhaps with the personal traits and learning styles of the people drawn to social work—may give the profession pause. The pressures generated by this new initiative may open further cracks in the meaning of professionalism. There is reason to believe that in order to avoid becoming managers many service workers might be willing to assume a more political definition of themselves and that social work leaders, at least, might begin to explore whether to become leaders of a social democratic political movement rather than of an eroding profession.

Self Help. As we noted in chapter 3, the self help movement also poses a significant challenge to the authority of professional expertise and the legitimacy of professional autonomy.[49] Of course, many efforts have not been self-consciously antiprofessional and have been supported under professional auspices. But all question the necessity for professional intervention and many leave the individual service worker unsure as to the appropriate professional role.

Indeed, the attempts to include self help approaches into the battery of professional skills may be another sign of the professional confusion in regard to its own self-interests. Any serious review of the underlying premises of self help and citizen action movements must acknowledge them as, in Peter Leonard's words, "an assault on professionalism itself," an attempt to shift the balance in regard to defining problems and determining appropriate responses and a clear alternative to the ideology of professionalism.[50] In place of an emphasis on knowledge it poses an acceptance of experience and feelings, it proclaims the value of subjectivity over objectivity, the value of identification over "controlled warmth." It challenges the very idea that a reserved, standardized encounter is better than spontaneous sharing and mutual discovery. While, as we suggested earlier, there can be other drawbacks to self help—the most important being the continued self-definition of participants as victims—as an assault on professionalism it is total.[51] Social work professionals may have tried to coopt self help groups, or to support them only for clients in whom they have no interest. But by opening the door they may have themselves given credibility to a fundamental undermining of professional authority.

Unions. Unionization raises other critical doubts about the benefits of professionalization. In many ways it embodies an opposite strategy for reaching similar ends. Both embody self-organization and stress their members' value to workplace goals. But, as Larson observes, no matter how much some unions may support internal hierarchy they still, finally, focus goals and strategies on collective benefits and serve to deemphasize the unique skills of particular workers. Professional organizing, on the other hand, engages in collective action only to advance the autonomy of individual professionals and suggests no notions of class interests and class discipline, much less the solidarity among all types of workers, which is implied by progressive unionism.[52]

Unions, then, even at their most conservative, would force professionals to make new kinds of alliances and to forgo the illusion of their autonomy for the benefits accruing from worker solidarity. Indeed, when Wagner and Cohen suggested a strategy for giving up the "myth of professionalism" their first step was unionization, as a means to "draw a line between us as social workers and our agencies."[53] It is such arguments which lead radical social workers in this country and in Britain to pose unions as a crucial means for defeating the privilege of professionalism and for giving service workers another, more politically acceptable identity.

Here, however, many professionals are not confused. Perhaps test of how much one really adopts the professional ideology may be one's reaction to unions. In a study by Haug and Sussman, 65 percent of those who opposed unionization did so because it was "unprofessional." The authors commented:

One possible explanation is that the individual who perceives himself as a professional, having taken on the imagery of the role, uses a rhetoric which is basically different from the pro-union occupation holder. Both want the best wages and working conditions for themselves and their colleagues. The latter employs an open dialogue of rights, demands, grievances, needs and privileges while the former cloaks his hidden agenda of higher pay and ideal work environment behind the words of service, reward, skill, mystery and privilege.[54]

Union drives may consequently serve two purposes. They may allow service workers the chance to directly acknowledge their material needs, without the smokescreen of professionalism, and may also identify those co-workers who, through their insistence on a professional identity, really cannot be trusted.

We will discuss the implications of unionization further in chapter 6. Here we suggest that human service workers may be able to preserve one aspect of what has been viewed as professionalism to the benefit of their new unions. The commitment to service and awareness of the needs of clients, which are the most admirable goals of the ideology of professionalism, may be brought into union activity. By taking up such questions within their unions, activists may address the legitimate professional fear about a narrow business unionism and also help to develop a notion of unionism that is more in harmony with the radical roots of industrial unionism.

Professionalism Under the Microscope. The last ten years have brought forward several theoretical critiques which should inform any attempts to oppose professionalism, even if we cannot expect them to influence the behavior of most professionals—as have the other challenges presented here. For our sake, and for the sake of collective political education, the works of Ivan Illich, John McKnight, Barbara and John Ehrenreich, and Margali Sarfatti Larson need to be encountered and considered.

First, Illich and McKnight, in *Disabling Professions* (1977) and elsewhere, pose the most radical opposition to all professionalism, and perhaps to any efforts at human service work. While Illich's attacks are more specifically focused on medicine and McKnight's concern is for social services, both see the "domineering professions" as weakening citizens and are forthright in arguing that public acceptance of their power "is essentially a political event."[55] McKnight goes on to raise chilling questions about whether all human services, provided as they are in the interests of the dominant class, can do anything but benefit that class—by defining needs, turning needs into individual deficiencies, and presenting professionals as the only hope for addressing the deficiencies, preferably with a technology and language which cannot be understood by the citizen turned client.[56]

McKnight and Illich raise questions that must be addressed not just by those social workers who define themselves as "professionals" but also for any of us who try to take the helping role. Their criticisms of "modernized professionalized services" ring true for the worst of the large public bureaucracies, or for the most elite professionalized care giving. But, they also suggest an inevitable lack of reciprocity which serves to undermine all helping efforts, especially because

. . . this mask of service is *not* a false face. The power of the ideology of service is demonstrated by the fact that most servicers cannot distinguish the mask from their own face. The service ideology is not hypocritical because hypocrisy is a false pretense of a desirable goal. The modernized servicer believes in his care and love, more than even the serviced.[57]

Here McKnight and Illich caution against feeling too arrogant about the potential of a political perspective to save us from the abuses of our service role. They question elitism in "political practice" which may still deny the rights of citizens to define their own problems. But they also assert that all these issues are not just questions of improving services. Rather than being technical problems regarding how to give quality care, they are all *political* problems that force us to look at and change how power is distributed at all social levels.

Barbara and John Ehrenreich have written a brief study of the rise and roles of what they call the professional managerial class (PMC), which is also provocative and not quite so troublesome. In "The Professional Managerial Class," they trace the history of professional development as the evolution of this new class which came into being because it "took on roles which had been performed for itself by the working class" and then proceeded to serve as "buffers between working class and capitalists."[58] They challenge service professionals to look at the class functions and uses of their work. They highlight material differences from the working class which cannot be denied by political goals but also which do not rule out political alliances if PMC members become critical of the role they have been forced to play for the capitalists.

Again, as with the Illich/McKnight arguments, the Ehrenreichs suggest that giving up an identity as social work professionals will not solve all problems. They suggest that the social relations of PMC life may have created aspirations and standards that are objectively different from those of working-class people. Such differences must be shared and understood before a radical alliance—rather than one built only around narrow economic issues—can be defined. In short, whether one is defined by the ideology of professionalism or not, the social role assumed by service workers has affected consciousness in critical ways that cannot be ignored.

Finally, Larson has written *The Rise of Professionalism,* a highly intelligent and insightful study, although written in turgid academic prose. She analyzes the development of professions in Britain and the United States and is especially helpful in explaining the special place of "organizational professions" like social work.[59]

Like the other writers considered here, Larson suggests personal dangers that formal professionalism creates. The desire for status and respect in one's work is a powerful lure of professionalism and one which few can give up lightly. The dream of a career, of a "life plan," is a "powerful factor of conformity" which supports a professional identity long after the belief in one's special skills or one's organized profession may have dimmed. She goes on to show the ways in which those who adopt the "special prestige" of career "can easily mystify themselves regarding actual power. Moreover, they are locked into conformity with the role society offers them to play—locked in by vocational choice, by the particular mystique of each profession and by their whole sense of social identity."[60]

Like the Ehrenreichs, Larson suggests the isolation that comes from these roles and the danger of the false meritocracy they they seem to represent. Many people, both professionals and nonprofessionals, see professional roles as open to all who take advantage of education. In fact, class structure already limits access, but the door seems open enough so that professionals can believe they made it "on their own." A sense that one is special—rather than lucky—can divide professionals from others and can make them feel that to give up the internal sense of prestige is to give up doing their work. Instead, Larson suggests that we need to get back to the socially desirable, useful, root functions of such work and to acknowledge that any power we have from performing such roles is either illusory or in the service of the capitalist class. Her final recommendation may be the root ethic of a political practice: "To separate the progressive human meaning of one's work from the ideological functions inscribed in one's role is a task of personal salvation."[61] And we would add, political salvation for workers who have lost their social potential in the ideologically deceiving morass of professional identity.

Radical Social Work. By now we have anticipated most of the criticisms of professionalism that have been made by the growing literature on radical social work practice.

Briefly, there are six main problems with social work professionalism which are examined by British and American writers.[62] All are socialists of some sort and all finally embody the conclusions of this book—that the only hope for social workers is to develop a political consciousness and an involvement with political struggle as the base from which they continue to do service work.

First, all see the substance of social work professionalism as supporting a capitalist ideology. The criticisms of casework are most explicit. Casework theory stresses the individualism of the client and the influence of social factors is ignored or taken as given. The worker

144 THE LIMITS OF PROFESSIONALISM

is portrayed as able to act in autonomous ways, while in fact there is often very little a worker can do. In other branches of the profession the "knowledge base" also consistently leads people to try to help groups and communities adjust to prevailing norms or to emphasize the role of the individual social planner. Both explicitly and implicitly, then, the profession serves to perpetuate the myth that capitalist social relations are natural, normal functions of industrial society. By presenting its knowledge base as apolitical, social work professionalism masks the highly political way in which all branches of its theory accept the capitalist status quo.

Indeed, this criticism is so basic to the radical analysis of social work that it is often assumed. Criticisms of social work professionalism often pass over it very quickly to get to other points which seem less obvious.

Second, all agree that professionalism divides social workers from other workers. It makes them avoid unions and advocate hierarchies. The supervisory structure creates dependency and isolates workers from each other. The inability of social workers to work on equal terms with "less professional" workers becomes a major barrier to unionization and to other collective actions.

Third, most writers are especially concerned about the way in which professionalism fosters a self-image that defeats workers in their attempts to help others. Professionalism blinds workers to issues of class and, especially, to their own class position and class function in relation to clients. The goal of autonomy and the myth of professional competency put workers in the position of doing harm to people through ignorance or social naiveté.

Perhaps the worst aspect of the mystification of the service role as seen by radical critics comes from the professionals' expectation that they deserve trust, as Geoffrey Pearson points out.[63] Professionals are taught to believe that they have special commitments and talents that call them to their profession, so they should be trusted. They should be trusted further because of their expertise and their specialized training. Their service ethic assures them of their own good will and allows them to see lack of trust only as a problem "for the client." Finally, since there is very little material basis for trust between professionals with such attitudes and working-class clients, the slim chance that any real assisance can occur is lost.

The fourth common criticism comes from an understanding that professionalism leads workers to identify with their agencies. Piven and Cloward see this as leading to an unquestioning assumption that "what is good for the agency is good for the client."[64] Especially when coupled with a political ideology that does not acknowledge the functions of the capitalist welfare state, such attitudes make social workers true agents of social control. Furthermore, the often stated ethic of professionalism—that one should not express one's personal criticisms of agency policies in public—can lead to self-censorship of whatever political opinions the loyal professional does develop.

Fifth, all critics agree that self-image engendered by professionalism limits social workers' ability to engage as equals in collective struggle. To borrow from Illich's phrase, it is also the social worker who becomes "disabled," who is always "on-duty" and unable to collaborate with others—especially working-class others—as a peer. When organizing efforts are made—with social workers as "facilitators," of course—the apolitical content of the ideology keeps a lid on the development of a full analysis of the situation. So, any collective activity developed by professional social workers is likely to be characterized by a lack of connection to other issues and broader struggles.

Finally, all radical critiques of social work professionalism become criticisms of social work education, which is viewed as providing the ideological and practical base for all the above problems. Most important, the schools are responsible for engendering the myth of professionalism into new social workers, of insisting upon the development of an identity as well as the acquisition of a collection of skills and theories. Many radical writings, indeed, are drawn from what happens to social work graduate students in "the field" and in the classroom.

Taken together, these criticisms constitute a strong radical consensus that professionalism is the major barrier to the politicization of individual service workers. Giving up the professional ideology and privileges—deprofessionalization—is an essential aspect to developing a politically effective practice. While the institutions and ideology of capitalism may make the objective results of even the most progressive service work problematic, it is professionalism that keeps workers from trying. Because of this, it is often easier for radicals to become personally more frustrated with professional social workers who do not accept their analysis than with the ruling class. Such attitudes, while understandable, limit mature political action and development. Before proceeding with a discussion of the relationships between radical practice and professionalism, I should, then, consider briefly the positive appeal of professionalism for many service workers.

THE ATTRACTIONS OF PROFESSIONALISM

For people who do not share a radical critique of capitalism or who are not already alert to the nature of class society, there are some honorable and undeniable benefits to identifying themselves as social work professionals. Furthermore, even for those who share such analyses but who remain skeptical about the possibility for collective change, professionalism may retain some appeal. If we are to replace a professional practice with a political practice, we must understand the appeal of professionalism and consider how to incorporate its genuinely positive aspects into an alternative model.

In criticizing lofty social work principles, radicals often begin by showing how they deny the reality of the experience of life in the capitalist welfare state. But if we grant our listeners at least our level of intelligence we must acknowledge that they may spot some hypocrisy in our argument.[65] Many activists are very critical of most "socialist" countries, yet they are always quick to argue that their practice does not invalidate the principles of socialism. Professional social workers may feel that the analogy holds for the relationships between their values and the way they are practiced. With such people we will not get far by simply exposing the failures of professionalism. Instead, we must show how the best goals of professionalism are defeated by the worst aspects of its class position under capitalism. We must suggest how to build those positive aspects into a more socially and politically satisfying practice.

Next, radical critics know how the pressure of life under capitalism tends to isolate and fragment people, to alienate them from their work and from meaningful social relationships.[66] The ideal of professionalism offers a sense of identity and even of community that is not available through most modern work. Employment studies show that most workers aspire to the autonomy, usefulness, and sense of fulfillment that are associated with professionalism.[67] We cannot deny what Barbara and Al Haber recognized in 1967:

"Middle-class aspirations" are not the only reasons why people want to teach, practice medicine, do intellectual work, be artists. There are good reasons for wanting to develop a particular skill or practice in a particular craft . . . there is (even) no reason to assume that motivation cannot be transformed and that skills once acquired cannot be put to important social use.[68]

In other words, radicals need to separate a criticism of the class implications of a professional identity and of the capitalist functions of a professional ideology from an appreciation that much of the *work* service workers do can be socially useful and personally rewarding. Indeed, one could start with respect for service workers because they have retained the strength to seek rewarding work in the face of all the pressures of a capitalist job market, even for "middle-class" people. Further, one could acknowledge that such workers seek professional identities exactly because they put forward the promise of real competence and clear standards for what "good work" entails. In this society where work is often so devalued, the quest to measure oneself against meaningful standards must surely be recognized as an indication of rare courage and self-respect.

Certain professional goals may be understood in this light also. Autonomy may, in fact, be an illusion in modern bureaucracies, and the demand for it can be an assertion of privilege. But all commentators also note that discretion can also be used for good purposes as well as bad. The desire to have control over one's work, if one holds oneself accountable to a broader community rather than to a narrow range of professional colleagues, *can* lead to better service.[69] Similarly, the desire for distance between oneself and clients can foster elitism and close off the possibility of political alliances. However, as Hirschorn argues in his study of alternative service institutions, the nature of the needs themselves creates a search for some type of "professional armor," for some ability to psychologically separate oneself from the pain. There can be a danger that comes from the "collapse of distance" and which leaves the most caring workers unable to help because they become so overwhelmed with the problems.[70] Feminists in health clinics and rape crisis programs noted the same need.

Unfortunately professionalism built upon such basic problems and offered the solution of class identity as the source of distance: professionals do not get overly involved because they have a special knowledge base, because they are privileged. Radicals perhaps can substitute a less devisive and less total source of distance—political perspective. Around certain issues service workers can help clients because of a political analysis that explains some of the pain and suggests some strategies for change. Around other issues they are in the same place as clients, and politics can help make this clear also.

In the current struggle between professionals and managers in human service bureaucracies, we are often on the side of the professionals. For all the puffed-up snobbism of their opposition to managers, professionals are often able to find ways to resist bureaucratic rationality using their demand for "professional autonomy in the service of clients." Michael Lipsky found this one ray of hope in his bleak world of the street-level bureaucrat.[71] Here even the much maligned "knowledge base" of professionalism may be a tool. As more and more public agencies are run by managers and lawyers, the one defense many service workers have is "their knowledge of the field." One cannot easily ask service workers to give up this defense totally in favor of a political critique. Professional jargon may be a better way to bamboozle administrators than socialist jargon. The need to be recognized for one's competence and knowledge of the problems in one's field, however, does not imply that one also has to take on all the accoutrements of professionalism. If we truly accept a role as skilled workers we may be able to continue to challenge management without having to adopt the condescending we-know-betterism that obscures so many management-professional debates. Indeed, in Massachusetts such superior attitudes on the parts of professionals have sometimes driven clients, workers, and the general public to feel sympathy for managers.[72]

Finally, we return to an old theme. Part of the appeal of professional social work is that it claims to value the process of helping individuals on a daily basis. Granted, it is off the mark in seeing social betterment as simply the sum of all these individual changes, and it does serve the broader aims of capitalism by atomizing society into a set of individual problems. On the other hand, the desire to do what one can to help alleviate pain and to value the social nurturance that comes from efforts to help others are strong, basic human urges. If becoming a professional is the only way to gain meaningful recognition for helping others, people will continue to choose professionalism. It offers legitimacy for performing roles which are the basis for a better society—indeed, too much legitimacy. Quickly professionalism renders an honest social value into a sign of class superiority. But a politicized alternative must also truly respect such caring activity and value it as a critical part of a broader change effort. Without this base we cannot appeal to those who want to see signs of love before they will consider accepting a new version of the truth. Can we really blame them?

ACHIEVING A DEPROFESSIONALIZED POLITICAL PRACTICE

As we have seen, the rise of professionalism performed a classic masking function of ideology—it served to convince workers, clients, and the broader public that services were not a political, value-laden activity. Instead, the practice of social welfare—whether one identified as a professional social reformer or a professional case worker—became one of creating a technocratic, bureaucratic, apolitical conception of both the substance and the function of social services.

To create an effective political practice we need to reject all aspects of this professionalized definition of the terms and see all work with clients as *political*. It involves individual power relations and it reflects broader power relationships in the society. All relations with co-workers are political: when one is a loyal professional one serves dominant interests; when one raises questions about agencies or about one's role as a worker, one begins to challenge existing power relationships. Social policies are not simple technical adjustments better left to the experts; instead, they are a basic arena of public conflict over what social resources are spent on whom for what purposes.

By rejecting professionalism we politicize all areas of our activity, we open everything up for debate and political scrutiny. This is threatening and frightening. It can make us, as Pearson says, "dizzy" when we stop "dodging the moral-political issues" imbedded in our work.[73] On the other hand, it can wake us too from the frustrating professional dreamworld in which we believed we had to have power to do good and make change because we had the knowledge and the skills, but nothing ever seemed to work and we did not know whom to blame but ourselves.

As we have noticed, social welfare professionalism is weak, perhaps based on the inherently radicalizing nature of the work and on the profession's failure to develop a truly professionalized workforce with enough status to be really legitimate—as opposed to simply *asserting* professional legitimacy. Its confusions may suggest that certain high level professionals might benefit from a politicization of their roles also. Although it is unlikely they would become radical socialists, they might become self-proclaimed social democrats.[74] As such they could fight openly for the welfare state as part of a long-range, gradualist socialist social agenda. If the social work leadership presented its goals as openly political, rather than as a natural evolving function of industrial society, it might politicize issues of social welfare in the broader society. It could allow radicals to function as a true "left wing" of social welfare workers, rather than, as now, leaving them with the limited role of constantly asserting the political value of service work.

The Centrality of Class. The most important function of the ideology of professionalism is to hide the reality of class and class relationships. The central role of a deprofessionalized political practice is to highlight the functions of class in all aspects of the human service system.

A major task of political practice must be to abandon professional assumptions that one's merit is due to personal expertise and the attendant superior sense of self which then becomes exhibited in all social relationships, with other workers, with clients, with the general public. If we cannot do this we help to continue the inherent tensions between members of the PMC and working-class people, seen by the Ehrenreichs:

The activities which the PMC performs within the capitalist division of labor in themselves serve to undermine the positive class consciousness among the working class. The kind of consciousness which remains, the commonly held attitudes of the working class are as likely to be anti-PMC as they are to be anti-capitalist—if only because people are more likely in a day-to-day sense to experience humiliation, harassment, and frustration at the hands of the PMC than from members of the actual capitalist class.[75]

The purpose of an awareness of such class roles is not to induce guilt, or to suggest that one should "proletarianize" oneself and deny all aspects of middle-class privilege. Such actions are foolish and doomed to fail. Instead we need to remember that "class is a relationship and not a thing," in E. P. Thompson's words, and begin to explore the class relationships emerging in our current situation and to note how a heightened awareness of our own and others' class relations affects our ability to act, and to take seriously our responsibility to do good work.[76]

We can, by a simple sharing of our assumptions and our perceptions of our roles and our options, make more explicit the nature of our relationships with clients. In an excellent book, *The Client Speaks*, John Mayer and Noel Timms point out all the ways in which working-class clients are simply unaware of the methods of problem solving employed by professionals (or, we would suggest, many people of the PMC without a professional identity).[77] An open discussion of what we want out of human service relationships, what the power and goals are, can go far toward building the base for either a meaningful class alliance or, at least, a more honest negotiation.

Professionals exert their class power by denying their class power, by defining it as expertise. When they, in all good faith, "represent" clients with authorities they may be effective actually because of the unacknowledged force of their—not the clients'—class relationships. Radical service workers must avoid such subtle assertions of class power. If one is called upon to represent people, expectations should be discussed beforehand and everything done to encourage them to speak their own case. If the ends absolutely justify taking a role as spokesperson, radicals must avoid unnecessary signs of class power, for example, as speaking with officials about clients as if they were not present.

The implications of such activity are that workers come to see all aspects of their work as arenas for "class struggle"—as places where the opportunity for upper-class dominance is either taken or stopped through their actions and the actions of clients and other workers. As noted in chapter 4, such opposition cannot be conducted alone. The pressures are too great and the risks of becoming a moralistic crusader for others—a role unappreciated by anyone—are too high. One needs always to consider tactics of achieving heightened class awareness in terms of their effects on clients and to avoid manipulating clients to make a point. However, minor actions can give energy, at least—such as never identifying clients as such to co-workers or bosses so they have to treat them as equals for as long as possible, or using staff meetings to examine the class structure of office rearrangements.

On a more serious level, however, we must acknowledge that an acute awareness of class issues can be personally draining and highly threatening to co-workers. As Piven and Cloward note: "It is not easy to be a professional, to lay claim to professional authority and esteem and to side with folks, especially poor folks."[78] Co-workers may feel that one is siding with clients against them. Or, if we discuss class power at the workplace, professional co-workers may feel we are being "unrealistic about how the work gets done"—as one radical was told when she suggested a minor reallocation of tasks in order to create more democratic working conditions.[79] One can be, and feel, divisive and difficult when raising class issues—especially if these are combined with sensitivity to racial and sexual dynamics. Hectoring and martyrdom are to be avoided. However, any effective political practice can come only at the expense of professional elitism and as a result of a long, careful effort to build more honest and effective class relationships at the workplace.

Deprofessionalized Relations with Clients. If we are not helping people meet their social needs because we are professionals with a special expertise which allows us to be neutral about their situation and help them help themselves, then why are we doing so? One answer to be explored in the next chapter is that we do so because we are street-level bureaucrats, functionaries hired to perform a task deemed socially necessary: we are following orders. If that answer seems hardly enough, even if more honest, then we must keep working to elaborate on the core element of our political practice: we help others because they are potential comrades, because if we all help each other we may also be able to work together to achieve other desirable, more wide-ranging social goals.

We began in the last chapter to explore the specifics of what it means to work with people as potential comrades. Here we will only discuss a few issues that are highlighted by questioning the ideals of professionalism. Epstein and Conrad begin to sketch out some possible changes that could occur:

Despite the possibility that delicate elitist sensibilities might be disturbed by it, there is much to be gained by de-professionalizing our conception of social work. It would reestablish the legitimacy of social workers doing what they do best and what the public expects of them—locating and providing concrete services. It would help break down, or at least curtail, artificial, credential barriers to social work employment. It would clarify and demystify the relationship between the techniques social workers employ and the political purposes they serve. It would open the way to identifying, codifying, and teaching the kinds of organizational skills that enhance organizational responsiveness to clients and reduce social worker "burn-out." Finally, an empirically based, de-professionalized conceptual model of social work would enable us to identify more readily those factors which facilitate or obstruct social service delivery.[80]

As suggested above, we will need some way to distance ourselves from the immediate pain of people's lives without becoming neutral or without failing to identify with their feelings. This seems to be a crucial distinction. Studies of social work radicalism have suggested that, while structural position and training were not significant in predicting political persuasion, "those social workers who were committed to a neutralized ideology of professionalism *were* significantly more conservative than those who eschewed this ideology."[81] If there is a full "collapse of distance," not neutrality, however, workers can be "burned out by the complexity and stress of mutual interdependence and emotional interchange."[82]

As suggested earlier, a political analysis may be able to replace a professional one in order to create a healthier, less permanent distance. In sharing their analysis with clients workers may explain how it allows them to be supportive while seeing their concerns in a larger perspective. Clients may then be able to challenge workers who they think are becoming too cold—because it may be easier to disagree with someone's politics than their unexplained expertise. The experience of feminist services supports this approach:

Usually it helps that we're feminists. It gives us a way to listen to the stories [of battering] and be sympathetic and helpful, not just overwhelmed. At first we just listen to try to help on an immediate level and to identify as women with what they're feeling. But after a while we can talk about why battering happens and why the courts and the welfare system are so bad and it helps us and her to keep going.[83]

In *The Client Speaks,* almost all satisfied clients expressed a feeling that "good" workers were interested in them, trusted them, tried to help them. They clearly felt that—even when the interchange was primarily one of obtaining material resources—they had made a relationship with their worker. They wanted to end the connection "properly." Most expressed a desire for feedback and advice from workers even if the feedback was negative or the advice not taken. In short, clients were always trying to make sense of their interaction with a service worker, to ask "What is happening?" "Why?" They were hampered in answering their questions because workers were being neutral, or just did not think to explain why they were acting as they were.[84]

A deprofessionalized political practice means treating potential comrades with basic respect and acknowledging that they are deciding on the type of relationship they want with us, just as we are with them. Of course one must avoid objectifying "potential comrades," just as one must not treat people as "cases." Here the goal is to develop habits of equality which will allow workers to avoid the naiveté of one young radical:

I worked in a neighborhood health clinic with a group of older working-class and minority women. Boy, did I work hard, treating everyone like a person, discussing their problems in a caring way, being real with people. I was quite proud of my ability to "relate" to people.

Then I got sick and was out. When I came back workers and patients were really nice to me. They showed real interest in how I was feeling. All of a sudden I realized that they were just treating *me* nice because I was another person, not because they wanted to "make relationships across class and race lines." It sure made me feel foolish, making a political act out of being friendly.[85]

Some problems will inevitably arise from attempts to deprofessionalize, however. Some clients may *want* workers to act professional, to assert their authority, as a sign that they can expect "first-class service." Alternative services workers encountered this tension constantly. The dilemmas are hard ones. In some situations it may be possible to discuss the issue with people, to explain how one feels about doing good work, which is the essence of what they mean by "professionalism." Often, however, uneasy adjustments must be made. Radicals must struggle to be respectful of clients and to provide "good service." On the other hand, some want the type of conservative authority which could not be tolerated in other political alliances, so radicals must gently, but firmly, refuse to give up political principles. Here is how one social worker handles such problems:

Some people come in here [a mental health clinic] and really want me to act like a psychiatrist. They are really subservient, partly because that is how they have learned to be a patient. I try not to play into it. I ask them what they think should be done. I explain the options and I talk about myself more than usual to try to force them to see me as a person. It is hard. It takes more time and sometimes it just does not work. But at least I don't contribute to it.[86]

In radical service efforts the problems were intensified because workers had the power to create an environment that looked totally "unprofessional." Then issues arose over dress, over how informal was offensive and how neat was "professionalized," and over the impact of each wall poster. Such discussions were important but time consuming. They did, however, force radicals to consider what professionalism meant to them and to the group of users they wished to attract. For radicals working in bureaucracies the issues are more below the surface; to a large extent they do not control the environment and must work out our compromises more idiosyncratically. An important, and fun, caucus meeting can be spent, for example, on what it means to "dress for success" as a radical service worker.

Another difficult aspect of deprofessionalizing is more important and more difficult to resolve. Having a political analysis and avoiding professionalism does not guarantee that workers will get along well with all clients. Some will never see workers as anything but representatives of agencies, and will remain hostile and "difficult" no matter how many attempts are made to create a different form of interaction. Such situations are personal disappointments but are politically straightforward. There are perfectly clear reasons why people do not trust *anyone* who works for the welfare state. If we cannot find room for new alliances, our job still remains to provide as much of the resources demanded as possible, to inform people of all options, rights, benefits, and other client organizations, and to be as respectful and honest as we can be.

More difficult are those situations in which workers find themselves on really different sides from the client. Depending on the job this may happen more or less often. Teenagers may constantly want staff to act differently, whereas parents in a day care center may seldom disagree. Here the only hope—and there is no doubt such situations are difficult—is to handle disagreements as one would among political adversaries: through open, equal (even if hostile) negotiations. At all costs we need to avoid the "pushing clients around 'for their own good,' bullying, scaring, arm twisting, conning and putting to shame [that] have been considered worthy elements in the noble pursuit of helping people to help themselves."[87]

Finally, if we despair when a deprofessionalized, politicized practice seems no easier than any other, we might remember the admonition of the Habers as they suggested ways "to stay sane and stay honest while trying to be effective":

It is very hard to practice differently. It is difficult to define new standards of effectiveness, to invent and implement new ways of doing things. Most things we try fail—and often not because of the oppressive power structure, but simply because they are difficult and original and most of us have limited capacity.[88]

Good Work, Not Professional Privilege. The most threatening aspect of deprofessionalization may be the implication that one's work is no longer valued, that one cannot take it seriously. Such attitudes result from the "degradation of work" under capitalism and need to be opposed when we frame socialist alternatives.[89] Not identifying as a professional means identifying as a worker who does a good job, who is accountable to clients and to wider political movement; it does *not* demean the value of our work. It means working collectively with other workers to protect our right and capacity to do good work. It still allows us to build serious relationships with co-workers around our joint tasks, as Larson notes:

All occupations which involve special skills and special worlds of work change to some extent the worker's personality and self-presentation. The pleasure of "talking shop" is not restricted to professions, nor is the anticipatory socialization which prepares an individual to work and act like people in his chosen field are supposed to.[90]

By asserting pride in one's work because it is well done, rather than because we are such "smart experts," new avenues of sharing are opened. Opportunities emerge to fight the elitism which professionalism represents. Professionals were trained to react to new policies in terms of how correct they were, according to some theory or, more often, according to what was "appropriate practice." Politicized workers can consider the effects on co-workers of new policies and pay more attention to personal work needs. An apolitical student of worker burnout noted that as new professionals lost their "idealism" they became more open to unionization.[91] We might suggest that, instead, as workers became more aware that "the personal is political" they begin to realize the futility of "ideals" based only on self-sacrifice. As one radical unionist noted:

Despite my politics if it weren't for the union I would kill myself at work. I still feel like I should take every case, answer every call. They help me put it in perspective. Now I spend all the extra time going to union meetings trying to fight cutbacks so we don't all work ourselves to death.[92]

In conclusion only those who have wanted and used the professional identity may feel that they have something to lose by deprofessionalization. Of course, for those who value the status and privileges—if not the money—of a professional designation, there is little to be said. Except, perhaps, in these times to question the viability of their career choice and suggest a new career in management. But for what we believe are the great majority of social work professionals there may be more to gain that to lose, even if one's politics are not well articulated. The urge to change one's role—what some Marxists, in an inimitable style, call "role contestation"—may originate with a simple sense that the old professional constructs are no longer working:

Role contestation originates with a refusal to view one's work as an isolated technical function and an insistence on seeing it as part of a larger social process. This begins as an act of individual defiance. . . . [But] the second phase of role contestation involves the development of new norms and new criteria which are alien to capitalist logic.[93]

Every social work professional who has thought she was suffering "burnout," who has felt isolated in her work, or who has started to wonder why everything seems to get worse, not better, no matter how much expertise is applied, has begun one small piece of that "role contestation." Slowly—and perhaps not so slowly as the New Right brings politics rudely to professionalism—such professionals might begin to discover that their work has always been political; sometimes because it supported the existing power relations, at other times because it gave them and the people they worked with a vision of what a more caring society might be like. Once we accept the inherently social-moral-political nature of our work, the question becomes not "What is the best expert solution?" but "What is the most effective and wide-ranging political strategy for change?"

We cannot expect that everyone will come up with the same answers. But at least socialists, conerned human service workers, and deprofessionalized social workers will all be asking the same basic question. Bertha Reynolds wrote, "It is easy to refine one's techniques to the point that only relatively refined people can make use of them."[94] Our quest to define a simple, not simplistic, political practice moves us back from what has become an overly refined, and increasingly irrelevant, professional method. It gives us hope that by sharing an awareness of the political realities that inform our work we can come to a far more complex, and grounded, model for a truly political practice.

6

GUERRILLAS IN THE BUREAUCRACY?

Most human service workers are employed in bureaucratic agencies of one sort or another. Three million of the 4.3 million salaried "service professionals" work in the public sector. Only 11 percent are self-employed.[1] So the dominant reality for most service workers is bureaucracy, with its hierarchy, its specialization, its rules, and its constant quest for functional rationality. Even for workers who seek a professional identity, the most pressing facts of work life are the expectations stemming from the bureaucratic role. The task, for those without a desire for, or access to, an independent professional position, is one of developing ways to receive satisfaction and meaning as organizational functionaries. And political activists face the exceptionally difficult job both of working within the bureaucracy and of maintaining a political identity and practice that allows them also to dissociate from it and to consider alternatives. A group of radical British service workers have aptly posed the problem as one of being "in and against the state."[2]

Yet, many commentators have noted that service workers are ill-prepared for their organizational environment. Most enter their work because of a concern to help others, or out of an interest in responding to specific human problems. Even the most educated social workers are scarcely trained to deal with their role as "street-level bureaucrat," as we can see from the warning given to new service workers in a recent textbook:

Ready or not, you are expected to be a help giver and a bureaucrat. To state the issue directly, you have technical competencies and skills, but you are probably unprepared for organizational life. You need bureaucratic skills in order to capitalize on the possibility for organizational change as well as to neutralize stresses and strains that will be placed on you.[3]

Indeed, studies of social worker socialization show that it is adjustment to the bureaucratic reality of the job that causes the most discomfort among new workers and is the most responsible for the loss of "idealism."[4]

For those service workers who also seek to develop a critical, political practice the realities of organizational existence are especially complicated. Their analysis already makes them skeptical of whether the social control functions of public and private welfare agencies can be overcome. Many leftists have, as we have seen, dismissed all aspects of the welfare state as repressive and in the service of capitalism. So when activists decide to work within the system they are already somewhat unsure of their analysis that "contradictions" create a positive potential for service work. As they encounter bureaucratic policies and procedures, interorganizational politics, and the endless frustrations of agency operations it is predictable that they may think that there has been a mistake, that there is no hope for progressive work in the bureaucracy. At best, they may conclude that the only defensible activity is that of becoming a "guerrilla in the bureaucracy," of undermining the agency at every turn. Many feel that their only options are those, as Piven and Cloward once wrote, of "protecting the poor, the sick, the criminal, and the deviant against the agencies."[5]

But, not all agencies are alike and not all the negative aspects of human service can be attributed to their social control functions under capitalism. Many of the undesirable aspects of service work and service delivery are the result of the complicated nature of human need and our continuing inability to define what real caring means. Similarly, political values lead activists to provide services for a range of reasons: to better understand and respond to human pain; to work with people in order to build political alliances for social change; to gain a clearer vision for a more caring society; and to expose the limits of human service bureaucracies in this society. Therefore, a mature political practice depends upon developing a more complex understanding of specific organizational developments and options as well as of the nature of bureaucratic pressures in general. Only after such an inquiry can we determine whether political practice forces us to be bureaucratic guerrillas or whether sometimes we may be able to come up from the political underground and operate more openly and positively in combining our service work with our political goals.

BUILDING BUREAUCRACIES: TRENDS IN U.S. HUMAN SERVICES

Many workers and managers in human service agencies are not fully aware of the history of their own or similar agencies. Most have received even less training regarding the functions and behavior of complex organizations. Unfortunately, even when concerned workers try to understand bureaucracies they often find the literature to be inaccessible and static. So most workers and activists operate out of great ignorance regarding the purposes, goals, and history of bureaucracies, in the United States and elsewhere. Before we can review the development of the American human service system, then, we need to consider briefly the dominant assumptions about the nature of bureaucracy that have defined the expectations of managers, workers, and even of many socialists within that system since the end of the nineteenth century.

There are many intellectual and political problems with the sources that should help us comprehend bureaucracy, however. In the first place, even a cursory review of the extensive studies on organizational behavior yields a literature that abounds with pseudotechnical language, is extremely abstract and dry, and seems more relevant to profit-oriented institutions than to human service bureaucracies.[6] More serious than this stylistic critique, though, is the falsely apolitical presentation of the nature of bureaucracies. The dominant theme of organizational analysis has been that bureaucracies could be studied empirically, in a political vacuum. Bureaucracies were presumed to be operating according to their own laws, regardless of the social sector in control of government or the differing values defining different regimes. Such treatments leave service workers with little base for criticizing the daily environment in which they find themselves.

Yet, the standard expectations of bureaucratic theory form an ideology which seems to justify a workplace with built-in barriers to a political practice. Almost all contemporary organizational analyses have expanded and developed concepts which go back to Max Weber's "ideal type" of bureaucratic characteristics: (a) high degree of specialization; (b) hierarchical authority structure with limited areas of command and responsibility; (c) impersonality of relationships between organizational members; and (d) recruitment of officials on the basis of ability and technical knowledge. And, as Mouzelis notes, there is usually one "common, all-pervasive element" linking the above characteristics: "the existence of a system of control based on rational rules, rules which try to regulate the whole organizational structure and process on the basis of technical knowledge with the aim of maximum efficiency."[7] In the writing and thoughts of managers and organizational theorists, such categories have not been just descriptive categories; instead they have become goals to strive for—in the name of efficiency—which serve to limit and define the range of appropriate behavior in the workplace.

Although Weber himself was unsure about whether bureaucratization was supportive or destructive to capitalist development, most commentators have accepted it as the organizational form necessary for modern capitalism. Especially as modified by this century's management theorists, advanced industrial monopoly capitalism has become synonymous with bureaucratic organization. The catch, however, is that most theorists see this as some type of functional accident—modern economies require that vast amounts of complex tasks become integrated in order to produce unified goals; the "natural" form for accomplishing this is bureaucratic organization. The very fact that the Soviet Union and Eastern European countries have also developed a highly bureaucratized society is used to support the contention that bureaucracy is an economically and socially neutral means to achieve the complicated ends of modern society, regardless of dominant political values.[8]

Such positivist assumptions have served to dampen our understanding of the general development of bureaucracies, and particularly public agencies, as *political* phenomena. They have supported the claim that professionals serve an apolitical function in an apolitical system, which developed "naturally" in response to social and industrial change. And, because they were so accepted by the left and the right, such "principles" of bureaucracy served to limit the political vision of those who could have created a more vibrant, more creative vision of true "social welfare."[9] Nearly everyone was attempting to develop an "efficient" system that would meet standards of bureaucratic rationality, so few were able to question the nature of the public system of bureaucratizing which slowly developed or to challenge whether the forms of organized public responsibility that became the American welfare state were not inherently destructive to the achievement of any true capacity for public caring.

Before developing a critique of bureaucracy, however, we need to understand the specific ways in which the American human service bureaucracies developed and how even those who desired the growth of classic bureaucratic patterns were unwilling to openly proclaim their goals. Once again we shall see that the widespread inability to address the political impact of the growth of welfare bureaucracies weakened the ability of both the proponents and the progressive opponents of those bureaucracies to respond to conservative attacks on the system.

The Building of a Bureaucracy: Early Patterns. Until the 1930s there was no national system of human service bureaucracies in the United States.[10] Instead, building on the localist traditions of American politics, each city, town, or county gradually created its own particularistic pattern of social welfare programs. The Progressive Era had brought some state-level centralization and coordination, but, again, patterns varied from state to state. There was little sense of the need for national bureaucracies, and even state and local programs were highly idiosyncratic.

As we have seen, the newly emerging social work profession tried to provide intellectual and methodological coherence. It did serve the critical role of defining the common self-image of professionals within agencies, and of establishing shared goals and values for bureaucratic behavior, but the very eclectic nature of social programs defeated any general effort to establish common patterns of bureaucratic development. By 1930 only veterans' services, some limited children's programs, and small vocational rehabilitation programs could be identified as a federally supported system. State patterns, while growing more similar over time, still varied widely in accordance with local history and the influence of different professional groups.[11] Most agencies were too small for specialization and their hierarchies were quite flat, often including a board, a director, a supervisor, and a few "street-level" workers. Larger state institutions were often run more like warehouses than standard bureaucracies with defined rules and regulations.

The Depression and the New Deal changed that, forever. By the end of the decade national patterns had been established which served as the basic skeleton for the system of human service bureaucracies we encounter today.[12] By 1940, most direct relief programs and other scattered service programs had adopted mechanisms that demanded all the standard characteristics of Weberian organization: hierarchy, specialization, a system of rules and paperwork flow, a defined set of program expectations. Although in the early days it is not clear how much monitoring and control was exercised, the model was set, just waiting for further sophistication.

What is important about the development of this national system (which was further clarified when the needs of a war economy brought even greater standardization) is that it was never proclaimed as such. In fact, the reverse is true. Each program was seen as a very separate entity and most were instituted with very careful language identifying them as "temporary" measures. Watchful conservatives in Congress were ever careful to oppose bureaucratic, "welfare state" programs, and the dominant leadership in the Roosevelt administration itself was not supportive of strong, planned, systematic service programs. Even the basic welfare programs—Dependent Children, Old Age Assistance, and Disability Assistance—were originally pushed as short-term measures, which would become unnecessary when Social Security was fully operational.

So we see, then, a bureaucratic paradox, as noted in chapter 1. Programs developed to provide financial and social relief, generating similar bureaucratic procedures and structures all across the country. But national leadership would not claim and put them in the spotlight—for the inevitable praise or blame. The welfare state was presented, in the words of liberal defenders, as "neither creeping socialism nor moribund capitalism. It was not coherent philosophy because its policy is one of improvisation to meet evils rather than one of enlightened planning to prevent them. Its wisdom such as it is is always ex post facto."[13] The tendencies of civil servants to work behind the scenes, out of public scrutiny (and accountability) were exacerbated. Many of the politicians who voted for such programs also did not want to claim them: they were still viewed as "weakening the work ethic" and "fostering dependence." Those who supported the development of such programs learned to be quiet and unassertive about their commitment to a public social responsibility.

Consequently, the national system of social welfare bureaucracies developed in hiding, under a climate of suspicion that it represented socialism and certainly with the assumption that it would be inept and bungled, even as it tried to follow standard bureaucratic principles. Here there were fewer social democrats of the English variety, who would openly push for the expansion of the state and for the continued development of new programs as an inevitable social good.[14] Bureaucratic values were assumed for agencies which developed incrementally as "necessary responses" to crises, but the climate was not conducive to open and responsible debate about the nature of the bureaucratic state, because the very existence of such a developing entity was being denied.

Unfortunately, one sure way to bring out the worst of bureaucratic patterns is to force organizations to operate in isolation, within a hostile climate and without ever being able to articulate legitimate needs and problems. Yet this is the pattern that dominated the development of American social service bureaucracies.

Bureaucrats were not even able to give themselves a proper name. In 1953, the Eisenhower administration proposed a cabinet-level agency to oversee, and finally acknowledge, the range of federal programs which had developed. The first Secretary, Olveta Culp Hobby (no radical, by any means), proposed that the new agency be entitled the Department of General Welfare. She drew this from the goal of the Preamble to the Constitution which proposed a government to "form a more perfect Union, establish Justice, insure domestic tranquility, provide for the common defense, promote the general welfare. . . ." However, Hobby soon discovered that the words "general welfare" suggested "socialist doctrines" and were "unthinkable." She quickly backed down—it *was* 1953, after all—and, after discussion, accepted the suggestion of Senator Robert A. Taft that it be labeled "Health, Education, and Welfare." As one commentator noted, because welfare was still in the title it was often abbreviated to just HEW, "sounding not unlike a sneeze or a deep sigh."[15]

By 1960, then, publicly supported social welfare programs had quietly grown to account for 5.434 million dollars' worth of federal, state, and local expenditures. Another 2.753 million was spent on private services.[16] Most of these agencies operated as traditional bureaucracies within hierarchies, increasing specialization, and ever-growing regulations and guidelines. Slowly, most attempted to "professionalize" their services and to reorganize to achieve greater efficiency. Except for a few flashy private agencies, most sought to keep an apologetic, low profile, the better to practice their bureaucratic trade and to avoid the hostility of a society which, knowing little about them, saw them as examples of social failure, as programs set up to deal with those who would not or could not achieve the American dream. So a system was in place, but one which was most often unexamined and unwilling to defend itself, even in terms of bureaucratic rationales.

Changes in the 1960s. As we have seen, the 1960s changed much of that. Social services and most social welfare programs came out of their self-imposed closet with a vengeance. Some bureaucrats seemed happy for the transition; others resisted it every bit of the way, looking back with longing to the days when they could do what they wanted with little scrutiny from workers, clients, or the general public.

As we saw in chapter 3, the Poverty Programs were a critical catalyst for the change. Fiercely antiprofessional and antibureaucratic in the early days, they served as an important model for a public organization that was activist, experimental, and client-oriented, even if still fundamentally supportive of the existing social order. They introduced structural involvement by clients in agency operations and in some places they went quite far in defining services as a right, not an intervention deemed necessary from above. When linked with the activists of legal service attorneys and local community groups, CAPS served as a prod to traditional agencies, both private and public. They gave clients new expectations, which they learned to carry into other settings.[17] By the early seventies, Poverty Programs and their imitators among contracted services (see below) had begun to suggest to a whole range of young people, both former service recipients and not, that there might be exciting work to be done in human services—work that was neither that of a snooty social worker nor that of a boring bureaucrat.

While less spectacular, and perhaps to some extent even a side effect of the Poverty Program efforts, the increase in welfare-related social services and in community services for deinstitutionalized populations also served to highlight and even change expectations about the nature of human service bureaucracies. Three major developments occurred in the early 1960s. One was the passage of the 1962 social service amendments. Another was the passage of Medicaid in 1965. The third was the enactment of the Community Mental Health Centers Act in 1963.[18] Taken together, all three fostered a new federal approach to services. Both in the legislation and in the implementing regulations, all suggested that individuals might need a range of soft and hard services in order to achieve change goals and all contained a bias against institutional care. All (with 1967 service amendment's federal job training programs added) were used to justify the development of more "community"—often meaning less professional and bureaucratized—services. Most importantly for our point here, all pushed public agencies into the role of broker for clients in relation to a set of available services. By doing so they forced readjustment of older, more stable and internalized relations within public agencies and between public bureaucracies and large private providers.[19] Finally, the result of all these changes was to involve the federal government more in social services delivery than it had been since the days of the WPA.

Here is not the place to review the substantive implications—or lack of them—of all these new programs. Some would argue that their purpose was to create the illusion rather than the reality of change. For us the point can be made that as a result of these changes (and others which could be mentioned, including the Older Americans Act and the new Special Education legislation), the range of options for human service organizations expanded. Before the 1960s human service workers could work in large, highly bureaucratic state agencies with low pay, low status, myriad rules, and lots of job security. Or they could work in a private agency with more status, less specialization, an emphasis on counseling services, a more "professional" atmosphere, and—usually—a less desperate client population. With professional training they might become administrators or planners in one of the few, prestigious social planning agencies.

By 1970 these options remained, but others appeared. One could work in a federally funded poverty agency where many of the staff were "from the community" and most of the services were noncounseling, hard services, with an advocacy orientation. Or one could work in a range of indigenous "community services" which grew up based on an uncertain mix of private and public funding and aimed at a particular population: youth, children, ex-offenders, and elderly. And, as we have seen, there were even explicitly political services to work in if one wanted to work for no or very low pay.

Such options meant that organizational forms became less fixed. Old notions of requirements for social work supervision did not always apply. Flat salary scales meant that directors were often not as disproportionately paid as in older organizations. Also, the system, for a time, was porous. Staff moved from agency to agency. Because of increased emphasis on referral and service brokering many service workers encountered many more different types of workers and were introduced to different expectations regarding their work. Indeed, had we thought about it, some of us might have thought the system was becoming debureaucratized. However, before we could really recognize and solidify the breakthroughs, the system was moving, like a great bureaucratic amoeba, to incorporate all these new organizational forms into itself. Before we knew we had it, the initiative was lost. From all sides came calls for better monitoring, more uniformity, more controls. Even though different structural models continued to exist, they were reconstituted into a new system of bureaucratic controls.

Here, then, is a good example of how a better understanding of bureaucracy, and a more political critique of it, could have helped activists keep their options alive. For all their attendant social control functions, the new programs of the sixties served to expose the problems of large-scale public bureaucracies and, often unwittingly, to offer options which contained the potential for less hierarchy, more community input, and greater social accountability. At this time, however, most progressives in social welfare only saw the system in simple outlines: if it was public money it must represent ruling-class and state power; if it did not restructure the economic system and only offered service—even in a potentially more humane way—it still was maintaining the social order. Instead of seeing the potential for more accountable and fluid organizational forms, and for services to become recognized as desirable rights, only the negative side of the contradiction was recognized. So, the traditional bureaucratic system was able to move—without fanfare—to regain its hegemony, and progressives were left wondering why we felt such a loss when the programs of which we had been so critical were gone.

Purchase of Service and the Entrepreneurial Spirit. One of the mechanisms which had allowed for the development of new organizational norms was the widespread institution of contracted services, or purchased services, which occurred across the country during the 1960s and early 1970s.[20] Ironically, it was through further development of the system of purchased services that the bureaucracy would regain firm control by the 1980s.

In social services, mental health, and certain areas of ancillary health care public agencies began, by the late sixties, to arrange for small private agencies to deliver services to eligible populations. Originally this process was a simple billing procedure: certain agencies would be designated as "vendors" and allowed to bill for reimbursement of allowable costs. (This is the mechanism that has often remained with Medicaid.) Gradually vendors were given budgetary ceilings, and later they were required to sign contracts that were highly specific regarding the service to be delivered. In social services a "donated funds" mechanism allowed private agencies to pay the matching amount required before reimbursement was allowed, so services could be provided with little or no state expenditure.

There are many reasons why such a system developed. Officially, state bureaucrats argued that it allowed them more "flexibility" in responding to "local needs," and it was supported by community agencies for the same reasons. Flexibility meant that small, innovative programs would begin without the "red tape" involved when state personnel and resources were used. For small alternative programs,

it meant that they could get public support for the services they wished
to provide without—especially in the early days—great "bureaucratic
hassle."

In addition, purchasing allowed states to take advantage of increased federal funding without having to expand the number of state
workers. Senior-level bureaucrats would argue for this as "bringing
new blood" into the system, while others would see it as a way to avoid,
or even break, public sector unions.[21] The new programs were cheap
and could provide "more efficient programs for the service dollar."
Even though some agencies saw this as exploitation, many of them,
especially the new agencies which were established for the explicit
purpose of receiving public contracts, saw it as the price they paid
for freedom.

In short, although there were always opponents of public purchase—both within and outside the bureaucracy—in the beginning it
was a system which was pursued by many. Just as Poverty Programs
were beginning to wane as the dominant activist community agencies, a whole new set of day care, youth, halfway house, and elderly
programs (to name just a few) began to grow in response to the
availability of state (with federal reimbursement) funding.

During the 1970s there were great increases in the amounts spent
on purchased social services.[22] Yet the great expansion did not bring
greater satisfaction. Early on, some state bureaucrats had begun to
realize that purchase-of-service mechanisms were jeopardizing state
control and accountability. Conscientious bureaucrats followed their
Weberian principles and began to develop more standardized systems of program monitoring and review. Especially in states where
deinstitutionalization had been rapid, some contracted agencies had
literally "bailed out" the states by providing shelter and services. Only
after a few years did state officials begin to realize that they wanted
more information, at least, and more control—standard needs of any
well-functioning bureaucracy.

State workers' unions began to criticize contracting as a way to break
their unions and to weaken the ability of the workplace to pressure
the administration. They argued that all workers within state and
contracted agencies were made more vulnerable by the system. Contracted employees usually earned less and had few benefits. They could
lose their jobs if the management of their small agency was inept in

getting funding or if the state cut back and/or "changed funding priorities." They were usually without union or civil service protection. As money for services declined and as state controls increased, many workers in private agencies began to see their dilemma. Some attempts at unionization were made, but all were difficult given the small size of workplaces.[23]

By the 1980s the increase in purchase of service had served to discredit the public sector. Public agency leaders were often quite open about using contracted services because they were "better" than the public sector could provide. The quality of workers, the flexibility, the ability to be innovative were all cited. Finally, this approach began to support the conservative argument that the public sector could not do anything right and needed reforming. Some only suggested managerial innovations; others used the opening as a way to argue that we should not provide *any* services (and next, any contracted services) at all.

Similarly, the private sector lost credibility with purchasing. With such great dependence on public money, it lost legitimacy with legislators and the media as outside critics. But because private agencies had not brought their proclaimed "expertise" into the public sector, the public credibility did not grow. Bureaucratically, the state might have gained more control, but it would not claim to be represented by its vigorously self-proclaimed "private" contractees. So neither side won, nor seemed to know how to relate to the other, as one Boston welfare official commented:

I'm never quite sure how to relate to them [the private providers]. Many of them have better education and more expertise than we do here in the Department. Some of them are very well connected to legislators and the schools of social work. Sometimes they come in with all these professional judgments and demands about how we have to do better. But the next day they will be back trying to negotiate a contract which is vague and unclear and which doesn't tell the Department enough about what they are going to do for us to monitor them. They expect us to trust them but, in their professional role, they want us to "enforce accountability" on the whole system.[24]

By increased monitoring and tight contracting mechanisms the public bureaucracies have recently regained some control, at a high price. The new system is riddled with internal mistrust, both between contractees and state agencies and among private agencies in competition for contracts. The private agencies that can afford to withdraw from the system and revert back to all private money are disaffected, and many workers have found themselves forced into giving up the dreams of creativity and commitment which originally motivated them, as witnessed by one Boston youth worker:

> I used to be glad I worked in a private agency and wasn't a state worker. I wanted to help people, not be a bureaucrat.
>
> I've been in the children's network for four years, always working myself ragged doing what I could to advocate, coordinate, or somehow make the system work for children. I've been praised by supervisors for my energy, but I still have no security, a low salary, and a sense that the kids I work with are never going to get real help. My friends who can are going to graduate schools or moving. I've got a family and I guess I'm looking for one of those cushy bureaucratic jobs I've always criticized. What else can I do?[25]

For the elite, trained social worker, another option has emerged, that of going into private practice as a therapist/counselor. Since 1970 many states have passed or toughened licensure laws for social workers and most have, with the strong lobbying efforts of NASW, made third party payments from insurance companies available for licensed social workers. Hardcastle estimates that there may be as many as 20,000 social workers in private practice.[26]

In many ways licensure and private practice are an expansion of the entrepreneurial spirit awakened by purchase of service. Before, energetic, ambitious service workers could hustle government agencies to get contracts for their own small, independent agencies. Now, with that dream fading into the reality of running a small institution at the mercy of bureaucratic fiat and budget cuts, the next logical step is to hang out a shingle for oneself. A service will still be provided, albeit probably to a less needy client, and the worker will still have the option for meaningful work.

However, as suggested earlier, there are a number of problems with the model of private practice as the last frontier. First, the work itself is often isolating and difficult to sustain as full-time employment and it is only an option for a privileged group of highly trained professionals. More importantly, there seems to be no long-term protection. The more people go into it, the greater the competition, with all its effects on demand and pricing. If insurance companies change their policies in the future and choose only to fund "group practice," for instance, individual practitioner's are at risk, just as they may be if "malpractice" suits become more prominent. For radicals, private practice poses special problems due to its lack of contact with other workers, its inevitable creaming of clients, and its asocial nature. But for any service workers the "escape from bureaucracy" into a model of independent professionalism, which never existed for social workers in the past, is likely to be a short-run phenomenon, and one which will benefit only the most well-connected and highly trained workers. The rest must continue to find some means to fight within organizations or to define new, more collective organizational forms.

Again, a more political critique of bureaucracy could have helped isolate the issues. If public responsibility had not come automatically to mean poor services, provided in large institutions through the most rigidly bureaucratized forms, then the development of "purchased services" could have taken on different meaning. Private agencies might have been brought into the sphere of public accountability without the hierarchical and rigidly structured controls that seemed so "natural." Individual workers might have found more options besides either surrender to the "inevitability" of bureaucratic behavior or individualistic entrepreneurship. In short, the political options might have seemed more varied and therefore purchase of service could have been viewed in a more complex way. Instead, activists swung from naively embracing it as an option for "creative" services without the unavoidable hassles of the bureaucracy to totally damning it as they came to see its capacity to further fragment the system. Here again, we needed less exclusive options.

From Coordination to Integration to Management Systems. Various means have been used since the 1960s to bring the system under greater bureaucratic control. Taken together, these attempts have created a new structure of management in human service bureaucracies and have served to further alienate service workers from the people and the structures which define their work.

It all started innocently enough. In the early seventies the "proliferation" of community services led to concerns over "duplication of effort," while some clients "fell through the cracks." Deinstitutionalization and new programs for children and the elderly, as well as the array of contracted agencies, were confusing to anyone trying to understand the system. So the call came down from HEW to begin to develop efforts for better coordinated services, for better information systems. Local agencies received "capacity building" grants to consider co-location and shared computer systems and to develop the generalist case manager concept.[27] Demonstration projects grew up which sought to replace specialists and professional social workers with the type of human service case manager who would help broker for clients without providing the older, direct services.

As we can see, there were attractive features to this and some of us, including this author, were momentarily beguiled by what seemed like a chance to break out of old, specialized, condescending patterns. Social work schools, ever adaptable when grant money seemed available, began to attempt to build up their administrative sequences and to rejuvenate social work administration as a viable part of practice.

But before we got very far, however, the implications of the shift started to become clear. Small community agencies began to worry about the kinds of information they were newly required to gather on clients. The calls *for* generalists became attacks *against* "recalcitrant" workers, who were blamed for continuing problems. In some agencies whole new layers of managers were brought in. What had begun as a call for better management systems became a call for more managers. Professionals in the bureaucracy began to be pushed out in favor of a "new breed" of managers who understood new realities and tried to count "units of service," instead of evaluating whether anything worthwhile was happening.

"Spiraling costs" were the justification for the new approach, although a closer look at the nature of the increases is interesting. Federal and state service expenditures did increase from 1968 until 1978, but the trend was primarily due to inflation and to rises in Medicaid and Social Security costs.[28] But the urge to contain all human service costs and develop more efficient systems went on unabated through the late seventies. "Reforms" often were little more than new ways to cut costs or to develop more efficient control. In Massachusetts, for example, one statewide effort to decentralize service delivery began to be used by upper-level umbrella-agency administrators as a way to get information to be used against specific agencies.[29]

Unions began to recognize that "centralized" methods of case record keeping turned into speed-ups, where workers faced more clients with fewer long-term contacts.[30] One worker expressed the growing sense of frustration by remarking, "It always seems to be a question of how they can get *more* out of the workers with as little investment as possible from the agency."[31] Indeed, it is no surprise that the period launched a new spate of studies on the street-level bureaucrat. My own study of Massachusetts suggested that worker frustration increased along with heightened concern for "productivity."

Looking back, we can see that much of the worry and dismay over the disorganized, poorly managed state of human services was a ruse. Instead these "problems" simply allowed the bureaucracy to expand, as Claude Lefort suggests:

The more activities are fragmented, services diversified, specialized and partitioned, the more numerous the structural levels and the delegation of authority at each level, the more coordination and control sectors multiply because of this dispersion. Thus the bureaucracy prospers.[32]

The system of human service bureaucracies was undoubtedly under more control in 1980 than in 1970. In addition, in many states and at the federal level a new stratum of managers had been brought in to oversee the expanded bureaucracies. This new group was trained to accept the hierarchy, specialization, and formalism of large organizations without any of the contradictions of a "service ethic" that might plague social workers, even those from administrative concentrations. And their special asset was that, because many arrived with experience in the private sector, many of the new managers could claim to be the enemy of the very public bureaucracies they were helping to build.

Contemporary Divestiture of Responsibility. The new managers, though, may have made a serious mistake. As we have seen, in order to secure control over the newly expanded bureaucracy, they chose to discredit the old system. When the New Right vanguard arrived in Washington it was armed with an ideology and information to use against the human service bureaucracy, regardless of who was in control of it. They could assert positively that the "public sector has failed" and dismantle the bureaucracy, not in order to improve or control service delivery, but in order to stop any attendant increase in public responsibility. Neither the old professionals nor the new managers could launch a strong defense. At base, the hard-core conservatives want to *eliminate* all of the positive functions of the welfare system, not to stop bureaucratic inefficiency. As the leader of the Massachusetts Citizens for Limited Taxation group was quoted as saying, "The government should only provide prisons, courts, and police."[33] Since this position is not likely to win in an open debate, New Right theorists instead launched a two-pronged attack on social programs that skirts their fundamental opposition to all programs.[34]

First, the New Right leaders attacked the service ethic of the social welfare tradition. They cited the functions of welfare programs to show how they weaken the family, how they are disrespectful of people, and how they undermine individual initiative to go out and, at all costs, struggle for survival in the labor market. Here they used critics like Christopher Lasch as well as more acceptable conservatives and critics from among the human service managers.

Second, they then went after these same managers and criticized them for the very bureaucratic systems they have worked so hard to create. The rules, the red tape, the bureaucratic attempts to control costs became standard jokes at every conservative gathering. No matter that the bureaucrats thought they were creating an efficient and accountable system, according to all of the standard rules. The New Right used the inherent inhumanity of bureaucratic forms against the agencies in order to stop them from accomplishing what few humanitarian purposes they could still achieve. We can almost feel sorry for this new breed of bureaucrats, so briefly on the throne. Just as they started to get their systems in order, based in part on attacks on the "false humanitarianism" of traditional services that should please any conservative, they found themselves asked to dismantle. But it is unfortunate that progressives had not previously been in the forefront of separating social welfare goals from bureaucratic process in order to stage a more effective counterattack.[35]

The result of all this was, for the wrong reasons, to further discredit what bureaucratic systems were left and thereby to make the next round of cuts and changes more defensible. It placed all workers in the double bind of having to defend themselves and their services at a time when, due to bureaucratic "reforms" and New Right cutbacks, those services were less defensible and more oppressive than ever. It is within this depressing and debilitating bureaucratic environment that service workers must currently create effective political strategies and tactics.

CURRENT ISSUES WITHIN THE BUREAUCRACY

As I suggested earlier, many commentators have noted that a major source of difficulty for service workers comes from conflicts imbedded in their organizational position, coupled with their lack of awareness of the nature of such conflicts.[36] Here a sampling from the literature may give a sense of the range of the problem. Wenocur and Sherman note, in a perceptive paper on worker empowerment, that

> If one talks to workers—particularly direct service workers—they too will state that they face insurmountable problems from clients and from the bureaucracy, that they often feel unable to cope and perceive few options; in other words, they feel that they cannot control their work situation, and that they do not have the ability, authority, or influence to change that situation and to be able to truly help their clients.[37]

They go on to see that organizational contradictions produce stresses for midlevel managers as well as workers asked to recognize that "under such conditions, organizational survival becomes the preoccupation for management and individual survival the crucible of the worker."[38]

Many writers have tried to classify groups of workers by their types of responses to the agency milieu. While these classification systems often seem to blame workers for their "choice" of category, some of the typologies suggested are interesting. Kroeger sees a four-point grouping: apathetics, advocates, bureaucrats, and mediators. Forbes sees fatalists and functionaires. Wenocur and Sherman see capitulators, noncapitulators, niche-finders, withdrawers, and victim-martyrs. Patti sees three types of low-level administrators: conservers, climbers, and professional advocates. Other breakdowns are equally suggestive if less sharply descriptive. Russo sees that workers either identify with clients, identify with their jobs and co-workers, or identify with the organization. Brager and Holloway find responses of moral indignation, psychological isolation, or structural isolation. And

Lipsky sees workers responding by trying to limit demand, modifying the concept of the job, or modifying the concept of clients.[39]

Taken together, none of the patterns seems very promising. Most become self-defeating and even defeating of the organization's stated goals. All seem to stem from a combination of ignorance about organizational patterns, unreasonable expectations regarding worker and organizational power to make change, and large-scale social contradictions built into the nature of human service institutions in a capitalist society. Perhaps the saddest of all the descriptions of frustration is the judgment made by Michael Lipsky, that the nature of the bureaucratic workplace means that "it is dysfunctional to most street-level bureaucracies to become responsive."[40] Elsewhere I have called this situation a "circle game," set up so that no one can win.

One critical reason for developing a political strategy which includes tactics for understanding and dealing with bureaucracies is to help workers be responsive. Most of the researchers above seemed overwhelmed by the patterns they discovered. One way out may be to expand our expectations regarding organizational behavior. And a key reason for seeking another way to conceptualize human service organizations and options for practice is so that we can help ourselves. The quest for political practice means changing conditions that create a circle game, and achieving solidarity with clients and with other workers. But it means also a search for ways to improve the lives of human service workers, in order to achieve mutual support and energy instead of frustration and defeat. We need not be apologetic about this.

The Sabotage of Relationships with Clients. Just as current bureaucratic pressures restrict the sense of personal efficacy and reward, they also limit one's ability to relate to clients in a humane way, much less as the potential comrades demanded by political practice. In classic fashion, workers begin to "blame the victim," the client, for their own inability to function. More professionally oriented commentators would tend to suggest that part of the reason for this was the "overidentification" of workers with clients and then prescribe a healthy professional distance as part of the cure. More progressive observers would tend to see the problem stemming, instead, from workers' inability to have equal relationships with clients. But all agree that organizational difficulties are most often experienced by clients as hostility or neglect from workers.

The reason why this happens, however, is not simply a case of social-psychological displacement of frustration/aggression. In fact, many students of bureaucracy as well as radicals recognize that one of the major *purposes* of a bureaucracy is to separate clients from workers. Sjoberg and others, for example, are clear that "bureaucratic systems are the key medium through which the middle class maintains its advantaged position vis-à-vis the lower class."[41] Therefore it is essential to the functioning of the bureaucracy that workers *do not* understand clients but are separated from them by having very different (unstated) goals, attitudes toward the client's problems, and standards of success than clients. Otherwise, the worker may understand why clients act as they do. If this happens, the worker "is likely to recognize that they have valid reasons for objecting to his conception of reality or, more specifically, to some of the bureaucratic regulations."[42] Such mutual understanding could lead to joint action and could, by definition, undermine the bureaucracy.

Much of this process begins, as was noted in chapter 4, with the very process by which citizens seeking assistance become transformed into clients. From the beginning of the interaction, the bureaucracy seeks to objectify clients so that the worker can manipulate them, not relate to them as individuals:

The individual applying for service personally enters into an organizational arena in which organizational factors affect the manner in which his problem, and indirectly his self, comes to be defined. Organizational factors, then, to some extent shape the process by which people are transformed into clients and people with troubles are assigned new public identities.[43]

Once this occurs the normal bureaucrat can only relate to clients as the personification of their problem, not as individual people like herself. As Larson notes, it is not correct to see "technobureaucratic professionals" as "indifferent" to their clients, rather "they simply do not have any autonomous orientation toward the clients, except indirectly. The corporation which they serve mandates, in fact, the professional's relations to the clients as buyers or users of corporate services or products."[44]

Professional training and agency socialization work together then to undermine the ability of bureaucrats "to believe that their clients can be equipped to collaborate with them as equals."[45] As Lipsky notes, "Conceptions of the job imply conception of the clientele. One cannot practice without an implicit model of the people whom one is processing."[46] And a major function of bureaucratic structure and training—along with professional ideology—is to create an image of the client that is incompatible with the development of any equal alliance between workers and clients. At best clients are seen as victims, overwhelmed by their problems, dependent on the worker for support and guidance. At worst they are doubted, suspected of fraud before they walk in the door, and seen as both wily and fundamentally incompetent.

Such imagery, if internalized, justifies agency practices and functions. Also, since good clients learn that to get what they need from the bureaucracy they must "act their expected role," they may even become self-fulfilling prophesies. Indeed, if workers try to break the rules and expect something different than the expected norm of clients they may find themselves distrusted by clients, as one veteran of Massachusetts Youth Services recalled:

I once had this worker who kept telling me to speak my mind, to say what I wanted when I was angry. I see now what he was trying to do. Back then I didn't trust him; I figured he was going to get me in trouble. He wouldn't be around to pick up the pieces if I shot my mouth off to the wrong person.[47]

Finally, then, bureaucratic controls serve to keep both clients and workers in a hierarchical, often mutually self-destructive relationship. The worker who advocates too strongly for clients is breaking the rules, as is the client who acts on a different set of expectations. A major task for radicals is to find ways out of this bureaucratically imposed box that are not suicidal either for clients or workers.

Who's a Worker? The complicated bureaucratic structures that have emerged over the past ten years have created fundamental political problems for human service activists. One of the most central difficulties is that it is now no longer simple to answer the question, "Who's a worker?"

As we have seen, the ideology of professionalism has made some people so blind to the need for solidarity with other workers, much less with clients, that they cannot be trusted in the workplace. This attitude is, of course, sponsored by management, which likes nothing better than to have self-appointed representatives at the delivery level. One task of a political practice is to help would-be professionals see this identity as self-defeating and isolating.

At the other extreme, there may be a struggle with other human service workers about joining with "nonservice" staff. Even many employees who are willing to see themselves as workers may balk at meeting with secretaries, cooks, bus drivers, or "temporary" employees. Here the position can be clear, activists must just keep pushing to convince other ex-professional workers of the common cause in bargaining units, or other workplace concerns. However, one must be prepared, on the other hand, for rejection by such fellow workers. Years of separation between professional workers and other workers may have made people wary of coalitions with newly aware workers. As one legal services secretary put it,

They always wanted to be the big professional lawyers. Then they found out that they could be fired and ordered around just like they ordered us around. So they decided to become workers and join our union. We met and talked about it and decided they should organize themselves. We would see how they acted, and if they supported us, before we would just let them join us. No way could we automatically trust them.[48]

In such situations the task is to create trust through one's practice but not to push for a false unity based on the good intentions of a minority of "professional" workers.

Another type of problem arises out of the complexities of contracting. Sometimes, within the same office, workers doing the same job may be employees of different bosses—one may be on a grant or "contracted" line, the other may be a state employee. Or workers at one halfway house in an association may be subject to the terms of a state contract and workers in another may not. If all the workers share a common identity this may pose problems only around unionization. But sometimes, because of differences in benefits and work expectations, such differences in bureaucratic identity may divide workers from each other.

In short, the bureaucratic environment creates special pitfalls by dividing workers from each other and confusing them about natural solidarity. Simply wishing that all would act like workers together will not make it happen. As I suggested in chapter 4, any strategy for politicizing our work must begin with an analysis of everyone who works there in order to determine, specifically, who the workers are.

Who's a Boss? Similarly the structure of human service work has made it difficult to determine an even more basic question, "Who's a boss?"

In large and small agencies, for example, people have been classified as management because they do planning or information monitoring, or simply because a grant demanded it. Also, in smaller agencies one or two promotions can land someone in a "management" position. As suggested in chapter 4, such jobs need to be reviewed individually before a decision is made about someone's status. Not to do this risks missing the chance for building alliances with workers like the Boston welfare "administrator" who complained: "During the strike I was management. I had to cross the picket line or lose my job. But I didn't make decisions here. I hated crossing the picket line even more because I didn't have any real power."[49]

Even more complex is the problem of how to evaluate the pleas of people whose positions are clearly administrative but who claim to have no autonomy because of requirements of the contract, or because of the complex structure of a large bureaucracy. Here again the answer may lie in a structural review of job responsibilities and a collective history of how particular individuals—or predecessors— have acted in a given job. The nature of the human service job structure, especially during boom times, did move many trustworthy people into positions of some authority. Such people should not be rejected in a formalistic way; individual decisions can be made based on their behavior—do they share management information and keep worker confidences, for example? However, there are some jobs, especially in these times, which simply cannot be performed by anyone who wishes to be trusted by workers or clients. The choice to take such a position is real, and cannot be smoothed over by naive plans to "influence" the power structure.

Finally, some people who act as consultants or individual entrepreneurs (doctors, lawyers) may either objectively function as bosses or may have a role more akin to that of other workers. Especially in state systems, there may be a large number of such people on staff. Again, each needs to be reviewed individually.

People with much less political experience may find such scrutiny and labeling offensive. After all, shouldn't we welcome anyone who wants to join us? Those with battle scars left over from trusting professional "co-workers" who sold out for career advancement or who have seen "progressive" supervisors knuckle under to the "political realities" demanded by administrators, will have to share old tales. If anything, being political means careful review of material conditions in one's workplace. The divisions are not "personal" judgments; one can still be friendly and positive with an administrator who wants to be supportive to staff. And one can still push to see tangible signs of support. But, in self-defense, workers may have to learn never to trust such administrators, because in classic bureaucratic fashion, under pressure they will choose to follow their mandated roles rather than defend their "subordinates." Let us be surprised by exceptions in our favor, rather than betrayed by false hopes.

The Limits and Promise of Unions. As the above suggests, any workplace where there are such basic confusions regarding the identity of workers and bosses as well as regarding the nature of "good work" is both ripe for unionization and likely to pose problems for the development of an effective union. Because unionizing seems like such a clear political strategy, many radical service workers may jump into it without careful thought and preparation. After a year or so they may find themselves caught up in problems that could have been prevented had they taken the time to evaluate the advantages and difficulties associated with union activity in the human service workplace.

There are, of course, many good reasons why human service workers need a union, especially in times of cutbacks. The 1970s were a time of public sector union expansion, for good reasons.[50] Public agency work has become increasingly unstable and the addition of a middle layer of managers in many agencies has made the human service workers' lack of power over their work, and over agency policy, much more obvious. While it is not clear whether the "proletarianization" of human service work is any different from its increasing "bureaucratization," the daily reality is that human service workers are increasingly specialized, subject to more and more control, and less and less flattered by the illusion that they have much "professional discretion" over their work.[51]

The new breed of human service workers since the 1960s may be less skeptical of unionization than traditional professionals. Many New Leftists went into human service work and are naturally sympathetic to unionizing as a way to give their work more political validity. Other unions seem less skeptical of public sector and "professional" unions than they used to be, so it is possible to build alliances with other workers. Finally, unionization has been seen by some as a nice, clean way to break the identification that so many workers have with their agencies: "Unionization symbolically draws a line between us as social workers and our agencies. By organizing we proclaim that we do not blindly maintain allegiance to our agencies and do not believe administrators have the same interests as we do."[52] It allows human service workers to act politically in response to a situation that is created by overtly political decisions and has manifestly political effects on their clients as well as themselves.

In short, especially in large bureaucratic agencies, unionization seems like a natural, obvious, and healthy response to the current plight. And even in smaller agencies, unionization can help clarify roles and build workplace solidarity—although there are special problems. Some have even suggested that in times of cutbacks, union activity may even help administrators to fight for programmatic goals. In Massachusetts, for example, some administrators seemed all too willing to "blame their contractual obligations" with the unions when explaining to elected officials why they could not implement cuts.[53]

Unionization is not the solution to all the problems of human service workers, however. As workers, especially radicals, have learned over the past fifteen years of union experience, there are many problems that usually remain untouched by union activity. As much as workers need unions, activists cannot go into them without an awareness of their inherent limitations.

A major problem with unions is that they are often another bureaucracy to deal with and many times are defined by a narrow, business unionist approach borrowed from conservative private sector unions. Paul Johnston, in an important *Monthly Review* article, has explained this clearly:

Unfortunately, public workers and their unions have tended to apply mechanically the models of unionism inherited from the private sector. This inherited unionism has a poor track record in the private sector itself, where it serves to defuse and contain labor struggle through its narrow economic forms. When transplanted to the public sector it faces conditions for which its basic strategies are in effect irrelevant. And so the new public unions find themselves in a position comparable to that of a naval force trying to fight with land-battle tactics. The failures which necessarily result place these unions into deepening crises which can only be resolved by the rank and file's assertion of a unionism suitable to the public sector.[54]

Even when workers try to create alternative models the pressures are great, as described by one Boston area unionist:

> We did not want to be a union which just counted caseload numbers. Many of us originally started as part of a client-oriented caucus and saw the union being in existence to provide better, more responsive service.
> But it was hard, if not impossible, to do this. We *did* have to count caseload numbers and protect employees in a traditional way, before we could have any legitimacy with the membership. And with the new push for a "management approach" we often had to fight administrators over things that had been handled more informally in the past. But they couldn't seem really to figure out what to do with us either.[55]

Such experiences can be frustrating, especially if a group has subsumed all of its political work into union activity. The endless stream of meetings, the fighting to have other issues taken as seriously as "wages and benefits" by union officials, the struggle for democracy, all are part of the work of what one activist now calls "the union business."

Management has also increased its sophistication in dealing with unions. Workers in small agencies, with a "friendly" management, may be surprised to find the hard-nosed tactics that are brought into play when they try to organize.[56] As Maier notes, managements have learned to use "management rights" clauses to restrict the scope of bargainable issues and to play unions off against each other by favoritism and by insisting on large units in order to benefit from existing divisions among workers.[57] All of these tactics, coupled with the work of creating a responsive and representative union, can mean that "union work" becomes a major preoccupation for human service workers. This may be the escape from their daily pressures that some workers want. But others who still find satisfaction and political potential in their service work may feel frustrated and torn. If one enters a union to make one's work less contradictory and impossible, it can be demoralizing to find that union activity seems to become simply another task to perform in addition to one's job. Here the importance of a political caucus that is separate from union work is essential to maintaining balance and political priorities.

If these were the only difficulties with union activity, however, there would be less cause for worry. Essentially they are the frustrations of any political work. But the nature of the class position of human service workers and the social control functions of agencies add another, deeper reservation about union activity. If, by taking on the mantle of organized labor, workers forget their contradictory class role in relation to clients and their real conflict of interest with them at times, they subvert serious political goals. Some workers encounter this difficulty when they strike, or try to fight speed-ups. They find that clients may not be supportive, and that the general public surely is not. This hostility can be demoralizing, or worse, can lead to worker anger at clients. An especially depressing example of such tension occurred in Massachusetts when a group of welfare rights activists were pitted against the union, as one organizer remembers:

Last summer on Cape Cod something happened which makes me hesitate to build alliances with workers, no matter how "correct" that strategy is. We were fighting for summer housing, always a problem on the Cape. While we were outside demonstrating welfare workers were ordered to guard the doors against us. They did. A scuffle occurred and there was fighting between some welfare social workers and some clients. So the next thing we know we [the union and the demonstrators] were all in court charging each other with assault. How's that for class solidarity?[58]

Such encounters are not inevitable. Workers can refuse such orders. Unions can build alliances with advocacy groups. One progressive Michigan union was able to respond after a worker was attacked by a client with a demand for more workers and better office conditions, instead of for more guards with guns.[59] But developing such client-oriented practices has to be a priority for radicals; without them the union card can become a badge of class divisiveness, not class solidarity, and can serve to discredit political work and the goals for a better service system. This is one area in which activists cannot slack off, or the claim to political legitimacy is lost.

Recently activists have begun to posit a more radical vision of what public-sector unionism can accomplish, aside from just establishing that human service workers are workers and not professionals. These ideas are highly exciting and begin to converge with notions of the potential for political practice.

Essentially, a whole set of radical critics are calling for substitution of political goals for narrow economic ones, for a merging of human service workers' awareness of the needs which the state does not meet with their organized demands to be allowed to do so. It is worth quoting a few people at length here. First there are the British writers of *In and Against the State:*

The struggle of state workers is not simply about wages and conditions of work, or restoring the level of services of a few years ago. It has to be about the content of the work we do, too. The state, in order to maintain control over a situation, defines the everyday problems experienced by people in terms which reflect *its* needs and interests. Successful working class demands for better living conditions, whether housing, health services or education, have been translated into the language and needs of the state. They may be "our" hospitals, schools and council houses, but they have been shaped by the state according to *its* interests, the interest of maintaining the necessary conditions for capital to flourish, not the interests of those who use the services. Questions about the kind of services and whom they are for are central to furthering the interests of both the workers who provide the services, and the consumers on the receiving end, for they are often the same people.[60]

And there is the hope of Michael Yates in *Crisis in the Public Sector: A Reader:*

By demanding public services for the working class and by showing clearly that government budgets can provide them, public-sector unions would put public employers on the defensive and ultimately force them to reveal through their actions that democracy in the United States is indeed a myth, that the purpose of our government is to preserve privilege by preserving capitalism. In other words, as the state refuses to serve the public when it has been clearly demonstrated that it could do so with existing resources, then the state may lose its legitimacy. But instead of this leading to worker apathy, or worse yet fascism, it could lead to a feeling among workers that they could and should organize to win control of the state and change it so that it does serve them.[61]

And, finally, the influential suggestions of Paul Johnston in *Monthly Review* are worth quoting extensively:

[The] immediacy of the meaning of the work in the context of the myth of democracy provides part of the basis for considering that there is an opening in the public sector for workers to begin critically defining the object of their activity (which, as pointed out above, is society itself). The workers can promote discussion, take a position, and demand democratic control of what should be done in connection with their work. When this notion—which is essentially that of a socialist unionism for the public sector—is placed into the framework of the need for political power, then we will understand that the community too has an interest in what is produced. . . .

The demand for democracy can also replace the politically counterproductive bargaining game over wages with a straightforward stand for something like: (1) equal pay with private-sector levels of unionized workers and (2) corrective adjustment of discriminatory pay levels (for example, clerical pay). Wherever possible, the union should seek forms which would tie the conditions and struggles of public-sector workers directly to those of private-sector workers, bringing them together in a common focus of struggle with state power . . . the bureaucracy is a structure of roles, which includes not only those at the top but those at the bottom. Workers who view the union as just another form of insurance—passive consumers without a sense of collective struggle—are an essential part of the bureaucracy. To the extent that those workers awaken and learn to organize themselves, the bureaucracy is vulnerable.[62]

Elsewhere, Johnston, an organizer himself, summed up the potential for this new brand of unionism:

Public workers are defined as public servants in a new sense: as responsible public servants intent upon serving the needs of the community. The intention is to serve the community and to participate in defining community needs and how they are to be served in opposition to government and business forces that stand in the way and define them according to capital instead of people.[63]

Such potential makes it all the more important that we overcome the difficulties with trade-union tactics and get on with the business of creating a wide alliance for true public service.

Agency Loyalty and Human Service Reforms. At the opposite end of the pole from unionism workers find themselves pulled toward greater defense of their agencies, or the broader policies they implement, because of the nature of current attacks. Or, they are urged to abandon efforts to improve the content of their work, because now is not the time for "idealistic" reforms. Liberals urge them to be realistic and not to air grievances at a time when all programs are so vulnerable. Indeed, workers may be asked to make public statements in support of their programs as part of a public campaign to keep funding. Subtle pressures may exist to "tone down the politics" for the good of the agency. All in all activists can feel in a double bind about how much to defend programs of which they are seriously critical.

As with so many of the dilemmas facing radical service workers there are no pat answers. Workers have a right to defend jobs and the benefits provided by agencies. But one must beware of sounding unaware of the problems which are faced in performing jobs under current circumstances. In union statements or other public appeals workers must find ways to combine demands that they be able to continue to provide services with a recognition of immediate problems. This must be done not only for reasons of political purity, but far more important, because clients and the general public are aware of the problems of agencies—to deny them is to lose credibility. Whenever possible, defense actions should involve clients and community supporters. Most important, administrators must be restrained from using clients and workers as shock troops to defend programs. Workers must push and pressure bosses to make public defense of programs, and not to play it safe. Many can be pressured into this from below, but will avoid it if they can.

Administrators are also apt to have rigged fights for resources, and fool workers into being their cheerleaders. In Massachusetts a predictable pattern has developed. The head of a department will make a public stand for more resources. He will go before the TV cameras and enumerate all the reasons why he needs a budget of a certain size. Then there will be a highly publicized meeting between the director and the head of the umbrella human service secretariat to resolve their differences. The director will emerge with a "compromise" and report back to all his staff that he had "gotten all he could." Maybe so. But the laws of bureaucratic hierarchy suggest that, since the director and the secretary were on the same side, and the director was accountable to the secretary, it was a pretty quick "compromise" dictated from above and engineered to convince workers and clients that they could not reasonably expect anything more. Agency loyalty does not mean falling for such tricks.

Sometimes agency loyalty becomes confused. In Massachusetts two public institutions were recently merged, one with higher professional status than the other. The staff at both were unionized. Instead of working together to fight for all jobs and to call attention to the net loss of service that was to result from the merger, the two locals (both part of the same public-sector union!) fought for themselves. The administration of the dominant institution was not satisfied, however. The director not only wanted "his" employees to fight for themselves but to support him in attempts to limit the number of other workers who would keep their jobs. Progressive union members from the two groups, who met to form a unified strategy, faced distrust from within both their institutions. Both administrators and fellow workers saw the only strategy as defending their institutions. The results of the conflict were demoralizing to the staff of both institutions and the lessons learned by one radical are highly pertinent:

> I learned how hard it is to do progressive organizing when everyone was frightened for their jobs. All people wanted was job protection. The fact that student slots were being cut by 30 percent, that job protections were being lost, that all remaining workers would be speeded up were not seen as immediately relevant.
>
> We couldn't unite with each other, so the only big winners were the upper-level administrators.[64]

Such experiences suggest that radicals have to be prepared to limit their loyalty to agencies to the extent that such loyalty hurts clients and other workers. They have to be prepared for the unpopularity of such stands, that, like the complexities of radical union activity, arise from a broader political awareness of the complexities of class.

Finally, activists have to be on the lookout for cutbacks clothed in the guise of "reform." Many service workers want to be in favor of "reforms"; few want to defend the status quo. But for the past decade, and even more so now, many "reforms," "reorganizations," and "new initiatives" have meant an objective decrease in direct services and in workers' ability to perform well. Administrators in the 1970s couched reforms as ways to improve services to clients and often blamed incompetent workers for the problems that brought the changes. Recently the climate is such that managers do not need to claim to better serve clients, all they are required to do is "save money." This makes obvious cutbacks easier to fight. But one can still be confused by appeals to a concern for long-range changes. One activist has developed a quick rule of thumb for evaluating such proposals:

After Vietnam I learned to be wary of schemes to "destroy villages in order to save them." I still am skeptical. When I hear someone tell me about the long-run benefits I get nervous. I want to know what this change will be like for me, my fellow workers, and clients on the first day it happens. If I would be worse off than I am now I try to oppose it. Anything else is a trick.[65]

For those with lingering professional illusions about their ability to plan change, such a position may still be difficult. Again, the best response may be to consult with one's caucus, to review any proposed changes together, and to consider how to respond to each point. Good elements may be mixed in with dangerous ones. If workers are well informed and organized there may still be some chance of fighting for certain small-scale reforms. And even without immediate victory, the collective campaign may help build alliances and raise the consciousness of workers and clients.

TOWARD A POLITICAL CONTEXT FOR BUREAUCRATIC ANALYSIS

The problems facing bureaucratic workers today cannot be addressed unless we begin to question the "natural logic" of bureaucratic behavior and attempt to identify options for accomplishing human service work which do not fall back on old expectations regarding the "rational" organization of work. Therefore, the first step in developing a political practice within bureaucracies is to devise a radical critique of bureaucracy itself. Here we must include a study of the role bureaucracies have come to play in existing "socialist" countries as well as under capitalism. Indeed, I suggest that we must question whether large-scale, bureaucratic forms can ever be adapted to more socialized egalitarian goals. Perhaps we must come to understand that, just as service work must be deprofessionalized to achieve more progressive aims, human service activity must be "debureaucratized" if we are ever to achieve a fully radical practice.

Here we are on even shakier ground than in criticizing professionalism. There is a new, but consistent left literature showing the danger of professionalism. And the general goal of worker solidarity—while vague—can offer the beginnings of an alternate form. There are far fewer sources for radical critiques of bureaucracy and an even less articulated vision of how to organize work and society without it. On the other hand, the depressing reality of the bureaucratic societies of Eastern Europe and the Soviet Union, as well as the overwhelming pressures on bureaucratized workers in the United States, suggests that we have to try. Here, of course, the state of the critical art and the limits of space allow us only to suggest some of the elements of a political critique and to pose some of the questions that must be answered by a debureaucratized alternative.

Beyond Bureaucratic Rationality: Sources for a Critique. As noted earlier, the socialist tradition—with its emphasis on the state and on centralized planning—has not led to a deep critique of bureaucracy. While capitalist management strategies were opposed as aiding the ruling class, there has not been a similar criticism of the limits of bureaucracy as a means to achieve socialist goals. Indeed, much of socialist practice—from Lenin's use of Taylorism to the development of modern socialist states—has assumed that somehow specialization, hierarchy, and technical rationality were apolitical means that could be used to achieve socialist ends as well as capitalistic ones.[66]

However, since the 1940s, other left thinkers have begun to question the appropriateness of bureaucratic means in the service of any humanitarian ends. Simone Weil's critique of large-scale bureaucracies—be they the Roman Empire, the Nazi Reich, or Stalinist Russia—led her to doubt whether the bureaucratic state could ever be anything but oppressive to human potential and social development.[67] Hannah Arendt's work on totalitarianism contained similar judgments, especially when augmented by her understanding of the "banality of evil" within bureaucratic hierarchies.[68] And Paul Goodman offered a witty and telling, even if unsystematic, critique of the inevitable dangers of trying to achieve the illusion of rational organization.[69] Finally, the attempt of French leftists Claude Lefort and Cornelius Castoriades to pose a viable Marxism in the face of Soviet failures has begun to suggest a new more thoroughgoing critique of bureaucracy as an organizational form, as the base for new class formations, and as the setting for a particular type of social relations. In the journal *Socialisme ou Barbaire* (Socialism or Barbarism) and in Lefort's later writings, the beginning basis for an attempt to abandon bureaucratic models is laid out.[70]

Lefort's ideas are most fully developed for our purposes. He contends that, in modern society, bureaucracy (meaning the people who direct and control dominant organizations) can develop relative autonomy, so that it both serves the ruling class and, "when the balance of social forces permits it," operates to create a set of social forces which support the continued expansion of bureaucratization. Thus bureaucracy can truly serve the capitalist class, or the ruling group in a society like the Soviet Union, but it does so not as a neutral mechanism. Instead, carrying out its own logic, bureaucracy seeks to include all social groupings within its hierarchical, homogenizing process:

Bureaucracy is a circle out of which no one can escape; that subordinates rely on their superiors to take the initiative and resolve difficulties, while the superiors expect their subordinates to solve particular problems which elude the level of generality where they have been conceived. This solidarity in incompetence goes quite far in tying the employee, situated on the bottom of the ladder, to the system of which he is a part. As a result it is impossible for him to denounce this system without simultaneously denouncing the vanity of his own function, from which he derives his material existence. Similarly bureaucrats seek the highest positions and work itself is subordinated to the gaining, or maintenance of personal status, such that bureaucracy appears as an immense network of personal relations.[71]

Such a process is similar to the "disabling function" of professionalism, denounced by Illich and McKnight. In fact, the development of professionalism and the development of bureaucracy can be seen in this light, not as the oppositional structures suggested by social work proponents of professionalism, but as mutually supportive, if different, formations. Here Larson, while not citing Lefort, seems to be on the same track when she argues that, in some cases, "Professionalism may be imposed from above." Management may attempt "to impose professionalism to maintain commitment on the part of those specialists who would ordinarily be considered failures for not moving up into management." Indeed, she goes on to argue that professionalism even allows bureaucracies the benefits of discretion without loss of control because it "makes the use of discretion predictable."[72]

Viewed in this light, bureaucracy becomes the beginning of a new form of the "incompetent" society, a form which can only develop so far under the controlling power of an external, capitalist ruling class.

But without the power of such a class it can become the dominant form of an oppressive social organization, as can be seen in Eastern Europe, where

bureaucracy exists only through bureaucrats and their common aim to form a nucleus apart from those whom they dominate, to participate in sociological power and to interdefine each other in a hierarchy which guarantees them either material status or prestige. . . . It multiplies positions and services, partitions various activities, generates artificial controls and coordination, and reduces an ever-growing mass of workers into merely mechanical functions in order to exercise its authority at every level.[73]

For those of us who wish to overthrow capitalist domination without replacing it with a bureaucratic stranglehold, Lefort and Castoriades suggest that the first step is to abandon the Weberian notion that bureaucracy is a neutral function. By supporting hierarchy, the "elimination of personal relations," and the "subordination of all activities to the application of a norm linked to an objective goal," it supports antisocial relationships and creates a base for a dehumanized social system even when profit and a capitalist ruling class disappear. Instead, they argue, "bureaucracy must be seen as a *social* formation, as a system of meaningful behavior, not merely as a system of organization. This implies an historical definition of the phenomenon as a human enterprise with its own goals."[74] It also implies that we must seek ways to organize work and society that do not recapitulate such problems. This process, they seem to hope without certainty, can begin simply by recognizing that we have created this bureaucratic monster by a process of human choice—not "natural," organic development—and that we may begin to find ways out by reexamining those prior choices.

Although such hopes may seem frail, without them we are left with the fatalism of many social welfare analysts. The literature in social work administration is full of criticism of bureaucratic behavior, all of which, finally, seem to suggest that its negative aspects—while not presented so starkly as by Lefort—are inevitable "facts of life." Many seem to agree with the rationale of William James, used by social work leader Porter Lee to defend inertia in the 1920s: "Most human institutions, by the purely technical and professional manner in which they come to be administered, end by becoming obstacles to the very purposes which their founders had in view."[75]

Some British activists, in trying to respond to the reality of their welfare bureaucracy, have gone a bit further than Lefort and Castoriades in suggesting the means to pursue in posing alternatives. As they see it, a critical means by which bureaucratic forms limit human potential is through the process of fragmentation, which divides co-workers from each other, clients from workers, both workers and clients from the larger social structure, and which serves to allow the general public, workers, and clients to see interrelated human needs as isolated from each other.[76] When nonradical critics observe such problems they usually pose a hodge podge of responses to better co-ordinate and integrate the bureaucracy. But the British Marxists who wrote *In and Against the State* see the nature of bureaucracy itself as causing the problem and as having to change before we can go "beyond the fragments." Their comments are worthy of extensive citation because they provide another small piece of the strategy that may begin to help us visualize alternatives to bureaucracy:

The processes by which the state fragments (or confirms the fragmentation of) society at large find their counterpart within the internal organization of the state apparatus itself. Just as the state deals with people in a fragmented manner as patients, social security claimants, or old age pensioners, so this is reflected in the internal division of labor within the state apparatus between those who deal with patients, those who deal with Social Security claimants, those who deal with old age pensioners. And just as the receipt of benefits and the definition of the claimant is bound up with a whole network of supervision and control, so within the state a massive system of hierarchical control ensures that the proper division of labor is adhered to. And just as the fragmentation of people's relations within the state obliterates the question of class, so, for those working within the state apparatus, the division of labor makes it virtually impossible to raise the question of class or exploitation. For a state worker to try to get to the roots of a problem would be to stray beyond her area of administrative competence.

So what is at issue here is not just a question of ideology is a simple sense. It is not just that our minds are constantly bombarded (as indeed they are) with the idea that we are living in a free, democratic society, that illness and poverty are individual problems. It is more than that. Even if we see through all this, even if we see or sense that illness or poverty are problems of society, we are still faced by the problem that any positive action by us seems to require us to jump through certain administrative hoops, to go through certain procedures which, whatever our beliefs, constrain us to act *as individuals* or as fragmented groups. The struggle against the state, therefore, is not just a matter of enlightening people, of showing them that the state is capitalistic. It is a problem of trying to develop alternative forms of organization which will counteract the fragmentation imposed by the state and give material expression to class solidarity.[77]

While far from a full-fledged strategy, the ideas expressed by British radicals and by Lefort and Castoriades do begin to suggest that, at least, we need to find ways to fight our human service bureaucracies that do not ask them to be more "efficient," in their own terms. Often, without thinking, through our criticisms we have helped bureaucracies become more specialized, more hierarchical, and more fragmented. (Once again I painfully recall my enthusiasm for integrated services.) Instead, we may need to find ways to argue for more small, overlapping, politically responsive, generalistic, and "inefficient" structures. To do this we will first have to rid ourselves of the very powerful ideas that have long convinced us that centralized, neutral, specialized, and streamlined structures were best. And then we will have to convince others, including fellow radicals, of our altered world view—no wonder we have discussed our task as a "long march through the institutions."

The Bureaucrat's Role Reconsidered. A more complex understanding of bureaucracy should also allow us to reconsider the stresses faced by service workers. Because service workers are responding to the dual demands of a capitalist social order and the developing, independent needs of bureaucratic rationality, they are often torn in two, not oppositional but slightly different, directions. In the service of reproducing capitalist social relations they are expected to convince clients that their problems are due to their own inadequacies and to help them accept responsibility for themselves. This takes time and "skill." In service to the bureaucracy's need for growth and interorganizational dominance the worker's task is to "process" clients as quickly as possible in the most formalistic manner, a style which may deliver the service but not "educate" clients to their ideological role. So the worker is conflicted, as Cherniss unwittingly observed: "In fact it often seemed that the real client was not the needy and/or suffering individual sitting before them asking for help, but the bureaucratic organization that paid the salaries and could hire and fire them."[78]

Therefore, workers, clients, and bureaucratic managers are often set up in three-way relationships that are complicating to all parties. Sometimes workers, as mentioned above, are expected to perform professionally and to "help" the client with a range of therapeutic interventions. The client may resist such assistance and appeal to management to force the worker "just to do the job" and not to "meddle." At other times workers may feel that their job is to advocate for clients just to obtain mandated services and then management becomes the common enemy, because it seeks, in Lipsky's words, to "hoard resources" that workers attempt to disperse to clients.[79] At still other times, bureaucratic management may take the leadership in programs that seem aimed at the best interests of clients—such as deinstitutionalization—and find themselves opposing workers, who are viewed as conservative and preserving the old forms of control. Finally, unionization can even elicit conflicting responses. Workers who wish to be professional upholders of the privilege of expertise may oppose it, while some high-level bureaucrats may be willing to "allow" it, under strict restrictions, as a means of controlling the workforce. And clients may become involved if they feel unsympathetic to the "plight" of workers whom they experience as oppressors.

Given such circumstances, neither simple, static analysis of the functions of bureaucracy, nor narrow Marxist equation of the state with capitalism will suffice. Instead we need to see bureaucratic workers as caught between the twin goals of capitalist ideological dominance and bureaucratic aggrandizement. Only by understanding the inherent conflicts of their situation and by seeking new ways out of the situation can workers find a progressive resolution. Ultimately, we can no more embrace the role of street-level bureaucrat—with all its attendant subservience to authority and mechanistic technology for processing clients—than we can accept the elitist professional identity of the socially detached care giver.

Here again, I come back to the notion that a political identity helps to form a way out, in the short and long range. In the immediate situation a political critique of one's specific roles, the organization, and its place in the unacknowledged jousting between bureaucracies and various segments of the ruling class should help. An identification with clients and fellow workers as political comrades should support resistance to both professional and bureaucratic identities—in large part because such a strategy will bring rejection from true professionals and true bureaucrats. In the long run, the development of a political critique of bureaucracy, as well as of capitalism, may help us find ways to articulate a new vision for helping a society to care for itself without the numbness of bureaucratic control or the terror of capitalist insecurity.

The Meaning of Debureaucratization. By viewing bureaucracies as, in Lefort's words, a "specific social stratum which in establishing a certain set of relations between its members generates its own history," we can begin to see new ways to consider human service organizations.[80] No longer need we study organizational theory in order to perceive how this neutral, mechanistic entity operates but we can look at specific historical, social, and political factors that serve to make some agencies more promising than others for radical activity and that suggest strategies and tactics appropriate to particular settings. Indeed, it may be that just by refusing to accept bureaucratic "rationality" as a given, but only as one option among many for getting work done, we have taken the first key step toward debureaucratization.

For example, many students of complex organizations complain that human service organizations are "flat," that it is difficult to achieve hierarchies within them because of the need to have skilled workers at the "front end." Even specialization, a second prerequisite of bureaucratic success, often seems counter to the holistic needs of agency clients. Such problems cause even traditional organizational theorists to doubt: "But the Weberian model may not be a rational or efficient organization for coping with many of the problems which have emerged."[81] Their solution may be to posit a subset model for human service bureaucracies, but ours may be to begin to question the hierarchy, the specialization, the belief in expertise, and the need for expansion which uphold the bureaucratic ideology. During the 1960s and early 1970s, as we have seen, some radicals tried to do this on a small scale. Although limited in scope and scale, such efforts do give some indications of areas for future activity, and some hope that the attempt to formulate new models is not impossible.

People come to agencies wanting immediate assistance and respect and to be told what is happening to them, among other things.

Workers want to be able to respond effectively, to do work which is valued, to be paid appropriately, and to have access to a variety of tasks and learning opportunities, among other things. Citizens have a right to some accountability from workers regarding their use of public money, and an assumption that fairness and justice are being carried out, especially if desirable services must be rationed. Neither a capitalist social and economic order nor an efficient bureaucratic system nor both of these working in tandem have been able to meet these needs. Perhaps the "long march through the institutions" means that as workers and clients we stop accepting the advice that Russo gives new human service workers:

No one has come up with a good substitute for bureaucracy as a means for organizing a group of people and, at the same time, checking on workers to see that they are doing what they are supposed to do. Many of the bureaucratic weaknesses that are detailed in this book and in many other places may not be caused by the structure but by the people who operate it.[82]

Instead, without yet having a clearly defined alternative, we may begin to resist the automatic acceptance of bureaucratic forms, as well as find ways to heighten tensions between capitalists and bureaucrats without taking sides. We can ask for full justification for bigness, for expansion, for specialization, for hierarchy, for all the bureaucratic "givens." Even more than deprofessionalization, debureaucratization will be a long-range, nascent goal, one which must be defined as we go along and as we experience attempts in different contexts. At this point it only means the choice to seek other alternatives and to train ourselves in the habit of questioning "obvious," "realistic" bureaucratic solutions to service problems. As radicals we have learned to stop accepting capitalist explanations of what constitutes the "good" economy and the "good" family. Now we need also to question definitions of what it means to be "well organized."

POLITICAL PRACTICE IN THE BUREAUCRACY

Perhaps the most difficult aspects of a political practice are those governing relationships with bureaucracies. Just to survive without burnout, bitterness, or suicidal gestures requires amazing patience, seriousness, sophistication, and complexity of analysis. The overriding goal must always be to politicize the workplace so that activists, clients, and fellow workers understand the political dimensions of the work and take the greatest advantage of the contradictions of the system. This can only be done by a self-conscious strategy that is sensitive to specific workplaces with their particular personalities, structures, and political imperatives and is aware of broader bureaucratic, economic, and social realities. What is needed is not a series of separate change efforts that arise whenever specific needs are perceived, but a long-range political strategy which includes such tactics as information gathering, analysis, identification of allies, neutrals, and enemies, as well as a set of specific and general changes we would like to see occur.[83] On the other hand, especially in the current crisis, radicals must not become so locked into one approach (for example, union organizing) that they lose the ability to react quickly to forced changes.

Such an approach assumes that one retain a belief in change. Nothing can be more demoralizing than an organizer who does not really believe that things can be better. It is easy, for example, to think that nothing can be done to affect the work of bureaucracies. But a look at the history of even the past twenty years suggests that this is not so.

At the same time one must maintain a sense of balance about how much can be done. Many activists tend to come to blame themselves or their comrades because all goals were not accomplished. They will feel this even though their own analysis tells them that capitalist institutions are strong and that it will take a congruence of powerful economic and social forces before conditions are created for basic change. Letting oneself get caught in this radical version of "blaming the victim" can lead to burning oneself out, frightening off potential comrades, and becoming brittle.

Exactly because bureaucratic forces are so powerful activists cannot forget that anything they do must have a collective base. The pressures are too great, the stakes are too high to work alone. As I suggested in chapter 4, the first task is to create a group of politically compatible people with whom to analyze information, develop strategy, and devise tactics. Criteria for unity should primarily focus on agreement regarding basic workplace issues and certain shared attitudes toward class, race, and sex. A workplace caucus that wants to spend a year designing "principles of unity" is avoiding politics.

As we have seen, the nature of bureaucracy is to divide workers from each other through hierarchy and specialization. A workplace collective is an essential tool in breaking down these divisions. It is also necessary for gathering the information workers need to understand their situation. One cannot underestimate how important good information is: workers need agency history, background on people, background on funding sources and expenditures, and a sharp picture of agency structure. Such data allow the development of an awareness of power within the organization. Workers need not only a sense of individual power relationships and opportunities but also an appraisal of how much power can be taken within the agency without selling out. In some organizations individuals or groups of radicals may honestly exercise a great deal of power—within a small program that is not central to agency goals, or because it is dirty work no one else wants, or just because of the nature of the institution. It takes collective support to take advantage of such potential power bases, collective support to resist offers for "power" that are really bribes for compliance with unacceptable norms. However, we must also recognize that powerlessness as well as power can corrupt.[84] If workers spend too long without any sense of collective or individual efficacy they may lose the ability to fight or to take advantage of real opportunities to make change. Here, too, collective evaluation and review of one's situation is crucial.

In the Belly of the Beast. To work in the large welfare agencies, the big mental health institutions, or certain juvenile justice or child welfare agencies is to work in the area of strongest social controls within the welfare state (short of prisons, which we will not consider as human service institutions here). Most of the clients are involuntarily connected to the agency, or at least not pleased to need the service. Often much of the workforce has been there for a long time and has been castigated for incompetence, laziness, or ignorance for years by clients, administrators, and reformers alike. The agencies themselves hold little public appeal and have not sought to represent themselves as a desirable social good to anyone.

Given such workplaces, it is no surprise that the notion of "guer-rilla in the bureaucracy" finds some favor. Even liberal critics like Brager and Holloway are willing to support "covert activities" within such environments.[85] For radicals in these bureaucracies the empha-sis in political work will be more narrowly defensive than in other settings. On the other hand, the very fact that these agencies are so central to the welfare state heightens the importance of political practice within them. If, in Johnston's words, workers within such agencies can find ways to perform "real public service," they may be able to provide leadership to all other human service work.[86]

The essential element of a political practice within the big bureau-cracies is the union, although it is in exactly such agencies that unions are apt to play an oppressive role with clients. In many states the workers in these agencies are the most likely to be unionized of all human service workers. If this is the case, a basic activity of radicals should be through direct participation in union activity and through caucus work within the union, if necessary. At all points political unionists will be looking to raise client concerns, to raise quality of service issues, and to oppose the kind of bureaucratic workplace con-ditions that force workers to hurt clients.

Passing information to the outside is another key role for radicals in big institutions. Exactly because these agencies are so large and complicated it is very difficult for client and community advocates to monitor their behavior, much less their plans. So workers willing to share rumors as well as approved policies can be invaluable to efforts to control the effects of agency policy.

Another major aspect of a political practice is to try to limit the lawless behavior of co-workers. This is a difficult task, which can un-dermine one's ability to do union work or to build honest alliances, but it needs to be a central task of any caucus and will probably be carried out informally in most cases. In his classic study of welfare workers, Blau noted that "anti-client statements were a mechanism for reaffirming social solidarity among colleagues" and were ex-pected in a subtle kind of social pressure to show that a worker was not "naive or sentimental about clients."[87] Without pomposity, it might be possible for more than one worker to turn such discussions around to become a show of solidarity against foolish or harmful policies that put clients and workers alike in double binds. If subtle pressures do not help, radical workers may finally have to resort to overt disapproval in order to stop such discussions, especially those which are also sexist, racist, and class biased. It is essential to stop overt behavior that demeans or degrades clients whenever one can. Sometimes all that can be done is to try to steer clients away from certain people and to discuss with client groups the workers to avoid. Other strategies may be to try to get a transfer for someone to a less dangerous place.

In addition to all of the general tactics for building client solidarity mentioned in chapter 4, activists in big bureaucracies need to try especially hard to support existing client advocacy groups, to help clients link with each other, and to be very visual, perhaps with a newsletter or letters to union or local papers, about client issues. There are two reasons for doing such things. One, naturally, is to make alliances with clients. The other is to indicate to other workers that it is possible to support clients' rights and be active in support of worker issues. Often workers will just be quiet when anticlient attitudes are expressed, or when hostile acts take place. The example of other workers (not one lone prophet) can give the quiet ones support for speaking up.

Finally, however, we must not abandon hope that anything positive can happen within the big bureaucracies. We must always be on the lookout for those new programs that may have a chance to help people, or those new workers *and* administrators who are able to accomplish some real, albeit small, innovations. Remember, analysis still shows that the system is contradictory, that it is not all oppressive. Constant intelligence must expose weak spots within the system, and allow efforts to expand them. Even in these mean-spirited times some opportunities can still be found to set up a colorful children's center in an office waiting room, to work with an administrator who really wants to monitor Medicaid vendors, or to turn administratively arranged training sessions into places of real sharing and support for workers.

The Middling Institutions. Many service workers, and perhaps most radical service workers, are employees of agencies that are not so uniformly controlling and bureaucratic. Many contracted agencies, community mental health centers, training programs, day care centers, halfway houses, multiservice centers, elderly programs, recreation centers, to name only a few examples, are much less total institutions and seem much more amenable to pressures for change. In fact, in many ways such agencies can be deceptively accessible. It is not until one starts to organize a union, or to raise political issues with clients, or to restructure office hierarchies that the underlying bureaucratic, control functions come to the surface (and then, of course, it is the radicals who are blamed for "polarizing issues").

In many ways most of the suggestions for political practice I have discussed thus far have been written with such agencies in mind, so I will not repeat them. Here I will only discuss a few special features of such organizations and their implications for political practice.

First, such agencies are most likely to have complicated funding patterns. Some may be fully funded by the state or by federal grants, but many may have money from different public and private sources, with different restrictions. It is essential that workers know about where the money comes from and the restrictions placed upon it. This may not be easy information to obtain, either because the agency management is inept (a not unlikely prospect in some small programs) or because the administration wants to keep such information to itself so that it can retain "flexibility." A key test, indeed, of the politics of agency management may be how easy it is to obtain this information.

Unions can be especially promising in these settings because they may be more able to move in the direction of becoming, in Johnston's terms, "public service" unions, addressing political issues as well as economic ones. Because the workforce may be smaller and more internally cohesive, the union may be able to be more democratic and to address a wider variety of issues. Workers who try to push such concerns may raise the ire of union staff from outside the agency—because we are being "unrealistic"—but an appeal to the membership may result in important inroads into the power of bureaucratic managements.

In such agencies the stance of "functional noncapitulation" developed by Wenocur and Sherman seems most applicable. In functional noncapitulation workers position themselves as

. . . active decision-makers in a reciprocal relationship with the various participants in the organization at all the different hierarchical levels. From this position workers have a right and a responsibility to attempt to influence the organization and to shape and influence attempts of others on them. Just as the organization transmits a constant downward pressure on workers to solve its organizational dilemmas, the worker constantly tries to reverse this pressure, transmitting responsibility back upwards to the organization where it must be shared with higher levels of authority.[88]

A caucus could help workers fill out the implications of such a stance and to monitor its effectiveness, given the balance of power in the agency.

The top leadership in middling organizations may be susceptible to politicization themselves, as suggested in chapter 5. Many may be aspiring professionals thoroughly bewildered by their current lack of technical effectiveness. It may be possible to pressure some of these people from the left, so that they will stand up and fight as social democrats for the political values they see in such programs. As I suggested earlier and will discuss again in the next chapter, if we can push social democrats, such as the heads of many middling agencies, to be more overtly political, in their terms, it will make our task of showing the limits of their politics more straightforward.

Finally, in such agencies activists may be able to build real alliances with co-workers and clients exactly because the work itself is less oppressive and the clients are less vulnerable. Indeed, workplace discussions about client issues may be as important a way to build solidarity with co-workers as unionization. Because there is more hope for better relationships, both clients and workers may be more willing to explore different kinds of nonprofessional relationships together. And both workers and clients may be able to quickly see the political and personal effects of cutbacks and policy changes—thus building a base for joint action.

But I should not paint too rosy a picture here. In the first place, some agencies of this type can be oppressively smug, professional, and happy with their own traditions. Politically active workers can be made to feel like bad children who have problems with authority. Secondly, even where all the potentials do exist we should not fail to realize that they do so because of a kind of organizational "creaming." If radicals choose to work and engage a political practice in such institutions they have essentially picked those organizations in which they are most likely to succeed. It may not be wrong to do so, but one, then, cannot be too arrogant about any successes. Instead activists have a special obligation to share what they have learned and to use their situation as a place of continued outreach, not simply as a safe haven from the hazards of less rewarding activity.

Alternative Services Revisited. In times of economic and social assault upon human services it may seem utopian to discuss the possibilities of political practice in alternative services. However, I would argue that exactly because times are so bad it is essential that we retain a vision of what we would want if we were in control, even if of only a small program. We need to keep our imagination and our hopes alive in the face of an ideology and a movement which seeks to convince people that social hope is unrealistic. Also, we need ongoing laboratories for developing alternatives to bureaucracy. Practically, there are still alternative—if not explicitly political—services that attract people, and they need support. Finally, any radical practice must include a consideration of positive as well as defensive strategies to truly deserve its name.

These days, it is still possible to find money for some services from government sources, either from contracts or federal grants. Getting and spending this money can cause grave difficulties, though, unless the political group requesting the money has clear political priorities.[89] All money has strings attached. Before applying for funding a political collective needs clarity regarding the degree to which it intends to follow funding guidelines and the degree to which it plans to use the money in ways that cannot be directly explained. All participants need to agree on this sense of accountability to the funding source and, if risks are to be taken regarding the "appropriateness" of expenditures, all must share them equally. All too often groups hire a bookkeeper or a financial manager to manage their money but do not share their full political strategy for using the money. This consistently leads to confusion, hostility, and even fear of reprisals on the part of the financial person. Equally destructive is the model where only one or two people decide to take risks and then staff later become very frightened when they discover the implications.

The lesson is that, just as in any bureaucracy, a political practice means sharing of all financial information. In an alternative institution it also means democratic sharing of decisions regarding money, and especially a shared sense of how accountable the group feels toward its funding sources.

Obviously, the core of what makes an alternative institution is this sharing of decision making. The experience of many groups suggests that one lesson of the sixties and seventies was that representative decision making probably works better than consensus decision making and that democratic votes have their uses in resolving disputes.[90] Whatever the explicit form developed, however, a key weapon in defeating bureaucracy is worker control of decision making and the absence of hierarchical and overly specialized structures. We tend to forget that a central obstacle to effective struggle in all workplaces is that workers often accept the legitimacy of hierarchical decision making. Successful and failed alternative institutions both are the building blocks by which we slowly learn how to conceive and operate the models of workplace democracy that will be a critical part of any basic social change.

Collective responsibility, however, does not mean that all will be rosy in alternative institutions. Sometimes a staff member just cannot do the work and action must be taken to protect the goals of the group. Such moments are the hardest of collective life, with no simple answers. Openness must be considered a goal in the process, achieved through firm discussion of all the issues. Sometimes radicals become protective toward a failing comrade and make the matter worse by not naming and explaining the problems. Speed is also a goal. Decisions to exclude a group member should be faced quickly. There should never be any organizational hesitation regarding covering unemployment benefits or perhaps other severance arrangements. The collective failed itself by choosing a member who could not manage and deserves to pay some of the costs. Most importantly, the remaining group needs to seriously consider, before bringing in a new person, how it went awry so as to avoid future mistakes, if possible.

As we can see, the operations of an alternative agency are quite similar to the inner operations of a workplace caucus—except that usually the focus is more constructive. But there needs to be plenty of time for staff discussion of ongoing concerns, goals, and operational issues. Meetings are serious political work, too. Initial agreement and then intense, isolated work cannot sustain an organization which seeks to avoid hierarchy, specialization, and overreliance on rule making.

The key element of an alternative service is that it embody the political values of its staff members in all aspects of its functioning. This is more easily said than accomplished for a range of reasons. One is that it is not always clear, concretely, what an antiracist, anticapitalist, feminist practice is in all areas of work. Another is that old habits die hard and committed radicals find themselves afraid to give up old habits of interaction with clients or organizational imperatives. To many a "well-organized" program would meet all Weber's criteria for bureaucracy. Third, standards for success are often too grand. Like good entrepreneurs activists often see growth and expansion as desirable in themselves and new areas of service as automatically to the good. So radicals have to struggle to set limits on what they try to do.

As with other service work, one can only retain political commitment if outside political connections are retained, otherwise broader goals are lost in the day-to-day pressure to provide service. One begins to reproduce old forms. Finally, just like workers within the bureaucracy, workers in alternative settings need constant reminders and collective supports to reach their goals.

But what is most exciting about radical services is that the goals are one's own; activists are not always tied to the role of critic or incremental change agent. Because the work is explicitly political from the beginning one can learn at a very fast pace and reaffirm the links between political values and the desire to do service work. Even if programs do not last they can have important effects, as Frances Piven has recognized:

Well, what if you can't build a stable organization? So what? We don't have any evidence, aside from unions, that anyone has ever been able to build a stable, enduring working-class (much less radical) organization. If that's the criterion, than I think the criterion is one of the problems.

One of the reasons organizers have dismissed historic organizing efforts is because they didn't last. So, many efforts that did achieve limited successes are dismissed as not good enough, because they didn't last. But although none may have lasted, some accomplished more than others, and are worth learning from.[91]

Finally, however, we need to see alternative efforts as not only teaching about what is truly valued for the future and as helping gain credibility in the attempt to be honestly concerned about existing pain, but also as ultimately limited. Their marginal nature in this society means that activists still have large, critical questions left to answer about how a radical vision addresses the needs of a whole society. We cannot claim to find full answers from such exercises; this is why people need to stay as activists in the bureaucracy even if times change and alternative services become more popular again. Moberg helps us understand this inherent duality of promise and limitation that is built into radical service efforts:

There is also a contradictory way in which the alternative institutions capitalize on the deep American distrust of the state as an instrument for change and justice. They demonstrate that socialism is not statism. They offer direct action and appeal to a native streak of anarchistic radicalism. That is one of their failings, too. Many poor people and blue-collar workers have come to look more to the state for redress of wrongs, and with good reason.[92]

So, once again, we can see that a choice will hurt political chances. We need to be in the state in order to understand it, fight its oppressive features, and assert the potential for a better public service. We need to be against the state in order to find options that are more curative than can ever be allowed by it and in order to strengthen ourselves for political struggle. It will take both strategies—not one or the other—to achieve Johnston's goal of "an alliance of [service] workers and community against government, instead of government and community against workers."[93]

7

ACHIEVING THE GOOD SOCIETY: SOCIAL SERVICES FOR SOCIAL CHANGE

The rise of social movements is also an indication that new social worlds have been conceived, new hopes are being expressed and faith has been renewed in the idea that humanity through its own efforts can make the world a better one.[1]

In the last quarter of the twentieth century many activists—be they socialists, feminists, anarchists, third world revolutionaries, or cultural radicals—have come to a broader conception of their political goals. No longer is the demand for "state power" enough, nor is control or redistribution of economic resources seen as a sufficient singular goal. From Eastern Europe, to Tanzania, to Nicaragua, to the United States, more radicals have come to see that their politics mean a quest for better collective and individual lives, that the argument that a centralized state will automatically guarantee social well-being is as bankrupt as the capitalist notion that unfettered economic accumulation will provide for all. European Marxist thought is more speculative and open to new suggestions than it has ever been. Non-westernized states seem more willing to question traditional capitalist *and* socialist arguments about the inevitable virtue and necessity for industrial economic growth. Women and other culturally down-graded peoples are questioning older definitions of success and progress in the United States and elsewhere. In short, the failures of traditional capitalist and socialist states, however disorienting and frightening they may be, have the potential of allowing a worldwide generation of activists to broaden its conception of what constitutes political tactics, strategies, and goals. As much as the pressures and fears can produce arguments for caution and conservatism they can, just as logically, produce a new rationale for experimentation.[2]

If anything, a major goal of this book has been to suggest ways in which a more political conception of social services and the practice of social work can be seen as central to such an expansive social agenda. Whether we try to create explicitly political service en-deavors, as with feminist or union services, or whether we try to act politically in our jobs as service workers, radical service workers are part of a critical effort to link concerns for the quality of daily life with broader political analyses and social progress. Such efforts are difficult but they have twofold benefits. On the one hand, they can help service workers and clients better understand and appreciate the fundamental social seriousness of their mutual endeavor. It is, in-deed, one skein of the threads that are necessary if we are ever to weave a healthy, caring social fabric within which people can come to be honestly interdependent because no one is ashamed of per-sonal need, and because we recognize that at times we all need the nurturing of good services and at other times we all have the capac-ity to provide that nurturing.

On the other hand, the closeness to daily human frailty *and* cour-age that comes from self-consciously political service work can help to strengthen political activity and theory by providing a deep grounding in the concerns of daily life. The purpose of this final chapter is to summarize the benefits of and necessity for such a merger and to discuss its implication for radical strategy and political prac-tice.

REFUSING THE CHOICE

Whatever their particular social vision, today's service workers and progressive movements will benefit from refusal to separate political values and goals from service activity.

First, by acknowledging their political purposes for providing services, workers will be more able to criticize the current unspoken but harmful connections between political goals and social programs. In the past, liberal technocrats, as well as some radicals, have criticized public and private service efforts by revealing the "bias" built into their treatment of different groups—minorities, women, the poor. While such revelations were, of course, usually true and helped to bring to light the ways in which the welfare state served the interests of the dominant classes, the very effort to expose discrimination often served to further the notion that services, and the state, could and should be neutral and apolitical. Such arguments served to mask the inevitable role of the state and its bureaucractic structures in maintaining social order and the perpetuation of the power of ruling and bureaucratic classes.

By insisting on our right to use services as a weapon for progressive social change we can show how social programs automatically serve political ends. The question is not whether they do so, but whose ends they serve. Certainly there is bias in the current structure and practice of service delivery; our task is not to eliminate the bias but to shift it.

In such a politicized climate people will disagree—some radicals will support compensatory education programs, for instance, and others will oppose them in honest controversy. But at least we can honestly debate the issues in terms of their effects on the relative power of different groups, on the opportunities created for individual social identity—in short, in political terms—instead of in the current political and moral vacuum.

Furthermore, the creation of lively, honestly political debates among progressives over the content and the process of social programs should allow more room to explore honestly what is meant by a socialist, or feminist, or nonracist social policy. Now, we find ourselves politically underdeveloped in terms of knowing what we really want, partially because we are forced to spend so much time exposing the bias of the dominant regime. How refreshing it would be, for example, to have wide-ranging debates about the best form of child care arrangements without the constant obligatory preoccupation with exposing the political bias of existing policies.

Second, in an immediate and personal way, the linking of service activity and political goals allows the individual service worker to create a more honest and reciprocal (rather than either falsely altruistic or antagonistic) relationship with clients. As we have seen, service work is inherently complex and demanding, regardless of one's political perspective. Without a self-conscious set of political goals and values, service workers are often thrown back on either bankrupt and elitist professional mores or demeaning bureaucratic "job descriptions" to find a sense of direction.

An explicitly political practice offers hope to individual workers. It can help them acknowledge and analyze the political forces that make their jobs difficult and can allow them to avoid personalizing their individual bosses, their co-workers, or their clients as the "enemy." It can permit radicals to test out their politics within their work and to evaluate professional practice in the light of political values. It can allow workers to acknowledge that, whatever the real class differences in access to service, they too have basic human needs which often require service—that they are not inherently "different" from their clients.

One feminist service worker expressed the benefits of her political perspective in a way that suggests the uses and the limits of a political practice:

It helps to have some better explanation for why things are so bad for women and why it's so hard to change. It helps to have other women to talk to about what can be done. It still hurts that we are so powerless to change things and to admit that even if we had power we don't always know what's best.

But at least I don't feel like everything is dead end, like I did when I worked in the hospital. At least I feel we are still learning and that we are trying, if not succeeding, to do something better.[3]

And another worker, from within the system, suggests how the application of a more political model of practice can make a difference, even within the biggest bureaucracies:

There are two kinds of people at my office. Some of us think that people without money have a right to food stamps and that our job is to help them get as much as they are eligible for. Some other people seem to think that people should be grateful for whatever they get and that our job is to make sure we don't give anybody any more than they absolutely need. It's funny but it makes a big difference how you look at it, even though none of us are trying to break the rules.[4]

Third, an acceptance of the political aspects of their work can give service workers a more definite identity in regard to co-workers and employers. Many have found that, although the label "activist" or "troublemaker" could be used against them, it could also serve to depersonalize conflicts and allow open discussion of different positions without so much personal animosity.

At my job people tease us about being the "feminists" and the "organizers" and sometimes it isolates and hurts us. But even doubtful co-workers will come up to one of us if they have a question about their rights on the job or about something that happened in the news. And at staff meetings, sometimes, we can get away with saying things out in the open which need to be said because it's not personal, it's because we are the "troublemakers."[5]

Of course, as we have noted, some workplaces are more tolerant than others, and in these times there may be more prejudice against radicals. But we may offer ourselves and other co-workers unconsidered options when we publicly discuss the political dimensions of service work. Galper has argued that one of the troubles facing even committed workers is that they "come to see problems from the perspectives of the solutions they have available" and therefore to "substitute technology for broadly based political action."[6] Simply by proposing a wider spectrum of alternatives activists may help to redefine the issues in the workplace, as well as to identify the range of possible political perspectives on the issues at hand.

Fourth, recognition of the political nature of social services should allow us to engage in meaningful political debate. Since social services have not been viewed as having political content, our ability to devise effective social strategies has been limited. A less apologetic comprehensive political agenda which includes the adoption of public social responsibility for meeting human needs should allow activists to criticize bad programs and still demand services be offered.[7] Here Gorz opened up important options when he suggested that a revolutionary reform strategy is one which may be in "the *beginning* a scaled series of reforms but which, as it unfolds, must grow into a series of trials of strength."[8]

Fifth, a conscious recognition of the politics of social services should support the development of the new ideology suggested at the beginning of this chapter. In the light of recent developments in socialist societies, many radicals are beginning to question the wisdom of avoiding consideration of the nature of basic human needs and the best ways to respond to them. They question the benefits of a work-oriented society and of a centralized state and are placing higher value on personal fulfillment and security as a driving force for social health. As veterans of the American welfare state, human service workers may have special insights that suggest the limitations of trying to "respond" to human need in a routinized, rationalized, narrowly materialistic way.

More importantly, the development of a political conception of social services may allow us to go beyond a critique of bureaucracy and the state—important as that may be—to consider the more fundamental meaning of social responsibility. In this book we have only been able to suggest the power that may come from an ethic of humanistic social reciprocity as replacement for the virtues of altruism, which permeate capitalist ethics, or the more rationalistic notion of societal justice, which has been identified with socialist countries.[9] Feminists and anarchists have begun to develop ideas of mutual aid, which allow people to share and grow together without developing either destructively dependent relationships or narrow, logical systems of who is owed how much by the society. Out of exploration of the political meaning of helping each other, based on actual experiences of doing just that, radical service workers may help other progressives to better understand both their ultimate goals and to develop strategies for change that inspire more trust than those heretofore developed.

The development of a more complex, political understanding of the nature of service work and social responsibility may also help radicals address the basic moral issues that elicit widespread popular concern without falling into the pietistic, individualistic moralism of the New Right or the cold-hearted rationalism of certain traditional Marxists. As Pearson has noted, the serious political consideration of service issues leads to "the rediscovery of social welfare as an activity which is grounded in moral-political choices."[10] If progressive service workers can begin to think more clearly about the underlying relationships between helpers and the helped, about the common human conditions that should justify social caring regardless of individual status (as capitalist producers or as socialist workers), and about the true nature of a social "necessity" that will allow people to develop their individual potential and support the growth of others to the fullest, then we may be able to define a political and social strategy which will have a broad mass appeal, no matter what its label. If radicals could be more united around such issues they might be more able to develop appealing social agendas for the distant future *and* to consider the types of programs that might honestly "prefigure" such new social formations.[11]

Currently, without a strong socialist understanding of such issues, we are "socially underdeveloped" in our visions of the future. We are unable to persuade skeptical workers who still reap some benefits from the droppings of capitalism that they should risk considering new social arrangements.

The special task of radical service workers may be to use their experience to build a movement which contains a more complex and far-reaching understanding of the web of social responsibilities and the hope for a fulfilled daily life than has been previously identified. Such an understanding could then inform their service work and thereby give ongoing credibility to the left's assertion that struggling for a better world is worth the risks.

Finally, avoiding the choice between a political conception of one's work and a serious attention to the daily concerns of providing service means recognizing that there never was a choice at all. How a society cares for itself is the result of *political* choices at every level, not of technical, value-free, expert decisions about the dispensation of economic and social responsibility. Conservatives have begun to come out of the closet and to frame their concerns about services and social responsibility in an overtly political context. If those who want radical social change also begin to do so, we may be able to force "apolitical" professionals and liberals to own up to their own political values about who deserves what kind of services, funded from what sources for which goals. As radicals we may not like all that emerges from such a political coming out party, but at least we will understand who is on which team, for what reasons, and we will be able to begin to play the game with a shared sense of the rules and the stakes.

DEFENDING THE VISION

The political pressures of the 1980s also serve, as has been suggested, to force a political defense of both the general goals of social welfare and the usefulness of particular methods of helping people. With the New Right has resurfaced the underlying critique of social programs which liberal politicians and professional leaders have avoided, rather than answered, for the past fifty years.[12] Now, all who wish to create and build a system of social services must defend their vision in overtly political terms. The intensity of the current attacks allows little room for burying basic differences of social vision under a plethora of apolitical, technocratic policy debates.

What makes conservative political arguments confusing, however, is that they are undertaken in the guise of *fighting* the "politicization of society," which, conservatives assert, has been the unproclaimed goal of the left. In attempting to reassert their vision, conservatives too wish to deny that they are political. Instead they present their perspective as "common sense," as the natural order which has been lost because of the political goals of progressives. Thus we enter into an Alice-in-Wonderland world of mirrors where political agendas are being proposed, but denied, by all sides—by the left out of fear of conservative political reaction, by the right in order to deny its desire to maintain political and economic power. Here the argument of conservative economic historian R. M. Hartwell, in *The Politicization of Society,* is telling:

Politicization can be defined as that now pervasive tendency for making all questions political questions, all issues political issues, all values political values, and all decisions political decisions. . . . Politicization can now be seen in the relationships between all people in a society: between parents and children, between teachers and pupils, between professors and students, between employers and employees, between producers and consumers, between races, between sportsmen, indeed between men and women. Where once individuals saw their problems as private and sought private solutions for them, now they seek political solutions. . . . Politicization thus takes the manifest form of increasing the power of the state, of increasing political power as against all other forms of power in society, of increasing the power of politicians and the bureaucrats as against the power of individuals, private institutions, and voluntary associations.[13]

The task for radicals is to expose the hypocrisy of such deeply political arguments. Thus far, the debate has not been clearly focused, although certain patterns are emerging. In spite of the pressures to make apolitical responses, oppositional positions are appearing which begin to define and defend differing visions of social welfare.

The dominant response is the least systematic, and the one which still attempts, as much as possible, to defend programs in the least political way. It is the standard response of most liberal politicians and professional practitioners, as well as some, but not all, of the professional social work leadership. As I mentioned in chapter 5, many of its proponents argue a "this too shall pass" position, that what we are undergoing is just another lurch in the democratic political process, not an attempt to make basic readjustments in political and economic priorities.

This liberal position, simply, is to defend most existing social welfare programs because they are necessary, because they help people, because the private sector cannot provide. They are not to be defended as redistributive of economic or social resources, as overtly political tactics to reach broader social ends. Service work is still seen as appropriately removed from the political fray. Essentially, this remains the technocratic response: there are ongoing social problems; we need quality professional services to respond to them; we cannot abdicate this responsibility. Here conservative critics are decried as ignorant of real needs and of the real activity of ongoing programs, but the basic threat is neither acknowledged nor answered. Often the "defense" is made that, of course, no one really likes such programs, but that we have to provide for those with no other options.

Indeed, weak as it seems, this is the dominant response one hears in the press, from politicians, and from agency leaders. Although at election time such arguments may be made in a "political" context, they do little to develop the basic political debate. Indeed, some commentators have even linked such liberal responses with the conservative critiques, as fundamentally similar positions which support the capitalist economy and ideology.[14]

On the other hand, it is only fair to admit that the power of the conservative assault, and the material impact of recent budget cuts, have begun to push many leaders of the social welfare profession into an explicit social democratic defense of the welfare state that is much more political and more public than we have ever seen in this country. Internal publications of NASW, the National Conference on Social Welfare, and the Council of Social Work Education have been more open about the political implications of the attacks and even about their own social visions. The full defenses do not often reach the wider public or even the legislative arena, nor do they usually involve an open discussion of socialism or the long-range benefits of the welfare state, but they do go beyond an ad hoc liberal defense of specific programs. Increasingly since 1980, we hear national leaders acknowledging their vision of an ongoing, increasing public responsibility for social security (broadly defined) and for their goal of a strong, activist state.

In Britain, where Thatcherism is older than Reaganism and where there is a much stronger tradition of social democracy within the Labor Party and of Fabian Socialism, this tendency is stronger. But here in the United States, too, old progressive arguments are recalled, as is the spirit of New Deal planners—limited as such traditions are. The rise of public-sector labor unions has been significant also. In defending their jobs, some national and local unions—most notably AFSCME and SEIU— have been willing to defend the general value of public human service programs for creating a better society. And the growing political power, and personal fear, of many organized advocates for the elderly have also meant that sometimes, even in the mass media, a ringing *political* defense of public programs is heard and the role of government in creating a more socially responsible society is proclaimed.[15]

Such broader political defenses of the welfare state are still tentative, and many proponents of them still seem to be hoping that the liberal Democrats will get back into power so that they do not have to continue to expose themselves politically. But they do reflect a trend which more outspoken socialists can only applaud. Every time social welfare leaders are willing, however cautiously, to proclaim their *political* values and goals they serve to change the terms of the debate. When, for example, a Dean of Boston University's Social Work School argues publicly that we must defend the welfare state because it serves political purposes of economic and social justice, because it helps create a better society, because it embodies desirable *political* goals--then it allows citizens more options for considering what they really want.[16] Such responses force conservatives to articulate their antisocial vision. They also allow more radical socialists to then go beyond that vision without having to deny its basic usefulness as a starting point.

Indeed, if the New Right serves to create a new breed of open, publicly identified social democrats who will fight for the political values which justify social services, we will have made a great step forward. Then socialists can question professionalism without seeming to undermine the importance of competent human services. Then radicals can begin to criticize the process and effects of large-scale bureaucracies without having always to simultaneously make the case for basic public accountability. Then the full terms of the debate will be out in the open and leftists will not have to be the only ones proclaiming the *political* importance of social services. Then we will be able to take up the harder questions of what a full socialist vision of the nurturing society should be. Then the challenge to defeat the choice really begins.

CREATING A POLITICAL STRATEGY FOR SOCIAL SERVICE WORK

The low, or nonexistent, level of political debate over the progressive value of social services has left most radicals with an underdeveloped sense of what we really want. The current crisis offers us the opportunity to develop a political strategy for integrating the goals and practice of social services into our theoretical and practical vision of how to achieve a better society. The following five aspects of a strategy have been mentioned throughout the book, and yet even now they still remain suggestions, not definitive recommendations.

Developing Public Responsibility. First, and probably most important, the goal of all our political practice and broader social activism must be to raise social expectations in this country. In every arena we must struggle to help people remember that we have some rights and deserve more, that it is possible to use collective social resources to benefit the majority of people. Such a stance is both defensive and offensive. Defensively, it is an absolutely necessary antidote to conservative attacks. If the Right is able to convince most people—as is its goal—that they can expect nothing from the broader society, that they have no social obligations because they can depend on nothing from anyone else, then we are in deep trouble. Then the whole basis for social solidarity is undermined and we face the prospect of an increasingly cruel, violent, truly reactionary society. So we have to defend our rights to expect social supports in order to protect ourselves from barbarism.

On the positive side, a radical call for public responsibility allows us to argue for good programs without falling into a dead-end defense of the capitalist welfare state. We could publicly acknowledge that a full achievement of social security is *not* possible under the limitations of the capitalist welfare state.[17] We could more honestly pose the real social choice—either we achieve only a very limited "social welfare" under the priorities of this economic system or we begin to seriously explore an economic and social order with different priorities.

Radicals, then, call for public responsibility not as a narrow demand for more programs but as a means to "break the bank," both economically and ideologically, of the capitalist welfare state. We can come to see ourselves as self-consciously engaging in what Gorz calls "progressive reform," without having to be responsible for the ongoing maintenance of the social order:

A socialist strategy of progressive reform does not mean that islands of socialism will emerge in a sea of capitalism. But it does mean the building up of the working class and popular power; it means the creation of centers of social management and of direct democracy . . . it means free products and services fulfilling collective needs; and this must inevitably result in intensified and deepened antagonism between the social production required by the needs and aspirations of the people on the one hand, and the requirements of capital accumulation and power on the other.[18]

In practical terms, the constant goal of developing public responsibility means that we do not accept the split between public and "private" services. Most "private" services, as we have seen, are now dependent on public money. Even those which are not, depend on public tax write-offs as a means of encouraging private giving. So we can hold "private" agencies just as accountable for serving general public needs as we hold public programs. This is especially important in all aspects of health care.

Similarly, we can watch public agencies with an eye toward making them as open as possible to all users. For example, we will be able to unambiguously oppose efforts to change youth service programs, which can serve many purposes, into "juvenile corrections" agencies, which are much less desirable social goods. Essentially, this means that our stance is an old one of favoring universalism, normalization, and generally the best care for all. We can now see the trap we were forced into when the Poverty Programs—useful as they were in many aspects—decided to "target" some groups as worthy of services, while others were deemed able to take care of themselves. Also we can now see that there is little reason to fear the dreaded "duplication of service" if such "duplication" means that more citizens are able to easily find places to help them out when they are in need.

Finally, the goal of achieving public responsibility means seeking ways to achieve real public accountability and a sense of collective ownership. Clearly, if there is any lesson from the development of our current bureaucracy, it is that the use of public money alone does not make most people feel that public agencies are "ours." In the words of British radicals, "The state is not 'our' state. It is 'their' state, an alien oppressive state."[19] Our task is to demand public services that reflect real public needs and are delivered in ways that make people pleased with what they get. This is the ultimate argument for a sound political practice, because if workers are doing a good job their work should serve to create increased demand and raised expectations. In addition, it is a strong argument for continuing to seek some form of creditable, meaningful "community control" and community involvement. Finally, only when people feel that public programs belong to them will services be valued. The ultimate satisfaction of this goal, I believe, can only be achieved when the economy and the state are truly socialized, but until then our job is constantly to raise public expectations about what they have a right to expect— even if they cannot get it yet—from the collective resources of the society.

Making Debureaucratization Complete. In many ways, a major factor in rasing social expectations of public programs will involve our capacity to define what we mean by debureaucratization and to convince people, including ourselves, that it is possible. Here we can only be suggestive and reaffirm that this aspect of our strategy reinforces the continued development of "alternative" service models, romantic as this may seem in the current climate. Only when we ourselves come to believe that recognition of competence and special skill does not necessarily justify hierarchy and special privileges *and* when we have some concrete examples of how work can be alternatively organized will we make much headway. All we can argue at this time is that we do not have to accept arguments for economies of scale, for rigid specialization, or for most "givens" of bureaucratic rationality. Here feminist concepts and practice are most instructive, as are the limited attempts at worker control and job redesign that have been made, even within a capitalist framework.[20]

Again we return to the idea that real "social services" should be universally available, and provided on the basis of constituency demand. Part of what makes bureaucratic work so alienating, to workers and clients, is that it is so often forced on people. One worker may have pointed to an important, often neglected aspect of bureaucracy when she noted that, as a result of a merger, her program for the first time was forced to serve a constituency who had not chosen to come to it for service:

It really made a difference when they didn't want to be here. Before we did exactly the same things, in the same way, but students had always chosen us, so they were more tolerant and we felt more like trying. Once the new group came in, nothing we did could please them and they had no tolerance for our inefficiency. Suddenly I felt defensive about doing the same things I had always done and I began to act more rigid, more like a bureaucrat, just to fend them off and keep them from complaining about everything.[21]

Community support and involvement, then, reemerge as an important way to achieve debureaucratization. The more a viable involved constituency can be identified, the more agencies may be able to fight the self-involvement and self-justification of bureaucrats, which was seen as so dangerous by Lefort. Johnston also argued that only when workers have a clear sense that their job is to "serve the democratically defined needs of the community" will they be able to resist "blind subordination to a state bureaucracy."[22]

Here we are exploring new territory, which has usually been the turf of anarchists, but we have few options. The credibility of our efforts to link organized social caring with progressive vision depends upon our ability to suggest models for providing services which do not dehumanize either workers or clients, or which do not—as in "state socialism"—raise the status of the bureaucrat above that of other workers and separate them from service users. This is a long-range goal, for now the first step in achieving it may simply be that of convincing ourselves, our unions, and our co-workers that it is possible to seek other options; in other words, to question the ideological basis of the bureaucratic ideal.

Doing Good Work in a Deprofessionalized Setting. Here again the underlying goal of our political practice is to break the grip of the professional consciousness, of the ideology that because one has learned special skills one therefore has assumed a special identity, which makes one somehow separate from others. The major task here involves helping co-workers, clients, and ourselves see that the acquisition of competence does not justify the assumption of privileges, either within the workplace or in the broader society. Much of our activity with co-workers should be geared to helping everyone develop and use their skills toward the best social goals without needing to hide behind those skills. We need to find ways, through workplace caucuses especially, to help us fight professionalism without seeming to disregard people's natural desire to do good work. Here we are fighting all the socialization which this society has heaped upon the middle class. People have grown up believing that even if they could not be rich they could have recognition, privileges, and respect if they would train themselves to be professionals. It is our political task to show that this was another trick, that assuming a professional identity—as opposed to becoming competent—is a sure way to *lose* the chance for solidarity and trust with most people in this society.

Once more we see the essential value in creating a sense of political accountability. If professionals could honestly experience the collective demands of a broader constituency, and could be clearer about what it would take to really provide services that were collectively demanded, they might be more able to give up the antisocial accoutrements of a professional identity. Bertha Reynolds recognized this, as did Cesar Chavez. As Larson notes, "Breaking with ideology, finding new norms for the social production of knowledge and the social uses of competence demands passion, vision, and hard work."[23] Only when we can show ourselves and other workers that the rewards of collective support and the opportunity for more equal relations with clients and co-workers are greater than the isolating self-importance of a professional identity will we be able to convince other activists that good services can be unqualified positive additions to the battery of tactics we use to achieve a better society.

Achieving Reciprocity. A major argument of this book has been that, even though achieving the broader aims of our strategy may be difficult for the individual service worker, there are ways to act politically in our daily work.

This is not naive personalism, as some would suggest.[24] Instead, it reflects the awareness that our personal activity is political and is, inevitably, linked to our achievement of broader goals. The things we learn as we try to define political practice help us provide better services and to develop a fuller, more grounded political analysis and strategy. As Cesar Chavez said, "All we can be sure of is what we are doing right now today. There is no such thing as means and ends. Everything that we do is an end, in itself, that we can never erase."[25] If this is so, our commitment to our political goals can best be measured by how well our daily service work embodies the values we wish to achieve in the broader society.

For me, this approach to political service work means developing an ethic of reciprocity in regard to our interaction with those who come to us for service. It means seeing that we have similar basic needs to our clients and that it is an accident of class, race, timing, or luck that they come to us, and not we to them, for service. Furthermore, reciprocity means that clients are potential comrades to whom we owe basic obligations beyond the particular service interchange. With potential comrades we must build alliances based on mutual disclosure of needs and mutual recognition of skills. We have the right to expect differences to be dealt with openly and fairly, because of their ability, otherwise, to undermine collective goals. Granted, the material conditions of how we are forced to relate to clients in most public settings differ from those in left services. But exactly because circumstances make it so difficult we should be able to see the long-term benefits of reciprocity as an ideal.

Finally, a nurturing society will be one where common human needs are recognized and great collective efforts made to meet them. It will be an environment where mutual dependence is the norm—not a feared state of ultimate degradation. It will be one where the ideal of altruism will have no meaning because everyone will acknowledge mutual needs. It will mean that we all offer help to others because we know we have a right to receive help in return. Although all this may sound utopian, it is ultimately the reason why the goals of social services cannot be separated from the hopes for socialism. Without such joint vision, services in a socialist society become just another "product" to be administered—by the state using collective re-sources, to be sure—without a sense of mutual obligation or accomplishment. Such a vision is not enough to warrant all the risks and pain it will take to achieve it. Instead, our new vision promises a more humane notion of reciprocal service, which may sustain us in the effort to create a better society.

Building an Outside Constituency. Important as they are, however, the efforts to maintain an effective daily political practice are probably impossible to achieve without outside support. As I have said before, it is the link with a broader movement that will allow us to remember where we are going. Also, we need to be part of broader efforts for social change in order to keep them attuned to the importance of social services in their strategy, tactics, and demands.

Here we can recall the important influence of the Rank and File movement in the 1930s. As a national presence it served to link service workers around the country and to sustain them in their political work. On the other hand, small as it was, it was able to influence the labor movement and the broader left organizations to pay more attention to human services.

For the same reasons, we need such a national movement today.

Perhaps a journal or newsletter—like *Social Work Today* was, or *Catalyst* may be today—can serve as a focal point, I am not sure. Maybe, too, progressive unionists have access to better means of getting people together. But, somehow, we must make alliances with each other which transcend professional associations. We also need city-wide organizations of progressive human service workers, both to build links and to help stop people from fighting each other over decreasing resources. At the local level, it should take only some careful organizing to build groups,* if the goals are general enough and there is a shared commitment to avoid overly bureaucratic organizational forms.[26]

No matter what the fate of conservative politicians, there will remain a reason for progressive human service workers to stay connected. The time is past due for us to create formal, flexible, collective means for doing so. Once, when I was teaching undergraduates at Brandeis, I managed to inspire a class to feel a real concern about the need for social change in this society. The whole group—about twelve young people—agreed that they wanted to "do something" about the issues we had been discussing. On the last day of class they were all insistent that I answer one question: "What career should we chose if we want to make change?"

Such young people, and many service workers today, have no experience of collective, political activity to help them reach their goals. They can only think in terms of jobs and careers. In our efforts to create a political practice we must not forget to reinforce our commitment to solidarity, to joint political struggle as a means to achieve our goals. It is time that we organize *ourselves*.

POLITICS FOR WHAT? THE END RESULT

Finally, we are making connections between social services and social change because we have to make them, because our service work is lessened unless it is informed by a broader political vision and our broader goals are diminished unless we understand the centrality of social services as both one means to achieve them and an important aspect of defining them. Andre Gorz has written:

That socialism is a necessity has never struck the masses with the compelling force of a flash of lightning. . . . It is no longer enough to reason as if so-

---

*Here the only word of caution is that initial organizers should begin carefully to assure that the group does not begin as an all-white organization. Initial planning groups should be strongly integrated and local minority networks activated to assure that, from the beginning, groups are not white-dominated. Once this happens it is very difficult to change the pattern.

cialism were a self-evident necessity. This necessity will no longer be recognized unless the socialist movement specifies what socialism can bring, what problems it alone is capable of solving and how.[27]

Our overall goal, then, is to allow what we learn from daily provision of service to influence our sense of political goals, and in turn, to allow our political values to affect the way we act as service workers. In revolutionary societies, or in developing nations, we can see the immediate benefits of such linking. In Nicaragua, teacher corps and other groups of service workers attempt to create a "revolutionary ethic" and to achieve the social goals of the revolution. There the problems lie with lack of expertise and lack of any liberating structures. In such situations it is easy—as we have seen in other revolutionary countries—to re-create oppressive forms of bureaucracy and professionalism out of a sense of immediate need to show "what socialism can bring" and of a lack of more creative options for how to organize social activity.

In this "advanced" society, which is far from a revolutionary state, our task may be different. We have both the frustration and the privilege that come from knowing that it is a long struggle. We are frustrated because all forces interact to make us doubt whether change can ever come, whether anything we do matters, especially anything which does not address questions of immediate economic injustice. On the other hand, we are privileged because we may have the time, and the resources, to create some better models.

During the 1960s many U.S. radicals made pilgrimages to revolutionary countries, or to meet third world leaders. Usually they would go with a sense of guilt as representatives of "imperialist America," the country that was causing so much economic and social hardship around the world. Often they would come back surprised and rejuvenated because the revolutionary leaders had given them a special charge, had said, in effect, that it was the duty of radicals within the United States—in the belly of the beast—to bring change here. American leftists were needed to stop the United States from hurting other countries, to educate the citizenry regarding the struggles of those in the Third World, and (important in this context) to use our own vast resources to create examples for how to bring needed changes.

As radicals working in the human services, it is perhaps not too arrogant to think of our task in this way. We can see the harm caused by injustice and misfortune and the futility of responding to it in a bureaucratic and professional manner. We may be able to help everyone to see the important political nature of our endeavors and to go beyond this to suggest some alternatives, which may be liberating to us but also to others around the world who seek a better society without going through all the hurtful social stages of "industrial development." In other words, by working to better define our dreams we may help ourselves in the everyday and offer to others some hope that they are not really faced with the cruel choices of separating the personal from the political, of separating daily caring from long-range goals, of separating the quest for economic and social justice from the ability to live a rewarding daily life.

Bertolt Brecht once wrote about the sadness which resulted when "we who would usher in the millennium of kindness found we could not ourselves be kind."[28] By linking the goals and practice of humane social services with the strategy and tactics for achieving broader social change, we may become a little more able both to "be kind" and to envision our own "millennium of kindness."

NOTES

INTRODUCTION

1. This was completed as my dissertation: "To Serve the People; An Inquiry into the Success of Service Delivery as a Social Movement Strategy" (Boston: Florence Heller School, Brandeis University) and summarized in "Surviving as a Radical Social Service Worker: Lessons from Movement History" in *Radical America,* vol. 12, no. 4.

2. See my recent publications: *The Circle Game: Services for the Poor in Massachusetts 1966–1978* (Amherst: University of Massachusetts Press, 1982); "Staying Alive: The Politics of Social Service Work," *C/O The Journal of Alternative Social Services* (Winter 1980), and "Beyond Realism: The Future of Social Services in the 1980s," *Catalyst: A Socialist Journal of the Social Services* (Winter 1983).

3. Interview with author, Fall 1975, Stoughton, Mass.

4. See George Gilder, *Wealth and Poverty* (New York: Basic Books, 1981) and *The Naked Nomad: Unmarried Man in America* (New York: Times Books, 1974); and Onalee McGraw, *The Family, Feminism, and the Therapeutic State* (Washington, D.C.: Heritage Foundation, 1980).

5. Andre Gorz, *Strategy for Labor* (Boston, Mass.: Beacon Press, 1964), p. 7.

6. See the discussion of the human service workforce in Betty Reid Mandell and Barbara Schram, *Human Services* (New York: John Wiley and Sons, 1983) and Robert J. Wicks, *Human Services: New Careers and Roles in the Helping Professions* (Illinois: Chas. C. Thomas, 1978).

7. Here I am generalizing from research done for *The Circle Game.*

8. There is a large literature on self help. Perhaps the best summaries are Alan Gartner and Frank Reissman, *Self-Help and Human Services* (San Francisco, California: Josey Bass, 1977); Alfred Katz and Eugene Bender, *The Strength in Us* (New York: New Viewpoints, 1976); and Alan Gartner, *The Self Help Revolution* (New York: Human Science Press, 1983).

9. See Withorn, "To Serve the People."

10. See Withorn, *The Circle Game.*

1. THE FORCED CHOICE: MAKING CHANGE VS. HELPING PEOPLE

1. Paul Halmos, *The Personal and the Political: Social Work and Political Action* (London: Hutchinson, 1978), pp. 32–33.

2. Here the best sources are: James Leiby, *A History of Social Welfare and Social Work in the United States* (New York: Columbia University Press, 1978); James T. Patterson, *America's Struggle Against Poverty 1900–1980* (Cambridge, Mass.: Harvard University Press, 1981); June Axinn and Herman Levin, *Social Welfare: A History of American Response to Need* (New York: Dodd Mead, 1975); Clarke A. Chambers, *Seedtime of Reform: American Social Service and Social Action 1918–1933* (Minneapolis: University of Minnesota Press, 1963); Nathan E. Cohen, *Social Work in the American Tradition* (New York: Holt, Rinehart, and Winston, 1958); and Walter I. Trattner, *From Poor Law to Welfare State: A History of Social Welfare in America* (New York: Free Press, 1974).

3. See Robert Wiebe, *The Search for Order, 1877–1920* (New York: Free Press, 1967); Harold L. Wilensky and Charles N. Lebeaux, *Industrial Society and Social Welfare* (New York: Russell Sage Foundation, 1958); Roy Lubove, *The Professional Altruist* (Cambridge, Mass.: Harvard University Press, 1965); and Chambers, *Seedtime of Reform*.

4. Especially useful here are Lubove, *The Professional Altruist*, and Chambers, *Seedtime of Reform*.

5. In addition to Lubove and Chambers, cited above, there are many helpful sources on the settlement house influence. See Allen Davis, *Spearheads of Reform* (New York: Oxford University Press, 1967); Ralph and Muriel Pumphrey, *The Heritage of American Social Work* (New York: Columbia University Press, 1961); Jill Conway, "Women Reformers and American Culture, 1870–1930," in *Journal of Social History* (1971–72), pp. 164–181; William L. O'Neill, *Everyone Was Brave: The Rise and Fall of Feminism in America* (New York: Quadrangle, 1961); and Amy Totenberg, "Women Reformers from the Settlement Movement 1889–1925," unpublished paper in the Schlesinger Library, Radcliffe College (1974).

6. Cited in Trattner, *From Poor Law to Welfare State*, p. 142.

7. See Murray and Adeline Levine, *A Social History of Helping Services* (New York: Appleton, Century, Crofts, 1970), as well as Leiby, *A History of Social Welfare;* Lubove, *The Professional Altruist;* and Chambers, *Seedtime of Reform.*

8. Review of yearly volumes of the *Proceedings* of the National Conference on Social Welfare (Chicago: University of Chicago Press) supports this, as does Leiby, *A History of Social Welfare;* Patterson, *America's Struggle Against Poverty;* and Trattner, *From Poor Law to Welfare State.*

9. For the best summary of social work in the 1930s, see Jacob Fisher, *The Response of Social Work to the Depression* (Cambridge, Mass.: Schenkman, 1980).

10. See Fisher, *The Response of Social Work*, as well as more general sources on New Deal social policy such as Paul Conkin, *FDR and the Origins of the Welfare State* (New York: Carvele, 1967); Donald S. Howd, *The WPA and Relief Policy* (New York: Russell Sage Foundation, 1943); Howard Zinn, ed., *New Deal Thought* (New York: Bobbs Merrill, 1965); and William Leuchtenburg, *The New Deal: A Documentary History* (New York: Harper and Row, 1968).

11. Again, see Fisher, cited above; Levine and Levine, *A Social History of Helping Services;* Leiby, *A History of Social Welfare;* Trattner, *From Poor Law to Welfare State;* and Axinn and Levin, *Social Welfare.*

12. Robert D. Vinter, "The Social Structure of Service," in Alfred J. Kahn, *Issues in American Social Work* (New York: Columbia University Press, 1959), p. 243.

13. For the best recent sources on social services see: Neil Gilbert and Henry Specht, *Handbook of the Social Services* (Englewood Cliffs, N.J.: Prentice Hall, 1981); Ilana Lescohier, "Identifying Trends in Social Service Provisions under the Public Assistance

Titles and under Title XX of the Social Security Act," Ph.D. dissertation, Brandeis University, 1979; and Sheila Kamerman and Alfred J. Kahn, *Social Services in the United States: Policies and Programs* (Philadelphia: Temple University Press, 1976).

14. There is a great deal of material on the Poverty Program. The most useful for our purposes are: Sar Levitan and Robert Taggart, *The Promise of Greatness* (Cambridge, Mass.: Harvard University Press, 1976); the *ANNALS* of the American Academy of Politics and Social Science, "Evaluating the War on Poverty," (September 1969), no. 385; Daniel Knapp and Kenneth Polk, *Scouting the War on Poverty* (Lexington, Mass.: D. C. Heath, 1971); Stephen M. Rose, *The Betrayal of the Poor: The Transformation of Community Action* (Cambridge, Mass.: Schenkman, 1972); Marc and Phyllis Pilisuk, eds., *How We Lost the War on Poverty* (New Brunswick, N.J.: Transaction Books, 1973); and Robert D. Plotnick and Felicity Skidmore, *Progress Against Poverty: A Review of the 1964– 1974 Decade* (New York: Academic Press, 1975).

15. Levine and Levine, *A Social History of Helping Services*, p. 5.

16. A range of writers has commented on this American ideology. For some of the most useful analyses, see Wilensky and Lebeaux, *Industrial Society and Social Welfare;* Joe R. Feagin, *Subordinating the Poor: Welfare and American Beliefs* (Englewood Cliffs, N.J.: Prentice Hall, 1975); Paul T. Therikildsen, *Public Assistance and American Values* (Albuquerque: University of New Mexico Press, 1964); and Robert Weibe, *The Segmented Society* (New York: Oxford University Press, 1975).

17. Wilensky and Lebeaux, *Industrial Society and Social Welfare.*

18. Interview with author for *The Circle Game,* Summer 1981.

19. See Lubove, *The Professional Altruist;* Chambers, *Seedtime of Reform;* and Leiby, *A History of Social Welfare.*

20. See discussion in Melvyn Dubovsky, *When Workers Organize* (Amherst: University of Massachusetts Press, 1968), and Bertha Reynolds, *Uncharted Journey: Fifty Years of Growth in Social Work* (New York: Citadel Press, 1953).

21. Quoted in Dubovsky, *When Workers Organize,* p. 26.

22. Samuel Gompers, *Labor and the Common Welfare* (New York: Dutton, 1919), p. 16.

23. We see this influence in the resistance to trade union services, to be discussed in chapter 2.

24. Gompers, *Labor and the Common Welfare,* p. 19.

25. Richard Titmuss, "Social Welfare and the Act of Giving," in Erich Fromm, ed., *Socialist Humanism* (New York: Doubleday, 1964), p. 388.

26. There is no hard evidence for such assertions, however, but the personal memories of Bertha Reynolds in *Uncharted Journey* and of other leftists do lend support to such speculation.

27. See Arthur Schlesinger, Jr., *The Coming of the New Deal* (Boston: Houghton-Mifflin, 1959); Howard Zinn, *New Deal Thought;* selected articles in Charles I. Schottland, ed., *The Welfare State* (New York: Harper and Row, 1967); George H. Nash, *The Conservative Intellectual Movement in America Since 1945* (New York: Harper and Row, 1976); L. J. Davis, "Conservatism in America," *Harpers Magazine* (October 1980); and Patterson, *America's Struggle Against Poverty.*

28. The experience of social workers during the McCarthy period was complicated and various. HEW banned Charlotte Tolle's booklet, "Common Human Need," and individuals were brought up on charges because they subscribed to *Social Work Today,* for instance. Voluntary agencies also conducted their own purges and in some areas,

like New York City, social workers with questionable backgrounds lost their jobs. There are few written sources about this; my sense of it comes from conversations with social workers like Bertha Reynolds, Norman Lourie, and Corinne Wolfe.

29. A good way to see the development of this approach is to read the yearly *Proceedings* of the National Conference on Social Welfare, published as *The Social Welfare Forum* by Columbia University Press.

30. See Wilensky and Lebeaux, *Industrial Society and Social Welfare*, and in Alfred J. Kahn, *Social Policy and Social Services* (New York: Knopf, 1973).

31. Here Wilensky and Lebeaux are most clear in their assertions about the natural, institutional nature of the development of social services, but this approach is reflected in most influential histories, including: Leiby, *A History of Social Welfare*, and John Romanyshyn, *Social Welfare: From Charity to Justice* (New York: Random House, 1971).

32. Kahn, *Social Policy and Social Services*, p. 18.

33. Kahn, p. 19.

34. Kahn, p. 20.

35. See Lee Rainwater, "The Service Strategy or the Income Strategy," *Transaction* (October 1969), vol. 4; Lewis Coser, "What Do the Poor Need? (Money)," in Joan Huber and H. Paul Chalfort, *The Sociology of American Poverty* (Cambridge, Mass.: Schenkman, 1974); and Levitan and Taggart, *The Promise of Greatness*.

36. Frances Fox Piven and Richard A. Cloward, *Regulating the Poor: The Functions of Public Welfare* (New York: Pantheon, 1971).

37. See their more recent work, *The New Class War: Reagan's Attack of the Welfare State and Its Consequences* (New York: Pantheon, 1982) and their "Notes Toward a Radical Practice," in Roy Baily and Mike Brake, eds., *Radical Social Work* (New York: New Viewpoints, 1975).

38. See Howard Zinn, *A People's History of the United States* (New York: Harper and Row, 1980); Roberta Ash, *Social Movements in America* (Chicago: Markham Press, 1972); and James Weinstein, *The Ambiguous Legacy* (New York: New Viewpoints, 1975).

39. James Weinstein, "The Left, Old and New," in *Socialist Revolution* (July/August 1972), 10:8.

40. Daniel Bell, quoted in Donald Egbert and Stow Persons, eds., *Socialism and American Life* (Princeton, N.J.: Princeton University Press, 1952), p. 217.

41. For examples of the differing views see: Weinstein, *The Ambiguous Legacy;* Roberta Ash, *Social Movements in America;* Paul Goodman, *Utopian Essays and Practical Purposes* (New York: Random House, 1952); Michael Harrington, *Socialism* (New York: Bantam, 1972); and Peter Clecak, *Radical Paradoxes: Dilemmas of the American Left, 1945–1970* (New York: Harper and Row, 1973).

42. See Ralph Miliband, *The State in Capitalist Society* (London: Weidenfeld and Nicolson, 1969); James O'Connor, *The Fiscal Crisis of the State* (New York: St. Martins Press, 1973); Ian Gough, *The Political Economy of the Welfare State* (London: Macmillan, 1979); Colin Pritchard and Richard Taylor, *Social Work: Reform or Revolution?* (London: Routledge and Kegan Paul, 1978); Vic George and Paul Wilding, *Ideology and Social Welfare* (London: Routledge and Kegan Paul, 1976); Norman Ginsberg, *Class, Capital, and Social Policy* (London: Macmillan, 1979); and Bob Deacon, "Social Administration, Social Policy, and Socialism," *Critical Social Policy* (Fall 1981), vol. 1, no. 1.

43. See David Wagner and Marcia Cohens's article, "Social Workers, Class, and Professionalism," in *Catalyst* (1978), vol. 1; and Paul Johnston, "The Promise of Public-Sector Unionism," in *Monthly Review* (September 1978), vol. 30.

44. For discussion of the bias against personalism see Jeffrey Galper, *The Politics of Social Services* (Englewood Cliffs, N.J.: Prentice Hall, 1975); Paul Halmos, *The Faith of the Counselors* (New York: Schocken, 1970); and *The Personal and the Political*, as well as the writings of Bertha Reynolds.

45. See Juliet Mitchell, *Psychoanalysis and Feminism* (New York: Random House, 1974), and Phil Brown, *Toward a Marxist Psychology* (New York: Harper and Row, 1974), for examples of efforts to bridge the gap.

46. Richard Flacks, "Making History vs. Making Life," *Working Papers for a New Society* (1974), vol. 2, no. 2.

47. Halmos, *The Personal and the Political;* also see Kahn, *Social Policy and Social Services*, ch. 7.

48. Here I am especially influenced by Carol Gilligan's work, *In a Different Voice: Psychological Theory and Women's Development* (Cambridge, Mass.: Harvard University Press, 1982), as well as more general treatments of women's "proper place," such as Sheila Rothman, *Women's Proper Place* (New York: Basic Books, 1980); Laurie Davidson and Laura K. Gordon, *The Sociology of Gender* (Boston: Houghton-Mifflin, 1979); Jessie S. Bernard, *Women, Wives, and Mothers: Values and Options* (Chicago: Aldine, 1975); and Joan Huber, ed., *Changing Women in a Changing Society* (Chicago: University of Chicago Press, 1973).

49. See Jean Giovannoni and Margaret Purvine, "The Myth of the Social Work Matriarchy," in *Proceedings* of the National Conference of Social Welfare (New York: Columbia University Press, 1974), and Elaine Norman and Arlene Mancuso, *Women's Issues and Social Work Practice* (Itasca, Ill.: F. E. Peacock, 1980).

50. See William O'Neill's treatment of social feminism in *Everyone Was Brave*.

51. Here again, I find Gilligan's recent work helpful in making concrete the intellectual and moral assumptions which underlie such separations.

52. Of course, we could view this as fulfilling the masking function of ideology, which is surely part of the problem. However, there are complex factors contributing to the situation which have been mentioned above and are covered with intelligence in Robert Weibe's *The Segmented Society*.

53. Interview for *The Circle Game*, Spring 1979.

54. For sources on planning see: Theodore Allison, *Toward a Planned Society* (New York: Oxford University Press, 1975); Alfred J. Kahn, *Theory and Practice of Social Planning* (New York: Russell Sage Foundation, 1969); Robert Morris, ed., *Centrally Planned Change: Prospects and Concepts* (New York: NASW, 1964) and his *Centrally Planned Change: A Re-Examination of Theory and Experience* (Urbana: University of Illinois Press, 1974); John Friedman and Barclay Hudson, "Knowledge and Action: A Guide to Planning Theory," in *Journal of the American Institute of Planners* (January 1974), no. 40; and Richard S. Boland, "Mapping the Planning Theory Terrain," in *Urban Social Change Review* (Summer 1975), no. 8.

55. See Theodore Marmor, *The Politics of Medicare* (Chicago: Aldine, 1973).

56. Gough, *The Political Economy of the Welfare State*, p. 65.

57. See Michael Lipsky, *Street-Level Bureaucracy* (New York: Russell Sage Foundation, 1980); Carole Joffee, *Friendly Intruders: Childcare Professionals and Family Life* (Berkeley: University of California Press, 1977); and Paul Halmos, *The Faith of the Counselors* and *The Personal and the Political*.

58. Sara Freedman, comment at presentation of her slide tape, "The End of the Corridor," a study of teacher burnout funded by the Massachusetts Foundation for the Humanities and Public Policy, 1981.

59. Halmos, *The Personal and the Political*, p. 117.

60. Reynolds, *Uncharted Journey*, p. 183.

61. These questions are typical of the attitudes I encountered in research on *The Circle Game*.

62. See Allen Hunter, "In the Wings: New Right Organizations and Ideology," in *Radical America*, (Spring 1980), vol. 15, nos. 1 and 2; and Linda Gordon and Allen Hunter, "Sex, Family, and the New Right," in *Radical America*, vol. 13, nos. 1 and 2.

63. Ralph H. Turner, "The Theme of Contemporary Social Movements," in *British Journal of Sociology* (December 1969), 20(1):391.

2. HISTORICAL PATTERNS OF OVERLAP: SOCIAL MOVEMENT SERVICES

1. For the best histories of American social movements see: Roberta Ash, *Social Movements in America* (Chicago: Markham, 1972); John J. Howard, *The Cutting Edge: Social Movements and Social Change in America* (Philadelphia: Lippincott, 1974); and Howard Zinn, *A People's History of the United States* (New York: Harper and Row, 1980). See also Murray Levine and Adeline Levine, *A Social History of Helping Services* (New York: Appleton, Century, Crofts, 1970).

2. Of course the main argument here is Frances Fox Piven and Richard Cloward's from *Regulating the Poor* (New York: Pantheon, 1971), but most other left-oriented commentators share this view, to some extent.

3. See Richard Titmuss, *The Gift Relationship* (New York: Random House, 1971), and Albert Fried, ed., *Socialism in America: A Documentary History* (New York: Anchor Books, 1976).

4. Again, see Ash, *Social Movements in America*, and Zinn, *A People's History of the United States*, as well as James Weinstein, *The Ambiguous Legacy* (New York: New Viewpoints, 1975). See also the social scientists John Wilson, *Introduction to Social Movements* (New York: Basic Books, 1972), and Luther Gerlach and Virginia Hines, *People, Power, and Change* (Indianapolis: Bobbs-Merrill, 1970).

5. Ash, *Social Movements in America*, p. 166.

6. There is an extensive and growing literature on the organizations of the women's movement. Most useful here are: Eleanor Flexner, *Century of Struggle: The Women's Rights Movement in the United States* (New York: Atheneum, 1971); William L. O'Neill, *Everyone Was Brave: The Rise and Fall of Feminism in America* (New York: Quadrangle, 1969); Aileen S. Kraditor, *Up From the Pedestal: Selected Writings in the History of American Feminism* (New York: Quadrangle, 1968); and Ellen Dubois, *Feminism and Suffrage* (New York: Schocken, 1978).

7. "Guide to Massachusetts Women's Organizations," Schlesinger Library, Cambridge, Mass., 1980.

8. For a discussion of the different ideological trends within the Woman Movement see William L. O'Neill, ed., *The Woman Movement: Feminism in the United States and England* (New York: Quadrangle, 1969), and Dubois, *Feminism and Suffrage*.

9. Frances Willard, *Do Everything* (Chicago: WCTU, 1895), p. ii.

10. See Samuel Ungar, "A History of the Women's Christian Temperance Movement," Ph.D. thesis, Ohio State University, 1933.

11. Willard, *Do Everything*, p. ii.

12. See Jill Conway, "Women Reformers and American Culture: 1870–1930," in *Journal of Social History* (1971–72); Flexner, *Century of Struggle;* and O'Neill, *Everyone Was Brave*.

13. See Dorothy Blumberg, "Florence Kelley: Revolutionary Reformer," in *Monthly Review* (November 1959), vol. 9; Flexner, *Century of Struggle;* and O'Neill, *Everyone Was Brave.*

14. For sources of general information about the black movement see: John H. Franklin, *From Slavery to Freedom*, 2d ed. (New York: Knopf, 1966); Robert Allen, *Black Awakening in Capitalist America* (New York: Doubleday, 1969); Francis Broderick and August Meir, *Black Protest Thought in the Twentieth Century* (Indianapolis: Bobbs-Merrill, 1971); and Joanne Grant, ed., *Black Protest* (New York: Fawcett, 1975).

15. Naomi Weiss, *The National Urban League 1910–1940* (New York: Oxford University Press, 1979), p. 58. See also Guichard Parris and Lester Brooks, *Blacks in the City: History of the National Urban League* (Boston: Little Brown, 1971), and William A. Simms, *The Urban League Story* (New York: National Urban League, 1961).

16. Weiss, *The National Urban League*, p. 65.

17. Weiss, p. 66.

18. Weiss, p. 85.

19. Harold Cruse explores the meaning of this split in *The Crisis of the Negro Intellectual* (New York: Morrow, 1967), p. 124.

20. David Cronin, *Black Moses* (Madison: University of Wisconsin Press, 1955), p. 7.

21. Cronin, *Black Moses*, p. 43.

22. Eric Lincoln, *The Black Muslims in America* (Boston: Beacon Press, 1961).

23. Lincoln, *The Black Muslims in America*, and Malcolm X and Alex Haley, *The Autobiography of Malcolm X* (New York: Grove Press, 1964).

24. For the best treatments of the history of the labor movement, see: Philip Foner, *History of the Labor Movement in the United States*, 4 vols. (New York: International Publishers, 1947, 1955, 1964, 1965); Joseph G. Rayback, *A History of American Labor* (New York: Macmillan, 1963); Richard O. Boyer and Herbert M. Morais, *Labor's Untold Story*, 2d ed. (New York: Cameron Association, 1965); and James R. Green, *The World of the Worker* (New York: Hill and Wang, 1980).

25. See Alfred H. Katz and Eugene I. Bender, "Self Help Groups in Western Society: History of Prospects," in the special "self help" issue of the *Journal of Applied Behavioral Science* (September 1976), vol. 13, no. 3.

26. Maximillian Hurwitz, *The Workmen's Circle* (New York: Workmen's Circle, 1936), pp. 13–14.

27. Hurwitz, p. 15.

28. Hurwitz, p. 196.

29. Foner, *History of the Labor Movement in the United States*, p. 136.

30. James Weinstein, "The IWW and American Socialism," in *Socialist Revolution* (September/October 1970), 1(5):25.

31. Arthur Stone and Mark Kahn, "How Flint Strikers Got Relief," in *Social Work Today* (March 1937), 18(6):10.

32. Stone and Kahn, "How Flint Strikers Got Relief," p. 10.

33. Bertha Reynolds, *Uncharted Journey* (New York: Citadel Press, 1956), p. 237.

34. Reynolds, *Uncharted Journey*, p. 229.

35. John L. Lewis, "Welcome to the Ranks of Labor," in *Social Work Today* (January 1938), 5(4):8.

36. Reynolds, *Uncharted Journey*, pp. 253, 255, 263–264.

37. Reynolds, p. 247.

38. Bertha Reynolds, "Labor in Social Work," in *Social Work Yearbook* (New York: National Association of Social Workers, 1945).

39. See Joseph Bevine, "Labor and Social Welfare," in *Social Welfare Forum 1956* (New York: Columbia University Press, 1956).

40. For a sense of how services developed within the AFL-CIO context see publications of the AFL-CIO, Community Services Division, Washington, D.C., especially the writings of the first director, Leo Perlis.

41. For literature on the history of the American Left, see Zinn, *A People's History of the United States;* James Weinstein, *The Decline of Socialism in America, 1912–1925* (New York: Monthly Review Press, 1967) and *The Ambiguous Legacy;* Theodore Draper, *The Roots of American Communism* (New York: Viking, 1957); Sidney Lens, *Radicalism in America* (New York: Crowell, 1969).

42. See Stanley Feldstein, ed., *The Ordeal of Assimilation* (New York: Anchor Books, 1974), p. 81.

43. For the best sources here, see Roy Rosensweig, "Organizing Among the Unemployed," *Radical America* (July/August 1976), vol. 10, no. 4, and Frances Fox Piven and Richard Cloward, *Poor People's Movements* (New York: Pantheon, 1977).

44. C. R. Walker, "Relief and Revolution," in *Forum and Century* (September 1932), 2:156.

45. Walker, "Relief and Revolution," p. 158.

46. Communist Party, U.S.A., "Toward Revolutionary Mass Work" (New York: Workers' Library Publishers, 1932), pp. 11, 46.

47. Boyers and Morais, *Labor's Untold Story,* p. 260.

48. Art Preis, *Labor's Giant Step* (New York: Pathfinder Press, 1964), p. xix.

49. My source on the IWO is an older ex-member of the Communist Party who wishes to remain unnamed.

50. Roberta Ash, *Social Movements in America,* p. 210.

51. Paul Halmos, *The Personal and The Political* (London: Hutchinson, 1978), p. 47.

3. LEGACY OF THE 1960s: JOINING THE PERSONAL AND THE POLITICAL

1. There remains to be written a comprehensive intellectual and social analysis of the 1960s. At this point the most helpful sources are earlier materials which offer firsthand accounts and basic narrative such as: Mitchell Goodman, *The Movement Toward a New America* (New York: Knopf, 1970); Edward Quinn and Paul J. Dolan, *The Sense of the Sixties* (New York: Free Press, 1968); Michael Miles, *The Radical Probe: The Logic of Student Rebellion* (New York: Atheneum, 1971); Priscilla Long, *The New Left: A Collection of Essays* (Boston: Porter Sargent, 1969); George Fischer, ed., *The Revival of American Socialism* (New York: Oxford University Press, 1971); Debbie Louis, *And We Are Not Saved: A History of the Movement as People* (New York: Doubleday, 1970); and Richard Cluster, ed., *They Should Have Served That Cup of Coffee* (Boston: South End Press, 1980).

2. Lawrence Ferlinghetti, "I Am Waiting," in *A Coney Island of the Mind* (New York: New Directions, 1958).

3. For some of these sources see Langston Hughes' autobiography *The Big Sea* (New York: Hill and Wang, 1940) as well as *Fields of Wonder* (New York: Knopf, 1947), and *Laughing to Keep From Crying* (New York: Holt, Rinehart, and Co., 1952); W. E. B. DuBois, *Dark Water* (New York: Harcourt, Brace, and Howe, 1952), *Black Reconstruction* (Philadelphia: Albert Saifer, 1935), and *The Souls of Black Folk* (New York: Blue Heron Press, 1953); Frantz Fanon, *The Wretched of the Earth,* Constance Farrington, trans. (New York: Grove Press, 1963), *Black Skins, White Masks,* Charles L. Markman,

trans. (New York: Grove Press, 1967), and *Studies in a Dying Colonialism,* Haakon Chevalier, trans. (New York: Monthly Review Press, 1965).

The most influential left works were C. Wright Mills, *The White Collar* (New York: Oxford University Press, 1951), *The Power Elite* (New York: Oxford University Press, 1956), *The Sociological Imagination* (New York: Grove Press, 1961), and *The Marxists* (New York: Dell, 1962); William A. Williams, *The Contours of American History* (New York: Quadrangle, 1961), *The Great Evasion* (New York: Quadrangle, 1964), and *The Tragedy of American Diplomacy* (New York: Dell, 1959); and Paul Goodman, *Utopian Essays and Practical Proposals* (New York: Vintage, 1952), *Growing Up Absurd* (New York: Vintage, 1960), and *People or Personnel* (Washington, D.C.: Institute for Policy Studies, 1963).

For feminist sources, see Simone de Beauvoir, *The Second Sex* (New York: Knopf, 1953); Doris Lessing, *The Golden Notebook* (New York: Simon and Schuster, 1962); and Betty Friedan, *The Feminine Mystique* (New York: Norton, 1963).

4. Such values could be seen as a general "prescriptive ideology," which informed the goals and the hopes of activists, if not their actual practice. See John Wilson, *Introduction to Social Movements,* for a description of how such ideology functions.

5. Peggy Hopper, "I Don't Want to Change My Lifestyle, I Want to Change My Life," pamphlet (Boston: New England Free Press, 1971).

6. Quoted in Kirkpatrick Sale, *SDS* (New York: Random House, 1973), p. 107.

7. "Program," ERAP Summer Institute (1964), from George Abbot White collection (Boston, Mass.).

8. Chicago ERAP "Report" to national office (May 1964), from George Abbott White collection (Boston, Mass.).

9. Letter from Richard Rothstein to Rennie Davis (March 15, 1965), from George Abbott White collection (Boston, Mass.).

10. Cleveland ERAP "Report" to national office (June 1964), from George Abbott White collection (Boston, Mass.), pp. 2–4.

11. Cleveland ERAP "Report" (July 1964) and letter from Cleveland ERAP to Rennie Davis in Chicago (Summer 1965), from George Abbott White collection.

12. "An Evaluation of the Trenton Project," report from Trenton ERAP to national office (Fall 1964), from George Abbott White collection (Boston Mass.).

13. Stanley Aronowitz to Rennie Davis (April 22, 1964), from George Abbott White collection (Boston, Mass.).

14. Sar Levitan and Robert Taggart, *The Promise of Greatness* (Cambridge, Mass.: Harvard University Press, 1976), remains the best source of analysis on the Poverty Programs. See also Robert D. Plotnick and Felicity Skidmore, *Progress Against Poverty: A Review of the 1964–1974 Decade* (New York: Academic Press, 1975); "Evaluating the War on Poverty," The *ANNALS* of the American Academy of Politics and Social Science, (September 1969), no. 385; Daniel Knapp and Kenneth Polk, *Scouting the War on Poverty* (Lexington, Mass.: D. C. Heath, 1971); Stephen M. Rose, *The Betrayal of the Poor: The Transformation of Community Action* (Cambridge, Mass.: Schenkman, 1972); and Marc and Phyllis Pilisuk, eds., *How We Lost the War on Poverty* (New Brunswick, N.J.: Transaction Books, 1973).

15. Useful sources here are Sanford Kravitz and Ferne K. Kolodney, "Community Action: Where Has it Been? Where Will it Go?" The *ANNALS* of the American Academy of Politics and Social Science, and Martin Rein, "Community Action: A Critical Assessment," in his *Social Policy: Issues of Choice and Change* (New York: Random House, 1970).

16. See Charles Brecher, *The Impact of Federal Anti-Poverty Policies* (New York: Praeger, 1973), and Kenneth B. Clark, ed., *A Relevant War Against Poverty: A Study of Community Action Programs and Observable Social Change* (New York: Metropolitan Applied Research Center, 1968).

17. Kravitz and Kolodney, "Community Action: Where Has It Been?" p. 37, and Lewis Coser, "What Do the Poor Need? (Money)," in Joan Huber and Paul Chalfant eds., *The Sociology of American Poverty* (Cambridge, Mass.: Schenkman, 1974), p. 19.

18. Here my argument is taken directly from that of Levitan and Taggart, *The Promise of Greatness.*

19. Quoted in Robert J. Lampman, "What Does It Do for the Poor? A New Test of National Policy," in *The Public Interest,* (Winter 1974), 34:75.

20. Levitan and Taggart, *The Promise of Greatness,* p. 9.

21. The best source on SNCC is Clayborne Carson, *In Struggle: SNCC and the Black Awakening* (Cambridge, Mass.: Harvard University Press, 1982); also see Cleveland Sellers, *The River of No Return* (New York: Morrow, 1973); Howard Zinn, *SNCC, The New Abolitionists* (Boston: Beacon Press, 1965); Allan J. Matuson, "From Civil Rights to Black Power: The Case of SNCC, 1960–1966," in Lawrence Levine and Robert Middlekaff, eds., *The National Temper* (New York: Harcourt, Brace, and Jovanovich, 1972); and Bruce Payne, "SNCC: An Overview Two Years Later," in Cohen and Hale, eds., *The New Student Left: An Anthology.*

22. Unsigned aphorism in *The Black Panther* newspaper (August 13, 1969), p. 12. The best sources on the Panthers are still primary sources and primary accounts, there being little serious literature. See Philip S. Foner, ed., *The Black Panthers Speak* (New York: Lippincott, 1970); Bobby Seale, *Seize the Time: The Story of the Black Panther Party and Huey P. Newton* (New York: Random House, 1970); and Terry Cannon, *All Power to the People* (San Francisco, Calif.: People's Press, 1970). Reginald Major's *The Panther Is a Black Cat* (New York: Morrow, 1972) is a bit more analytical than the other works cited.

23. *The Black Panther* newspaper, March 3, 1969, p. 12.

24. Huey P. Newton, "On the Defection of Eldridge Cleaver from the Black Panther Party and the Defection of the Black Panther Party from the Black Community," Black Panther Party pamphlet (Fall 1970).

25. "East Oakland Community Information Center Report," in G. Louis Louis, ed., *The Black Panther Leaders Speak* (Metuchen, N.J.: The Scarecrow Press, 1976), p. 5.

26. *The Black Panther* newspaper (April 27, 1969) and (March 3, 1969).

27. *The Black Panther* newspaper, Oct. 11, 1969.

28. *The Black Panther* newspaper, May 31, 1969.

29. For general sources on the UFW and on the issues involved in farmworker organizing see: Joan London and Henry Andersen, *So Shall Ye Reap: The Story of Cesar Chavez and the Farm Workers' Movement* (New York: Crowell, 1970); Peter Matthiessen, *Sal Si Puedes: Cesar Chavez and the New American Revolution* (New York: Random House, 1973); Jacques E. Levy, *Cesar Chavez: Autobiography of La Causa* (New York: Norton, 1975); Sam Kushner, *Long Road to Delano* (New York: International Publishers, 1975); and the numerous sources cited in Beverly Fodell, *Cesar Chavez and the United Farm Workers: A Selected Bibliography* (Detroit, Mich.: Wayne State University Press, 1974).

30. Interview with Roberto Ybarra, UFW Services director, Calexico, California (January 1976).

31. This overview is taken from a series of interviews I conducted in California from

the summer of 1975 through the summer of 1976. It also incorporates a reading of many memos, unpublished documents, and the proposal which originally funded the Martin Luther King Fund.

32. Interview with UFW Services Director, Roberto Ybarra, Calexico, California (August 1975).

33. All quotes taken from unpublished record of the proceedings at the Service Workers' Training Conference held in Keene, California, in July of 1976. I did not attend the conference but I reviewed the written record of the conference (from which these quotes are taken) and interviewed many participants.

34. It is not necessary here to cite all sources on the early history of the current women's movement. A few basic texts include: Sara Evans, *Personal Politics: The Roots of Women's Liberation* (New York: Knopf, 1978); Jo Freeman, *The Politics of Women's Liberation: A Case Study of an Emerging Social Movement* (New York: McKay, 1975); Joan Huber, ed., *Changing Women in a Changing Society* (Chicago: University of Chicago Press, 1973); Judith Hole and Ellen Levine, *The Rebirth of Feminism* (New York: Quadrangle, 1971); Robin Morgan, ed., *Sisterhood Is Powerful* (New York: Vintage, 1970); and Vivien Gornick and Barbara K. Morgan, *Women in Sexist Society: Studies in Power and Powerlessness* (New York: Basic Books, 1971).

35. Probably the most widely read publication to come out of the current feminist movement is *Our Bodies, Ourselves: A Book by and for Women*, by the Boston Women's Health Book Collective (New York: Simon and Shuster, 1973), now in its third edition.

36. See Gail Sullivan, "Cooptation in the Battered Women's Movement," in *Catalyst* (Winter 1983), and Naomi Gottlieb, ed., *Alternative Services for Women* (New York: Columbia University Press, 1980).

37. See Barbara Ehrenreich and Deirdre English, *Witches, Midwives, and Nurses: A History of Women Healers* (New York: The Feminist Press, 1972), and Ellen Frankfort, *Vaginal Politics* (New York: Quadrangle, 1972), for early efforts to consider the politics of women's health.

38. Much of this overview is taken from a review of *Health Right*, a women's health newsletter published in New York in the mid-seventies, as well as from an analysis of two surveys conducted by that newsletter in 1974 and 1976. Finally, Naomi Fatt, an activist in *Health Right*, was especially helpful in sharing drafts of unpublished papers and recollections in the spring of 1977.

39. All quotes are from *Health Right* surveys, 1974 and 1976.

40. This analysis comes from conversations with Naomi Fatt at *Health Right* and from statements in *Health Right* surveys.

41. Hyde Park Chapter, Chicago Women's Liberation Union, "Socialist Feminism: A Strategy for the Women's Movement," widely circulated unpublished paper (1973), p. 14.

42. Again, the best sources for doing this are pages of *Health Right*, or of *Off Our Backs*, a Washington-based feminist newspaper. Helen I. Marieskind's and Barbara Ehrenreich's article, "Toward Socialist Medicine: The Women's Health Movement," in *Social Policy* (September/October 1975), vol. 6, no. 2, also provides useful background.

43. See the "Self Help Reporter," published in New York City (c/o National Self Help Clearinghouse, 33 W. 42d St., Room 1227, New York, N.Y. 10036) for basic bibliography and other updates on the self-help approach.

44. Martin J. Lowenthal, "The Social Economy of Low Income Communities," in Gary Galpert and Harold Rose eds., *The Social Economy of Cities*, UAAR (Beverly Hills, Calif: Sage Publications, 1975), vol. 9.

45. See Alfred H. Katz and Eugene I. Bender, "Self Help Groups in Western Society," *The Journal of Applied Behavior Science* (September 1976), vol. 12, no. 3.

46. See the two basic books (which are constantly being superseded by more particular texts) on self help: Alan Gartner and Frank Reissman, *Self Help and Human Services* (San Francisco, Calif.: Jossey Bass, 1977), and Aflred Katz and Eugene Bender, *The Strength in Us* (New York: New Viewpoints, 1976). Again, it is best to review the "Self Help Reporter" to keep up to date.

47. See Victor and Ruth Sidel, "Beyond Coping," in *Social Policy* (September/October 1976), vol. 7, no. 2 and my article, "Helping Ourselves: The Limits and Potential of Self Help," *Radical America* (May/June 1980) vol. 14, no. 3, for cautions regarding the benefits of self help.

48. Lowell S. Levin, "Self-Care: An International Perspective," in *Social Policy* (September/October 1976), vol. 7, no. 2.

49. See Mary Richmond, *Social Diagnosis* (New York: Russell Sage Foundation, 1917) and *What Is Social Casework? An Introductory Description* (New York: Russell Sage Foundation, 1922).

50. William Carlos Williams, *Paterson, Book I* (New York: New Directions, 1963), p. 65.

51. See Carl Boggs' *Gramsci's Marxism* (New York: Urizen Books, 1976), and Antonio Gramsci, *Selections from Political Writings 1910–1920,* Quentin Hoare, ed. (London: Lawrence and Wishart, 1977).

52. Levy, *Cesar Chavez*, p. 521.

53. Interview for dissertation, Boston, Mass., Summer 1976.

4. PERSONAL DIMENSIONS OF SERVICE: DEFINING POLITICAL PRACTICE

1. Unfortunately, the antinuclear movement does not go very far in considering the implications of this, nor in defining what it means, beyond spending for social programs rather than military budgets.

2. Here it is important to mention the special influence of Jeffrey Galper's work on my thinking. His two books, *The Politics of Social Services* (Englewood Cliffs, N.J.: Prentice Hall, 1975) and *Social Work Practice: A Radical Perspective* (Englewood Cliffs, N.J.: Prentice Hall, 1980), are sensitive to the needs and concerns of individual service workers and give support to all of us who try to link the personal with the political.

3. Interview conducted for dissertation, Boston, Mass., August 1976.

4. Interview conducted for *The Circle Game*, Boston, Mass., Summer 1979.

5. Here I am once again carrying on a continuing dispute with the late Paul Halmos, especially as he expressed himself in his last (posthumous) book, *The Personal and the Political: Social Work and Political Action* (London: Hutchinson, 1978).

6. For a good example see Hans Toch in "Collective Behavior," Gardner Lindsey, ed. *Handbook of Social Psychology* (Cambridge, Mass.: Addison-Wesley, 1968).

7. Hans Toch, in his *Social Psychology of Social Movements* (Indianapolis: Bobbs-Merrill, 1965), and Rudolph Herberle, "Observations on the Sociology of Social Movements," *American Sociological Review* (1940), vol. 14, are particularly critical, but the tone of most of the literature on social movements, especially before the 1970s, was uniformly

skeptical. See John Wilson, *Introduction to Social Movements* (New York: Basic Books, 1972), for a review of this literature.

8. Geoffrey Pearson, "Making Social Workers: Bad Promises and Good Omens," in Roy Bailey and Mike Brake, *Radical Social Work* (New York: Random House, 1976), p. 18. For other sources on the motivation of service workers see: Pranab Chatterjee and Darla Ginter, "Commitment to Work Among Public Welfare Workers," in *Public Welfare, (Fall 1972); vol. 30;* Paul Halmos, *The Faith of the Counsellors* (New York: Schocken Books, 1970); H. Prins, "Motivation in Social Work," in the British journal, *Social Work Today*, vol. 5, no. 2.

9. Paul Potter, *A Name for Ourselves* (Boston: Little Brown, 1971), pp. 147–148.

10. Joseph R. Starobin, *American Communism in Crisis* (Cambridge, Mass.: Harvard University Press, 1972), p. xiii.

11. Halmos, *The Personal and The Political,* p. 146.

12. I teach a twice-yearly workshop on "Learning Theory" to adult service workers. The direct service workers and the radical students (who are also usually service workers) tend to have very similar "learning styles," by most common measures. Of course, such observations are not presented as hard data, only as suggestive for our purposes.

13. Richard Titmuss, "Social Welfare and the Art of Giving," in Erick Fromm, ed., *Socialist Humanism* (New York: Doubleday, 1964).

14. For the best sources on the desire for nurturing relationships as a basis for social work, see Paul Halmos, *The Faith of the Counsellors* and *The Personal and the Political.*

15. Paul Halmos, *The Faith of the Counsellors,* p. 164.

16. Interview for this book, Boston, Mass. (Summer, 1982).

17. The Baroness Burdett-Coatts, ed., *Women's Mission* (New York: Scribner's, 1893), p. 315.

18. See Carol Gilligan, *In a Different Voice: Psychological Theory and Women's Development* (Cambridge, Mass.: Harvard University Press, 1982).

19. Mrs. S. R. I. Bennett, *Women's Work Among the Lowly: Memorial Volume of the First Forty Years of the American Female Guardian Society and Home for Friendless Women* (New York: American Female Guardian Society, 1880), frontispiece.

20. Some common analyses of the problems facing human service workers can be found in: Cary Cherniss, *Professional Burnout in Human Service Organizations* (New York: Praeger Special Studies, 1980); Herman Resnick and Rino J. Patti, *Change from Within: Humanizing Social Welfare Organizations* (Philadelphia: Temple University Press, 1980); Jeffrey Prottas, *People-Processing: The Street-Level Bureaucrat in Public Service Bureaucracies* (Lexington, Mass.: Lexington Books, 1979); Michael Lipsky, *Street-Level Bureaucracy* (New York: Russell Sage Foundation, 1980).

21. See Cary Cherniss, *Professional Burnout,* for a serious review of the problem of worker burnout. Less substantive material can be found in the numerous "how-to" guides published by University Associates.

22. See George Konrad, *The Case Worker* (New York: Harcourt, Brace, Jovanovich, 1978).

23. Despite its age, C. Wright Mills' critique of this literature is still the most telling. See "The Professional Ideology of the Social Pathologists," in *American Journal of Sociology* (September 1943) vol. 49, no. 2. Recent American writers especially helpful here are Jeffrey Galper, *The Politics of Social Services* and *Social Work Practice,* and Steve Burghardt, *The Other Side of Organizing* (Cambridge, Mass.: Schenkman, 1982). British writers: Paul Corrigan and Peter Leonard, *Social Work Practice Under Capitalism: A Marxist*

244 4. PERSONAL POLITICAL PRACTICE

Approach (London: Macmillan, 1978); Steve Bolger et al., *Towards Socialist Welfare Work* (London: Macmillan, 1981); Roy Bailey and Mike Brake, *Radical Social Work;* and Howard Jones, ed., *Towards a New Social Work* (London: Routledge and Kegan Paul, 1975); and London- Edinburgh Weekend Return Group, *In and Against the State: Discussion Notes for Students* (London 1979).

24. Typical cartoon by Koren, regular *New Yorker* magazine contributor.

25. Michael Lipsky, *Street-Level Bureaucracy,* p. 71.

26. Interview for *The Circle Game,* Spring 1979.

27. Interview for *The Circle Game,* Summer 1979.

28. Frances Fox Piven and Richard Cloward, "Notes Toward a Radical Social Work," in Roy Baily and Mike Brake, ed., *Radical Social Work,* p. xxviii.

29. Bertha Reynolds, *Uncharted Journey* (New York: Citadel, 1953), pp. 173–174.

30. See Corrigan and Leonard, *Social Work Practice Under Capitalism;* Stephen Bolger et al., *Towards Socialist Welfare Work;* Bailey and Brake, ed., *Radial Social Work;* Daphne Stratham, *Radicals in Social Work* (London: Routledge and Kegan Paul, 1978); Geoffrey Pearson, *The Deviant Imagination* (London: Macmillan, 1975); Jeffrey Galper, *The Politics of Social Services* and *Social Work Practice;* Steve Burghardt, *The Other Side of Organizing.*

31. Interview with author, Stoughton, Mass., Fall 1975.

32. During the McCarthy period there was red-baiting. People were reviewed and fired for left activity from public as well as private agencies. Within HEW, for example, it was possible to be reviewed because one was reported to have subscribed to *Social Work Today,* to have befriended Bertha Reynolds, and to have owned "socialist books." I learned of such activities, of course, not in the social work histories but in private interviews with Corrinne Wolfe (who worked in HEW) and Norman Lourie (who worked in private New York agencies).

33. Galper, *Social Work Practice,* p. 122.

34. Piven and Cloward, "Notes Toward . . . ," pp. xlvi–xlvii.

35. Richard N. Bolles' *What Color is Your Parachute?* (Ten Speed Press, 1980) is a best-selling manual for how to find job satisfaction.

36. Lipsky, *Street-Level Bureaucracy,* p. 23. For further discussion of discretion, see Jeffrey Prottas, *People-Processing: The Street-Level Bureaucrat in Public Service Bureaucracies* (Lexington, Mass.: Lexington Books, 1979), and Joel F. Handler, *The Deserving Poor: A Study in Welfare Administration* (Chicago: Markham, 1971).

37. Interview for *The Circle Game,* Spring 1980.

38. Bertha Reynolds, *Social Work and Social Living* (New York: Citadel Press, 1951), pp. 63–64; *Uncharted Journey,* pp. 253–255.

39. Prottas, *People-Processing,* pp. 3–4, 116–117.

40. Interview for *The Circle Game,* Fall 1980.

41. Here the work of Carole Joffee, *Friendly Intruders: Childcare Professionals and Family Life* (Berkeley: University of California Press, 1977), offers insights into the complex dynamics of worker-client relationships.

42. Steve Burghardt, *The Other Side of Organizing,* p. 215.

43. The rationale to exclude nonneighborhood residents—who were often feminists—in favor of "community women"—who might not be—was hotly debated. In November 1971, the clinic organizers published an open letter to the women's movement in *On Our Way,* the newsletter of the Cambridge Women's Center, which justified their position.

44. Galper, *Social Work Practice,* p. 131.

45. Betty Reid Mandell has noted, in a review of this document, that some working-class, or non-Anglo, people may feel constrained by the legalistic notion of contracts. While she has a point, it seems to me that, somehow, we must find ways to give up some of our power by letting clients know what to expect. See her excellent discussion of class and cultural factors in service delivery in her textbook, with Barbara Schram, *Human Services* (New York: Wiley, 1983), as well as Burghardt, *The Other Side of Organizing*, ch. 6.

46. Piven and Cloward, "Notes Toward . . . ," p. xlviii.

47. Jeffrey Galper, "What Are Radical Social Services?" *Social Policy* (January/February 1978), 8(4):88, and *Social Work Practice*, p. 149.

48. Interview for dissertation, November 1975.

49. Interview for *The Circle Game*, Summer 1979.

50. Corrigan and Leonard, *Social Work Practice Under Capitalism*, p. 102.

51. Paul Adams and Gary Freeman, "On the Political Character of Social Service Work," in *Social Services Review* (December 1979).

52. This notion of underclass is an uncharitable revival of the old "worthy poor" argument. Now a small group is deemed worthy because they are so socially marginal that we can rightfully expect nothing from them. The most important source for this is Ken Auletta, *The Underclass* (New York: Random House, 1982). For a review which demonstrates the danger of the argument, see Andrew Hacker's comments on the book in *The New York Review of Books* (August 12, 1982), vol. 23, no. 13.

53. Interview for *The Circle Game*, Fall 1981.

54. Here the suggestions of Corrigan and Leonard, *Social Work Practice Under Capitalism*, are especially helpful.

55. Most radical British social workers, especially, have been quick to point out the dangers inherent in the individualized supervision model so sacrosanct to social work. See especially Bailey and Brake, *Radical Social Work*.

56. Interview for this book, Summer 1982.

57. Interview for *The Circle Game*, Summer 1979.

58. Interview for this book, Summer 1982.

5. THE LIMITS OF PROFESSIONALISM

1. Interview for this book, Spring 1981.

2. There are many articles which consider the state of human service professionalism. Most useful is Irwin Epstein and Kayla Conrad, "The Empirical Limits of Social Work Professionalism," in Rosemary Sarri and Y. Hasenfeld, eds., *The Management of Human Services* (New York: Columbia University Press, 1978). See also all the articles in Paul Halmos, ed., *Professionalization and Social Change*, Sociological Review Monograph #20 (University of Keele, 1973); David Hardcastle, "The Profession, Professional Organization, Licensing and Private Practice," in Neil Gilbert and Harry Specht, *Handbook of the Social Services* (Englewood Cliffs, N.J., Prentice Hall, 1981); M. Haig and M. B. Sussman, "Professional Autonomy and the Revolt of the Client," in *Social Problems* (Fall 1969), vol. 17; David Wagner and Marcia Cohen, "Social Workers Class and Professionalism," in *Catalyst* (1978), vol. 1, no. 1; and George Summers, "Public Sanction and the Professionalization of Social Work," in *Clinical Social Work Journal* (Spring 1976), vol. 4, no. 1.

3. Quoted in Epstein and Conrad, "The Empirical Limits of Social Work Professionalism," p. 123.

4. Margali S. Larson, *The Rise of Professionalism: A Sociological Analysis* (Berkeley: University of California Press, 1977), p. 156.

5. Geoffrey Pearson, "The Politics of Uncertainty: A Study in the Socialization of Social Workers," in Howard Jones, ed., *Towards a New Social Work* (London: Routledge and Kegan Paul, 1976), p. 49.

6. The term "search for order" was first used by Robert Weibe in his book *The Search for Order* (New York: Hill and Wang, 1967). Other sources on the origins of professionalism are: Roy Lubove, *The Professional Altruist* (Cambridge, Mass.: Harvard University Press, 1965); James Leiby, *A History of Social Welfare and Social Work* (New York: Columbia University Press, 1978); Raymond Callahan, *Education and the Cult of Efficiency* (Chicago: University of Chicago Press, 1962); Eliot Friedson, *Professional Dominance* (New York: Atherton Press, 1970); Howard M. Vollmer and Donald L. Mills, eds., *Professionalization* (Englewood Cliffs, N.J.: Prentice Hall, 1966); and Barbara and John Ehrenreich, "The Professional Managerial Class," in *Radical America* (May/June, 1977), vol. 11, no. 3.

7. Wiebe, *The Search for Order*, pp. 111, 129.

8. Larson, *The Rise of Professionalism*, p. 8.

9. Wiebe, *The Search for Order*, p. 134. This whole discussion is influenced especially by pp. 129–134.

10. For a full historical discussion of this development see Lubove, *The Professional Altruist*.

11. Clarke A. Chambers, *The Seedtime of Reform: American Social Service and Social Action 1918–1933* (Minneapolis: University of Minnesota Press, 1963), provides the best history here. See also Allen F. Davis, *Spearheads for Reform: The Social Settlements and the Progressive Movement* (New York: Oxford University Press, 1967).

12. The major source for understanding this progression is Chambers, *Seedtime of Reform*, but it can be seen in the articles in all the standard social work journals of the period.

13. Lubove, *Professional Altruist*, p. 15.

14. Christopher R. Dykema, "Toward a New Age of Social Services: Lessons to be Learned from Our History," in *Catalyst* (1978), 1(1):63.

15. Dykema, "Toward a New Age of Social Services," p. 62.

16. For standard sources on the definition of professionalism see Harold Wilensky and Charles Lebeaux, *Industrial Society and Social Welfare* (New York: Russell Sage Foundation, 1958); Ernest Greenwood, "Attributes of a Profession," *Social Work*, (1957), vol. 2; Abraham Flexner, "Is Social Work a Profession?" in *Proceedings of the National Conference of Charities and Corrections* (Chicago: The Hilderman Company, 1915); Nina Toren, *Social Work: The Case of a Semi-Profession* (Beverly Hills, Calif.: Sage Publications, 1972); and Howard M. Vollman and Donald L. Mills, eds., *Professionalization* (Englewood Cliffs, N. J.: Prentice Hall, 1966).

17. Harold L. Wilensky and Charles N. Lebeaux, *Industrial Society and Social Welfare* (New York: Russell Sage Foundation, 1958), p. 184.

18. See Lubove, *The Professional Altruist*; Leiby, *History of Social Welfare*; Chambers, *Seedtime of Reform*; Nathan E. Cohen, *Social Work in the American Tradition* (New York: Holt, Rinehart, and Winston, 1958); and Murray and Adeline Levine, *A Social History of Helping Services* (New York: Appleton, Century, Crofts, 1970).

19. For typical left criticisms of casework, see Roy Bailey and Mike Brake, eds., *Radical Social Work* (New York: Pantheon, 1975); Howard Jones, ed., *Towards a New Social Work* (London: Routledge and Kegan Paul, 1975); Jeffrey Galper, *The Politics of Social Ser-*

vices (Englewood Cliffs, N.J.: Prentice Hall, 1975) and *Social Work Practice* (Englewood Cliffs, N.J.: Prentice Hall, 1980).

20. Quoted in Lubove, *The Professional Altruist*, p. 202.

21. Mary Richmond, *Social Diagnosis* (New York: Russell Sage Foundation, 1917), p. 25.

22. See Elaine Norman and Arlene Mancuso, *Women's Issues and Social Work Practice* (Itasca, Ill.: Peacock, 1980).

23. For a general review of the field of community organization and its links with social planning, see: "Social Planning and Community Organization," by Robert Perlman, and the section on "approaches" by Neil Gilbert and Harry Specht in *The Encyclopedia of Social Work*, issue 17, vol. 2 (New York: NASW, 1977). For a critique of community organization as a way to achieve "the containment of change," see Jeffrey Galper, *The Politics of Social Services*.

24. This point is also made by Galper, *The Politics of Social Services*, p. 111.

25. Larson, *The Rise of Professionalism*, p. 148.

26. For examples of this approach, see Schottland, "Social Work in the 1960s," p 40; Robert H. MacRae, "Social Work and Social Action," *Social Service Review* (March 1966), 11(1):6; Alan D. Wade, "Social Work and Political Action," *Social Work* (October 1963), 8(4):3–4; and Rudolph Danstedt, "The Assessment of Social Action," in *Social Welfare Forum* (New York: Columbia University Press, 1958), p. 205.

27. Porter Lee, *Social Work: Cause and Function* (New York: Columbia University Press, 1937), p. 264.

28. Of course, it is important to acknowledge that this confusion is one purpose of any ideology and that, in saying this, I am not blaming the individuals who assumed the ideology, which, indeed, serves many "useful" functions within a capitalist society.

29. Kenneth Reid, *From Character Building to Social Treatment* (Westport, Conn.: Greenwood Press, 1981), pp. 226–227.

30. This analysis is taken directly from Jacob Fisher's important book, *The Response of Social Work to the Depression* (Cambridge, Mass.: Schenkman, 1980).

31. Fisher, p. 91.

32. Dykema, "Towards a New Age of Social Services," p. 63.

33. Leslie Alexander and Phyllis Lichtenberg, "The Casework Notebook: An Analysis of Its Content," *Sociology and Social Welfare* (January 1978), p. 55. See also Bertha Reynolds, *Uncharted Journey* (New York: Citadel Press, 1953) and *Social Work and Social Living* (New York: Citadel Press, 1951).

34. For sources on the New Careers see: Arthur Pearl and Frank Reissman, eds., *New Careers for the Poor* (New York: Free Press, 1955); Charles Grosser et al., *Nonprofessionals in Human Services* (San Francisco, Calif.: Jossey Bass, 1965); and Robert Cohen, *New Careers Grows Older: A Perspective on the Paraprofessional Experience 1965–1975* (Baltimore, Md.: Johns Hopkins University, 1977).

35. For examples of cultural criticism of social work practice see: Barbara B. Solomon, *Black Empowerment: Social Work in Oppressed Communities* (New York: Columbia University Press, 1976); Joe R. Feagin and Clairece Booker Feagin, *Discrimination American Style: Institutional Racism and Sexism* (Englewood Cliffs, N.J.: Prentice Hall, 1978); Andrew Billingsly and Jeanne Giovannoni, *Children of the Storm* (New York: Harcourt, Brace, and Jovanovich, 1972); Shirley Jenkins, *The Ethnic Dilemma in Social Services* (New York: Free Press, 1981); and Felice Perlmutter and Leslie Alexander, "Exposing the Coercive Consensus: Racism and Sexism in Social Work," in *The Management of Human Services*.

248   5. THE LIMITS OF PROFESSIONALISM

36. One drawback in this effort was the disdain which the New Left held for social work. So few serious radicals went to social work schools, as one activist recalls, "I was the only leftist I knew who *chose* to go to social work school in community organizing. Everyone else studied sociology and learned to organize by doing it."

37. Danny L. Jorgansen, "The Social Construction of Professional Knowledge: Social Work Ideology 1956–1973," *Sociology and Social Welfare* (June 1979), vol. vi, no. 4.

38. See David Hardcastle, "The Profession, Professional Organizations, Licensing, and Private Practice," Neil Gilbert and Harry Specht, eds., *Handbook of the Social Services* (Englewood Cliffs, N.J.: Prentice Hall, 1981).

39. I am referring here to the useful, but politically compromised, *New England Journal of Human Services,* published in Boston since the fall of 1980.

40. See Irwin Epstein and Kayla Conrad, "Limits of Social Work Professionalism," in Rosemary Sarri and Zeke Hazenfeld, eds., *The Management of Human Services* (New York: Columbia University Press, 1977).

41. There was a recent NASW conference held in Washington, D.C., on issues of women and social work, and national meetings of social work professionals have shown an increasing public recognition of women's issues, at least. See Elaine Norman and Arlene Mancuso, *Women's Issues and Social Work Practice* (Itasco, Ill.: Peacock, 1980), and the NASW newsletter: "Women's Issues and Social Work Practice."

42. J. R. Cypher, "Social Reform and the Social Work Profession," in Howard Jones, ed., *Towards a New Social Work,* p. 21.

43. Clarke Chambers, "Introduction," to Jacob Fisher, *The Response of Social Work to the Depression,* p. xi.

44. Roy Lubove, "Social Work and the Life of the Poor," in *The Nation,* (May 23, 1966), 220(21):610.

45. Willard Richan and Allan Mendelsohn, *Social Work: The Unloved Profession* (New York: New Viewpoints, 1973).

46. Richan and Mendelsohn, pp. 49, 146.

47. See Betty Reid Mandell's forthcoming article, "Blurring Definitions of Social Services: Human Services vs. Social Work," in *Catalyst* (Spring 1983).

48. For further sources on this trend see back issues of *The New England Journal of Human Services* and numerous publications of "Project Share," a federally funded clearinghouse of information on human services (P. O. Box 2309, Rockville, Md. 20852).

49. Project Share, cited above, has even published a bibliography on self help in human services and the "Self Help Reporter" serves as a monthly source of information on expanding programs.

50. Peter Leonard, "Professionalization, Community Action, and the Growth of Social Service Bureaucracies," in Paul Halmos, ed., *Professionalization and Social Change,* Sociological Review Monograph #20 (University of Keele, 1973).

51. See my article, "Helping Ourselves: The Limits and Potential of Self Help," *Radical America* (May/June 1980), vol. 14, no. 3, for a discussion of the political problems with self help.

52. Larson, *The Rise of Professionalism,* pp. 156–157.

53. David Wagner and Marcia Cohen, "Social Workers, Class, and Professionalism," in *Catalyst* (1978), 1(1):25 and 52.

54. M. Haug and M. B. Sussman, "Professional Autonomy and the Revolt of the Client," *Social Problems* (Fall 1969), 17:533.

55. Ivan Illich, ed., *Disabling Professions* (London: Marion Boyars, 1977), p. 20.

56. John McKnight, "Professionalized Service and Disabling Help," in *Disabling Professions.*

57. McKnight, "Professionalized Service . . . ," p. 73.

58. Barbara and John Ehrenreich, "The Professional Managerial Class" and "The New Left and the Professional Managerial Class," in *Radial America* (March/April 1977) vol. 11, no. 2 and (May/June 1977), vol. 11, no. 3. See also Pat Walker, ed., *Between Labor and Capital,* (Boston: South End Press, 1979). For our purposes this anthology is limited because it chooses to argue primarily with the technical definitions of class raised by the Ehrenreichs rather than with the functions of the PMC, whether they are a "class" or not.

59. Larson, *The Rise of Professionalism,* chs. 4 and 5.

60. Larson, pp. 229–236.

61. Larson, p. 243.

62. See Galper, *The Politics of Social Services, Social Work Practice,* and "What Are Radical Social Services?"; and see also Wagner and Cohen, "Social Workers, Class, and Professionalism." In Britain see: Corrigan and Leonard, *Social Work Practice Under Capitalism* (London: Macmillan, 1978); Geoffrey Pearson, "Making Social Workers" and "The Politics of Uncertainty;" John McKinley, ed., *Processing People* (London: Holt, Rinehart, and Winston, 1975).

63. Pearson, "The Politics of Uncertainty," pp. 69–70.

64. Piven and Cloward, "Notes Toward . . . ," p. xxii.

65. Paul Halmos, "Introduction," *Professionalism and Social Change.* Halmos here is typical of other more socially democratic professionals who simply cannot accept the implications of a more fully radical critique of social work and of capitalist social, *not economic,* relations. See here Alfred Kahn, *Social Policy and Social Services* for an American example, and read Bolger et al., *Towards Socialist Welfare Work* (London: Macmillan, 1981), and Colin Pritchard and Richard Taylor, *Social Work: Reform or Revolution?* (London: Routledge and Kegan Paul, 1978) for analyses of why this happens.

66. Here the major source is, of course, Herbert Marcuse, but the collected work of Erich Fromm is also relevant.

67. See Larson, *The Rise of Professionalism,* ch. 8.

68. Barbara and Al Haber, "With a Little Help from Our Friends," "Radicals in the Professions," pamphlet published by the Radicals Education Project of SDS (1967), pp. 50–51.

69. Here all commentators seem to agree. See Cherniss, *Professional Burnout;* Michael Lipsky, *Street-Level Bureaucracy* (New York: Russell Sage Foundation, 1980); Joel Handler, *The Deserving Poor* (Chicago: Markham, 1971); as well as the standard professional textbooks.

70. Larry Hirschorn, "Alternative Services and the Crisis of the Professions," in John Case and Rosemary Taylor, *Coops, Communes, and Collectives* (New York: Pantheon, 1979), pp. 170–173.

71. Lipsky, *Street-Level Bureaucracy.*

72. I saw this unfortunate tendency exhibited over and over again during my research for *The Circle Game.*

73. Pearson, "The Politics of Uncertainty," p. 87.

74. See the sources cited in note 65 for a review of the content of British social democracy.

75. Ehrenreich and Ehrenreich, "The New Left and the Professional Managerial Class," p. 22.

76. Quoted in Harry Braverman, *Labor and Monopoly Capitalism* (New York: Monthly Review Press, 1974), p. 411.

77. John Mayer and Noel Timms, *The Client Speaks* (London: Routledge and Kegan Paul, 1970).

78. Piven and Cloward, "Notes Toward . . . ," p. xiii.

79. Interview for this book, Summer 1982.

80. Epstein and Conrad, "Limits of Social Work Professionalism," p. 179.

81. See Epstein and Conrad, "Limits of Social Work Professionalism," p. 176.

82. Hirschorn, "Alternative Services," p. 177.

83. Interview for the dissertation, Spring 1977.

84. See Mayer and Timms, *The Client Speaks.*

85. Interview for the dissertation, Summer 1976.

86. Interview for this book, Summer 1982.

87. Pearson, "The Politics of Uncertainty," p. 52.

88. Haber and Haber, "A Little Help from Our Friends," p. 60.

89. Of course, the major source for this concept is Braverman, *Labor and Monopoly Capital.*

90. Larson, *The Rise of Professionalism*, p. 228.

91. Cherniss, *Professional Burnout*, p. 93.

92. Interview for *The Circle Game*, Spring 1979.

93. Quoted in Larson, *The Rise of Professionalism*, p. 244, taken from Albert Szymanski, "Technicians and the Capitalist Division of Labor," *Socialist Revolution*, (May/June, 1972), vol. 2.

94. Quoted in Joan L. Goldstein, *Bertha C. Reynolds—Gentle Radical* (New York: Yeshiva University, 1981).

6. GUERRILLAS IN THE BUREAUCRACY?

1. Dale L. Johnson and Christine O'Donnell, "The Accumulation Crisis and Service Professionals," in Kenneth Fox et al., eds., *Crisis in the Public Sector, A Reader* (New York: Monthly Review Press/Union for Radical Political Economists, 1982), p. 34.

2. See London-Edinburgh Weekend Return Group, *In and Against the State* (London, 1979).

3. Robert J. Russo, *Serving and Surviving as a Human Service Worker* (Monterey, Calif.: Brooks/Cole, 1980), p. 134.

4. For sources on worker socialization see Cary Cherniss, *Professional Burnout in Human Service Organizations* (New York: Praeger Special Studies, 1980); David Street et al., *The Welfare Industry: Functionaries and Recipients in Public Aid* (Beverly Hills, Calif.: Sage Publications, 1979); H. S. Becker et al., *Institutions and the Person* (Chicago: Aldine, 1968); Arthur C. Cyrns, "Social Work Education and Student Ideology: A Multivariate Study of Professional Socialization," *Journal of Education for Social Work* (1977, vol. 13; and Irwin Epstein, "Organizational Careers, Professionalization, and Social Worker Radicalism," *Social Service Review* (1970), vol. 44.

5. Frances Fox Piven and Richard A. Cloward, "Notes Toward a Radical Social Work," in Roy Bailey and Mike Brake, *Radical Social Work* (New York: New Viewpoints, 1975), p. xii. Their recent book, *The New Class War, Reagan's Attack on the Welfare State and Its Consequences* (New York: Pantheon, 1982), suggests a more complex understanding of the welfare state and its workers.

6. Relevant sources on bureaucratic behavior are: Douglas Yates, *Bureaucratic De-*

mocracy: The Search for Democracy and Efficiency in American Government (Cambridge, Mass.: Harvard University Press, 1982); Fred A. Kramer, ed., *Perspectives on Public Bureaucracy*, 3d ed. (Cambridge, Mass.: Winthrop Publishers, 1981); Anthony Downs, *Inside Bureaucracy* (Boston: Little Brown, 1967); Peter Blum and W. Richard Scott, *Formal Organizations* (San Francisco, Calif.: Chandler, 1962).

7. This discussion is drawn from the excellent summary of bureaucratic theory by Nicos P. Mouzelis, *Organizations and Bureaucracy: An Analysis of Modern Theories* (Chicago: Aldine, 1968), p. 39.

8. This is the predominant view expressed in the literature cited in note 6. Left critics sometimes take a more sophisticated view, however. See Richard Bendix, "Socialism and the Theory of Bureaucracy," *Canadian Journal of Economics and Political Science* (1980), vol. 16; Andrew Arato, "Understanding Bureaucratic Contradiction," *Telos* (Spring 1978), no. 35; and Fred Block, "Beyond Relative Autonomy, State Managers as Historical Subjects," *The Socialist Register 1980* (London: Merlin Press, 1980).

9. Contemporary Marxist theorists are beginning to go beyond this acceptance of bureaucracy, even if their ways of writing about their new insights leave them inaccessible to most of us. See the following examples of important, if sometimes unintelligible, current thinking: Franco Ferrarotti, "The Struggle Against Total Bureaucracy," *Telos* (Spring 1976), no. 27; Ferenc Feher and Agnes Heller, "Forms of Equality," *Telos* (Summer 1977), no. 32; Noberto Bobbio, "Is There a Marxist Theory of the State?" *Telos* (Spring 1978), no. 35; Angelo Bolaffi, "The Crisis of Late Capitalism and the Future of Democracy: An Interview with Habermas," *Telos* (Spring 1979), no. 39; Andreas Wildt, "Totalitarian State Capitalism: On the Structure and Historical Function of Soviet-Type Societies," *Telos* (Fall 1979), no. 41; and Stuart Hall, "Nicos Poulantzas, State Power, and Socialism," *New Left Review* (January/February 1980), no. 119.

10. See again the historical sources cited in chapter 1, especially James Leiby, *A History of Social Welfare and Social Work in the U.S.* (New York: Columbia University Press, 1978); James T. Patterson, *America's Struggle Against Poverty 1900–1980* (Cambridge, Mass.: Harvard University Press, 1981); and Harold L. Wilensky and Charles N. Lebeaux, *Industrial Society and Social Welfare* (New York: Russell Sage Foundation, 1958).

11. Again, see Leiby and Patterson, cited above, and many articles in the National Conference of Social Work *Proceedings* of 1932 (Chicago: University of Chicago Press, 1932), especially Harry L. Lurie, "Developments in Public Welfare Programs," pp. 253–266, and C. A. Dykstra, "The Partnership of Public and Private Agencies," pp. 65–82.

12. See Jacob Fischer, *The Response of Social Work to the Depression* (Cambridge, Mass.: Schenkman, 1980); Patterson, *America's Struggle Against Poverty;* Donald S. Howd, *The WPA and Relief Policy* (New York: Russell Sage Foundation, 1943); and Leiby, *A History of Social Welfare.*

13. Sidney Hook, "Welfare State: A Debate That Isn't," in Charles Schottland, ed., *The Welfare State* (New York: Harper and Row, 1967), p. 170.

14. For a better understanding of the British concept of social democracy, see: Colin Pritchard and Richard Taylor, *Social Work: Reform or Revolution?* (London: Routledge and Kegan Paul, 1978); Vic George and Paul Wilding, *Ideology and Social Welfare* (London: Routledge and Kegan Paul, 1976); Steve Bolger et al., *Towards Socialist Welfare Work* (London: Macmillan, 1981); Norman Ginsberg, *Class Capitalism and Social Policy* (London: Macmillan, 1979); Daphne Stratham, *Radicals in Social Work* (London: Routledge and Kegan Paul, 1978); and London-Edinburgh Weekend Return Group, *In and Against the State* (London, 1979).

15. John Upton Terrell, *The United States Department of Health, Education, and Welfare: A Story of Protecting and Preserving Human Resources* (New York: Meredith Press, 1965), pp. 9–10.

16. See National Association of Social Workers, *Encyclopedia of Social Work*, 17th ed., (New York: NASW, 1977), 2:1642 and 2:1645.

17. See Sar Levitan and Robert Taggart, *The Promise of Greatness* (Cambridge, Mass.: Harvard University Press, 1976), and Robert D. Plotnick and Felicity Skidmore, *Progress Against Poverty: A Review of the 1964–1974 Decade* (New York: Academic Press, 1975).

18. See Neil Gilbert and Harry Specht, eds., *Handbook of the Social Services* (Englewood Cliffs, N.J.: Prentice Hall, 1981) for an updated review of the programmatic effects of such legislation.

19. See Ilana Hirsch Lescohier, "Identifying Trends in Social Service Provisions under the Public Assistance Titles and Titles XX of the Social Security Act," Ph.D. dissertation, Brandeis University, 1979; Bill Benton et al., *Social Services: Federal Legislation vs. State Implementation* (Washington, D.C.: The Urban Institute, 1978); and Martha Derthick, *Uncontrollable Spending for Social Service Grants* (Washington, D.C.: Brookings Institution, 1975). For a more popular understanding of what such changes meant in one state see my book, *The Circle Game* (Amherst: University of Mass. Press, 1982).

20. See sources in note 19 for an overview of changes. For critiques of purchase of service see Massachusetts Taxpayers Foundation, Inc., *Purchase of Service: Can State Government Gain Control?* (Boston: Massachusetts Taxpayers Foundation, 1980); Arnold Gurin and Barry Friedman, Project Directors, "Contracting for Services as a Mechanism for the Delivery of Human Services: A Study of Contracting Practices in Three Human-Service Agencies in Massachusetts," unpublished report, OHDS Grant No. 18P–0017011–01 (1980); and Suzanne Sankar, "Contracting Out: Attrition of State Employees" in Fox et al., eds., *Crisis in the Public Sector, A Reader*, pp. 275–280.

21. Sankar, cited above, is especially useful here, as is the Massachusetts Taxpayers study, *Purchase of Service, Can the State Government Gain Control?*

22. See Paul Terrell, "Financing Social Welfare Services," in Gilbert and Specht, *Handbook of the Social Services*, as well as Ilana Hirsch Lescohier, "Identifying Trends in Social Service Provisions," and Arnold Gurin and Barry Friedman, "Contracting for Services as a Mechanism for Delivery of Human Services," OHDS Grant No. 18P–0017011–01, Brandeis University, 1980.

23. See Andrew McCormick, "Union Organizing in Day Care," pp. 281–288, as well as Sankar, "Contracting Out, Attrition of State Employees," both in Fox et al., *Crisis in the Public Sector, A Reader.*

24. Interview conducted in Spring 1979, as part of research for *The Circle Game.*

25. Interview conducted in Summer 1979, as part of research for *The Circle Game.*

26. See David Hardcastle, "The Profession, Professional Organizations, Licensing, and Private Practice," in Gilbert and Specht, eds., *Handbook of the Social Services.*

27. See Research Group, Inc., *Integration of Human Services in HEW* (Washington, D.C., 1972), vol. 1; Gerald Horton et al., *Illustrating Services Integration from Categorical Bases,* Project Share Monograph No. 3 (Washington, D.C.: HEW, 1976); Sidney Gartner, *Roles for General Purpose Governments in Services Integration,* Project Share Monograph No. 2 (Washington, D.C.: HEW, 1976). These and other efforts are criticized in an unpublished talk given by Robert Morris and Ilana Hirsch Lescohier, "Services Integration: Real vs. Illusory Solutions to Welfare Dilemmas" (conference on Issues in Service Delivery in Human Service Organizations, June 1977).

28. *Social Security Bulletin* (May 1980), 43(5):5.

29. See W. Robert Curtis, *Area-Based Human Services* (Boston: SMRI Publications, 1979), and Withorn, *The Circle Game*.

30. One example of such a process was demonstrated in an unpublished study done for the Massachusetts social workers union, SEIU 509, by the Massachusetts Labor Research Group, "An Analysis of Proposed Productivity Methods and Standards for Assistance Payments and Medical Assistance Units of the Massachusetts Department of Public Welfare" (Boston: SEIU, 1979).

31. Henry W. Lawton and Anthony Magarelli, "Stress Among Public Child Care Workers," *Catalyst* (1980), no. 7, p. 61.

32. Claude Lefort, "What Is Bureaucracy?" *Telos* (Winter 74/75), 22:44.

33. Walter V. Robinson, "Taxcurb Backer Wants Services Cut," *Boston Globe*, May 10, 1979.

34. Here I am drawing directly from the work of Allen Hunter in "The Ideology of the New Right," in Fox et al., eds., *Crisis in the Public Sector: A Reader*, pp. 309–332, and his "In the Wings: New Right Organizations and Ideology," in *Radical America* (Spring 1980), vol. 15, nos. 1 and 2.

35. For an overview of the range of current assaults see Alan Gartner et al., eds., *What Reagan Is Doing to Us* (New York: Harper and Row, 1982).

36. Many writers have tried to examine workers' experiences in human service organizations. See Elihu Katz and Brenda Danet, eds., *Bureaucracy and the Public: A Reader in Official-Client Relations* (New York: Basic Books, 1973); Herman Resnick and Rino J. Patti, *Change From Within: Humanizing Social Welfare Organizations* (Philadelphia: Temple University Press, 1980); Naomi Gottlieb, *The Welfare Bind* (New York: Columbia University Press, 1974); Michael Lipsky, *Street-Level Bureaucracy* (New York: Russell Sage Foundation, 1980).

37. Wenocur and Sherman, "Empowering the Social Worker," p. 1.

38. Wenocur and Sherman, p. 10.

39. See Naomi Kroeger, "Organizational Goals, Policies, and Output: The Dilemma of Public Aid," Ph.D. dissertation, University of Chicago, 1971; Richard P. Forbes, "Socialization of the Public Caseworker: Resolution of Uncertainty," Ph.D. dissertation, University of Chicago, 1973. I learned of both dissertations from reading David Street et al., *The Welfare Industry: Functions and Recipients in Public Aid* (Beverly Hills, Calif.: Sage Publications, 1979). Also see Rino J. Patti, "Organizational Resistance and Change," in Herman Resnick and Rino J. Patti, eds., *Change From Within: Humanizing Social Welfare Organizations* (Philadelphia: Temple University Press, 1980); Russo, *Serving and Surviving as a Human Service Worker;* Brager and Holloway, *Changing Human Service Organizations;* and Lipsky, *Street-Level Bureaucracy.*

40. Lipsky, *Street-Level Bureaucracy*, p. 101.

41. Gideon Sjoberg et al., "Bureaucracy and the Lower Class," in Elihu Katz and Brenda Danet, *Bureaucracy and the Public* (New York: Basic Books, 1973), p. 61.

42. Sjoberg, "Bureaucracy and the Lower Class," p. 65.

43. James R. Greenly and Stuart A. Kirk, "Organizational Characteristics of Agencies and the Distribution of Services to Clients," in Resnick and Patti, *Change From Within*, p. 69.

44. Marlagi S. Larson, *The Rise of Professionalism: A Sociological Analysis* (Berkeley: University of California Press, 1977), p. 189.

45. Donald Klein, "Some Notes on the Dynamics of Resistance to Change: The Defender Role," in Resnick and Patti, *Change from Within*, p. 151.

46. Lipsky, *Street-Level Bureaucracy*, p. 152.

47. From interview conducted in Spring 1979 for *The Circle Game*.

48. From interview conducted in Spring 1982 for this book.

49. From interview conducted in Summer 1979 for *The Circle Game*.

50. See numerous articles in Fox et al., eds., *The Public Sector Crisis, A Reader*.

51. See David Wagner and Marcia Cohen, "Social Workers, Class, and Professionalism," in *Catalyst* (1978), vol. 1, no. 1.

52. David Wagner and Marcia Cohen, "Social Workers, Class, and Professionalism," p. 52.

53. See the exchange on human service unions, edited by me in *The New England Journal of Human Services* (Fall 1981), 1(4): .

54. Paul Johnston, "The Promise of Public Sector Unionism," *Monthly Review* (September 1978) vol. 30, 1–2.

55. From interview conducted in Spring 1979 for *The Circle Game*.

56. See McCormick, "Union Organizing in Day Care."

57. See Mark Maier, "Public Sector Labor Relations," in *Crisis in the Public Sector: A Reader*.

58. From class presentation given on worker-recipient relationships given by welfare rights activist in Winter 1980 and used in *The Circle Game*.

59. See Judith Transue, "Collective Bargaining on Whose Terms," *Catalyst* (1980), no. 5.

60. London-Edinburgh Weekend Return Group, *In and Against the State*, p. 1.

61. Michael D. Yates, "Public Sector Unions and the Labor Movement," Fox et al., eds., *Crisis in the Public Sector: A Reader*, p. 232.

62. Johnston, "The Promise of Public Sector Unionism," *Monthly Review*, pp. 8, 14, 15, 16.

63. Paul Johnston, "Public Sector Unionism," in Fox et al., eds., *Crisis in the Public Sector: A Reader*, p. 212.

64. From interview for this book, Spring 1982.

65. From interview for this book, Fall 1980.

66. See Harry Braverman, *Labor and Monopoly Capitalism;* Claude Lefort, "What is Bureaucracy?"; Herbert Marcuse, *One-Dimensional Man* (Boston: Beacon Press, 1964); Paul Goodman, *Utopian Essays and Practical Proposals* (New York: Vintage, 1952); and Michael Harrington, *Socialism* (New York: Bantam, 1972).

67. These ideas were most fully expressed in *Oppression and Liberty* (Amherst: University of Massachusetts Press, 1973) and *Selected Essays—1934–1943* (London: Oxford University Press, 1962). For a set of provocative essays on her work and a full bibliography, see George Abbott White, ed., *Simone Weil: Interpretation of a Life* (Amherst: University of Massachusetts Press, 1981).

68. See Hannah Arendt, *Totalitarianism* (New York: Harcourt, Brace, 1951), and *Eichmann in Jerusalem: A Report on the Banality of Evil* (New York: Viking, 1963). Here see an application of Arendt's concepts for the welfare system in Betty Reid Mandell, "Welfare and Totalitarianism—Part I, Theoretical Issues," in *Social Work* (January 1971), vol. 16, no. 1, and "Part II, Tactical Guidelines," in *Social Work* (April 1971), vol. 16, no. 2.

69. See Paul Goodman, *Utopian Essays and Practical Purposes* (New York: Random House, 1952), *People or Personnel* (Washington, D.C.: Institute for Policy Studies, 1963), and "Legitimacy," in *The New Reformation* (New York: Vintage, 1971).

70. Claude Lefort and Cornelius Castoriades have been introduced to the United States through *Telos*, a difficult to read but important journal of Marxist thought. See

Lefort, "What Is Bureaucracy?" in "Interview with Claude Lefort," *Telos* (Winter 1976–77), no. 30; and "Then and Now" *Telos* (Summer 1978), no. 36. Also see Cornelius Castoriades, "On the History of the Workers Movement," *Telos* (Winter 1976–77), no. 30.

71. Lefort, "What is Bureaucracy?" p. 34.
72. Larson, *The Rise of Professionalism,* pp. 193 and 198.
73. Lefort, "What is Bureaucracy?" p. 48.
74. Lefort, p. 37.
75. Quoted in Porter Lee, *Social Work: Cause and Function* (New York: Columbia University Press, 1937), p. 185
76. Morris Janowitz, *Social Control and the Welfare State* (New York: Elsevier, 1976), p. 235.
77. London-Edinburgh Weekend Return Group, *In and Against the State,* p. 37.
78. Cherniss, *Professional Burnout,* p. 71.
79. Lipsky, *Street-Level Bureaucracy,* p. 73.
80. Lefort, "What is Bureaucracy?" p. 43.
81. Sjoberg, "Bureaucracy and the Lower Class," p. 69.
82. Russo, *Serving and Surviving,* p. 65.
83. An overall, political, strategic approach to organizational change is what is lacking in such generally useful books as Brager and Holloway, *Changing Human Service Organizations,* and Resnick and Patti, *Change From Within.*
84. This point is well taken in Rosabeth Moss Kanter's book, *Women and Men of the Corporation* (New York: Basic Books, p. 164. In this book Kanter has many important insights into organizational behavior and how people are hurt by bureaucratic patterns, but finally, she opts to help people adjust to the structure rather than to suggest basic changes.
85. Brager and Holloway, *Changing Human Service Organizations.*
86. Johnston, "Public Service Unionism."
87. Peter Blau, "Orientation Towards Clients in a Public Welfare Agency," in Katz and Danet, eds., *Bureaucracy and the Public,* p. 240.
88. Wenocur and Sherman, "Empowering the Social Worker," p. 18.
89. See Gail Sullivan, "Cooptation in the Battered Women's Movement," *Catalyst* (Winter 1983).
90. See Joyce Rothschild-Witte, "Conditions for Democracy: Making Participatory Organizations Work," in *Coops, Communes, and Collectives.*
91. Interview with Frances Fox Piven, by Haymarket Foundation, Boston, Mass., May 1975.
92. David Moberg, "Experimenting with the Future: Alternative Institutions and American Socialism," in *Coops, Communes, and Collectives,* p. 307.
93. Johnston, "The Promise of Public-Sector Unions," p. 14.

7. ACHIEVING THE GOOD SOCIETY: SOCIAL SERVICES FOR SOCIAL CHANGE

1. John Wilson, *Introduction to Social Movements* (New York: Basic Books, 1972), p. 4.
2. A few examples of the stimulation caused by changed circumstances can be seen in: Rudolph Bahro, *The Alternative in Eastern Europe* (London: New Left Books, 1978); Andras, Hegedus et al., *The Humanization of Socialism: Writings of the Budapest School* (New York: St. Martin's Press, 1976); Ralph Miliband, *Marxism and Politics* (Oxford:

Oxford University Press, 1977); Raymond Williams, "Beyond Existing Socialism," *New Left Review* (March/April 1980), no. 120; David Beetham, "Beyond Liberal Democracy," *The Socialist Register, 1981* (London: Merlin Press, 1981); and Angelo Bolaffi, "The Crisis of Late Capitalism and the Fate of Democracy: An Interview with Habermas," *Telos* (Spring 1979), no. 39.

   3. Interview for dissertation, Boston, Mass., Summer 1976.
   4. Interview for *The Circle Game*, Spring 1979.
   5. Interview for this book, Summer 1982.
   6. Jeffrey Galper, *The Politics of Social Services* (Englewood Cliffs, N.J.: Prentice Hall, 1976), p. 93.
   7. This is what I tried to do, on a state level, with *The Circle Game* and what I urge my students to do in their own agencies.
   8. Andre Gorz, *Socialism and Revolution* (Garden City, N.Y.: Anchor Books, 1973), p. 136.
   9. Much more analysis needs to be done on the ethic of reciprocity vs. altruism. Some sources which are helpful, but which do not really make the point suggested here, are: Larry Blum, *Friendship, Altruism, and Morality* (London: Routledge and Kegan Paul, 1980); Alvin Gouldner, "The Norm of Reciprocity," in *American Sociological Review* (April 1960), no. 25; Claude Levi-Strauss, "Reciprocity: The Essence of Social Life," in Rose L. Coser, ed., *The Family: Its Structures and Functions* (New York: St. Martin's Press); and, of course, Richard Titmuss, *The Gift Relationship* (New York: Random House, 1972).
   10. Geoffrey Pearson, "The Politics of Uncertainty: A Study in the Socialization of Social Workers," in Howard Jones, ed., *Toward a New Social Work* (London: Routledge and Kegan Paul, 1975), p. 48.
   11. The value of "prefigurative communism" comes from the work of Antonio Gramsci and is key to maintaining our commitment to experimentation and the development of new forms of social organization.
   12. Here I am indebted to the analysis of David Stoez, "A Wake for the Welfare State: Social Welfare and the Neo-Conservative Challenge," *Social Service Review* (September 1981). See also George Gilder, *Wealth and Poverty* (New York: Basic Books, 1981) and *Naked Nomads: Unmarried Man in America* (New York: Times Books, 1974); Martin Anderson, *Welfare* (Stanford, Calif.: Hoover Institute, 1978); and Onalee McGraw, *The Family, Feminism, and the Therapeutic State* (Washington, D.C.: Heritage Foundation, 1980). Less obnoxious writers contribute to this argument also. See Christopher Lasch, *Haven in a Heartless World* (New York: Basic Books, 1979), and Robert Nisbet, *Prejudices* (Cambridge, Mass.: Harvard University Press, 1982).
   13. R. M. Hartwell, "Introduction" to Kenneth S. Templeton, in *The Politicization of Society* (Indianapolis, Ind.: Liberty Press, 1979), p. 14.
   I am indebted to Allen Hunter for this analysis and for his use of the quote in his article "The Ideology of the New Right," in Fox et al., eds., *Crisis in the Public Sector: A Reader* (New York: Monthly Review Press, 1982).
   14. See here the provocative forthcoming dissertation by Mary Jo Hetzel on the "Crisis in the Public Sector and the Response of Human Service Workers," University of Massachusetts/Amherst, 1984.
   15. My understanding of the increasing willingness of social welfare leaders to assert their political values is not based on academic research, but on reviews of the professional literature and my personal experience in Massachusetts. It was also, fairly,

called to my attention by John Romanyshyn in his highly critical review of a draft of this book.

16. Dean Hubie Jones has been exemplary in this regard. He has directly confronted Massachusetts conservative human service officials and has been vocal and clear about his sense that human services are an arena for *political* struggle. He remains a social democrat in his belief in the power of good professionals and well-run bureaucracies to provide for our social needs, and in his participation in the Democratic Party and politics, but his activity is exactly the type of political, social-democratic response we need if activists are ever to successfully pose a more radical alternative.

17. Gosta Esping-Anderson, "After the Welfare State," in *Working Papers* (May/June 1982), pp. 37–38.

18. Andre Gorz, *Socialism and Revolution* (Garden City, N.Y.: Anchor Books, 1973), p. 137.

19. London-Edinburgh Weekend Return Group, *In and Against the State*, p. 35.

20. The most useful sources on worker control are: Paul Bernstein, *Workplace Democratization: Its Internal Dynamics* (Kent, Ohio: Kent State University Press, 1976); Carole Pateman, *Participation and Democratic Theory* (Cambridge: Cambridge University Press, 1970); S. N. Eisenstadt, "Bureaucracy, Bureaucratization, and De-Bureaucratization," *Administrative Science Quarterly* (1959), no. 4; Louis E. Davis and James C. Taylor, eds., *Design of Jobs* (New York: Penguin Books, 1972); David Jenkins, *Job Power* (New York: Penguin Books, 1974); and HEW Taskforce, *Work in America* (Cambridge, Mass., 1971).

21. Interview for this book, Fall 1982.

22. Paul Johnston, "Public-Sector Unionism," in Fox et al., eds., *Crisis in the Public Sector: A Reader*, pp. 218–219.

23. Margali Larson, *The Rise of Professionalism* (Berkeley: University of California Press, 1977), p. 243.

24. Here I would actively disagree with Paul Adams and Gary Freeman, "On the Political Character of Social Service Work," in *Social Service Review* (December 1979).

25. Quoted in Joan London and Henry Andersen, *So Shall Ye Reap* (New York: Crowell, 1970), p. 183.

26. A very helpful source here is Renae Scott, "Race and the Shelter Movement," pamphlet written for the Massachusetts Coalition of Battered Women's Shelter Groups (Boston, 1981).

27. Andre Gorz, *Strategy for Labor* (Boston: Beacon Press, 1964).

28. Bertolt Brecht, "To the Unborn," spoken translation by Jerry Bedonis, 1966.

ACKNOWLEDGMENTS

B ECAUSE of its long history it is almost impossible to acknowledge the many people who helped create this book. In the early stages there were many people who helped in the research for my dissertation. I received critical help and assistance then from Roland Warren, Robert Morris, David Gil, Naomi Fatt, Anne McGregor, Roberto Ybarra and Rosina Becerra. At another phase many people helped me understand the broader implications of the research I was doing on the Massachusetts human service system. Here Nancy Aries, Lois Balfour, Donna Grimaldi, Ilana Lescohier and Rochelle Lefkowitz were especially helpful. Finally, as I have tried to develop my notions of political practice in human service other friends and associates have given critical readings and offered important help. They include: David Gil, Deanne Bonnar, Suzanne Sankar, Elliott Sclar, Miren Uriarte, Beryl Minkle and Anne Kaplan. I want to recognize the special ongoing support and critical attention I received from my associates and friends, Mary Jo Hetzel and Betty Reid Mandell.

In addition I have been lucky to have colleagues and friends who have supplied the sustaining support to keep me working. Here I can only mention a few of my friends at the College of Public and Community Service and on *Radical America* who were more helpful than they know: Joanne Pearlman, Jim Green, Vickie Steinitz, Gail Sullivan, Frank Brodhead, and Margaret Rhodes. Carol Nadelson kept me from running away. The students at my college, and especially the women of ARMS, kept me going because they also gave me a sense of purpose. Ruth Anderson and Elisa Nazeley were reliable and productive in typing the manuscript. Frances Goldin helped to make it all happen. And, most important, George Abbott White was the sustaining force who offered challenge when it was asked, support even when it was not, and helped to give a deeper meaning for all the work.

Finally, I wish to acknowledge Bertha Reynolds because it was the inspiration of her life and her writings which helped me to articulate my own vision. My own brief interviews with her in 1975 were critical moments in my political development. I hope that this book in some way carries on the work she began, almost alone, over fifty years ago.

INDEX